INTO THE ABYSS

Benedict Allen is the editor of *The Faber Book of Exploration.* For the past twenty-five years he has conducted solo expeditions through the Amazon jungle, along Namibia's Skeleton Coast and across Mongolia's Gobi Desert without the use of GPS, satellite phone or other means of outside support, as well as having written ten books of his adventures. He was the first explorer to bring the full experience of remote travel to television – taking the genre to its limits by not using a camera crew and so bring an immediacy to his experiences. Allen regularly gives lectures at the Royal Geographic Society.

by the same author from Faber

HUNTING THE GUGU
INTO THE CROCODILE NEST
MAD WHITE GIANT

as editor
THE FABER BOOK OF EXPLORATION

INTO THE ABYSS

EXPLORERS ON THE EDGE OF SURVIVAL

BENEDICT ALLEN

faber and faber

First published in 2006
by Faber and Faber Limited
3 Queen Square London WC1N 3AU
This paperback edition published in 2007

Typeset by Faber and Faber Ltd
Printed in England by Mackays of Chatham plc, Chatham, Kent

A CIP record for this book
is available from the British Library

ISBN 978–0–571–22395–4

2 4 6 8 10 9 7 5 3 1

To the memory of Charlie Forman, a dear friend

‘So, you’re now asking if it was clinging on to an idea that kept me alive in the Pacific? Look, I don’t know the answer to all your questions about survival, Mr Allen. You must keep on asking around: I know only that pursuing ideas has almost killed me.’
Thor Heyerdahl, not long before his death, at a lunch to celebrate the Kon-Tiki expedition and a life of adventure

‘At times it seemed to me that it was my destiny: that I was simply meant to live, Benedict. Other times I thought there might be something inside that we may call upon to sustain us – something ancient, perhaps carried with us from our first home in Africa.’
Laurens van der Post, asked what enabled him to survive while a Japanese POW and on journeys into the Kalahari and elsewhere

LIST OF ILLUSTRATIONS

1 Yasha and Tolia, with failing Soviet buildings behind them.

2(a) Anadyr, capital of Chukotka and seat of Governor Roman Abramovich; (b) Flashy White, the alpha male and guardian of team leader Top Dog.

3(a) Me, trying to get 'Bumbling' Bernard's attention; (b) Top Dog, inspecting his team; (c) Allegiances: Jeremy tucks in close to Bernard; Frank hides behind an ice block from the feared Mad Jack; Top Dog still eyes me.

4(a) Top Dog, the team leader, supported here by Mad Jack, the only dog ever hopeful of an encounter with wolves; (b) Over sea ice: Yasha lays down a trail for the other teams to follow. Tolia, with dogs trained to sniff for water, stays between my team and thin ice.

5(a) Tolia; (b) The constant winds which make the Chukchi Peninsula one of the least hospitable places man has settled in.

6(a) Raw walrus meat, awaiting consumption; (b) An abandoned outstation in the tundra.

7(a) Testing the courage of my dogs: Tolia's 'water-sniffing' team leads. The water opens up – and almost immediately stiffens as it freezes over again; (b) The cliffs of Sireniki: snow from the Siberian interior blows into the Bering Sea, where the ice has been parted by the gale.

8(a) Novoye Chaplino: a building, not quite buried; (b) My dog team: no bedding, no shelter, and able to cope at minus 50°C.

9(a) Towards the end: the formidable Flashy White now supplicating himself before the new alpha male; (b) Top Dog, with battle scars.

10(a) The traditional yaranga tent of Chukchi reindeer herders, as the wind gathers; (b) Wolf country: Top Dog looks back for reassurance. Young Basil has his tail characteristically high; Bernard is, as usual, not bothering to pull.

11(a) Discussing the oncoming weather at dusk; (b) About to leave for the Bering Strait: saying goodbye to Bernard, while his companion Jeremy looks on anxiously.

12(a) Heading off alone into the Strait. Bernard joins the team unharnessed, content just to be back alongside Jeremy; (b) Devoid of all 'back-up' in the Bering Strait; Top Dog as usual with his eyes on me.

13(a) Melting snow to drink, the tent up as a windbreak. The ice of the Strait is comparatively smooth as yet; (b) View from the end of Asia: about to head east from the Russian cliffs towards Alaska.

14(a) About to cross a pressure ridge: the lead dogs lie down, saving energy. Jeremy is about to take over, leading the strong rear dogs Dennis and Muttley; (b) Jeremy takes charge: Muttley and Dennis wait for my order to take the strain, Jeremy prepares to lead – and Bernard still daydreams.

15(a) A quiet word with the leader: Top Dog with me, while Flashy White looks on; (b) The dog team safety back in Lorino.

16 A Chukchi herder lassoing deer.

MAP: AUTHOR'S ROUTE THROUGH THE RUSSIAN FAR EAST

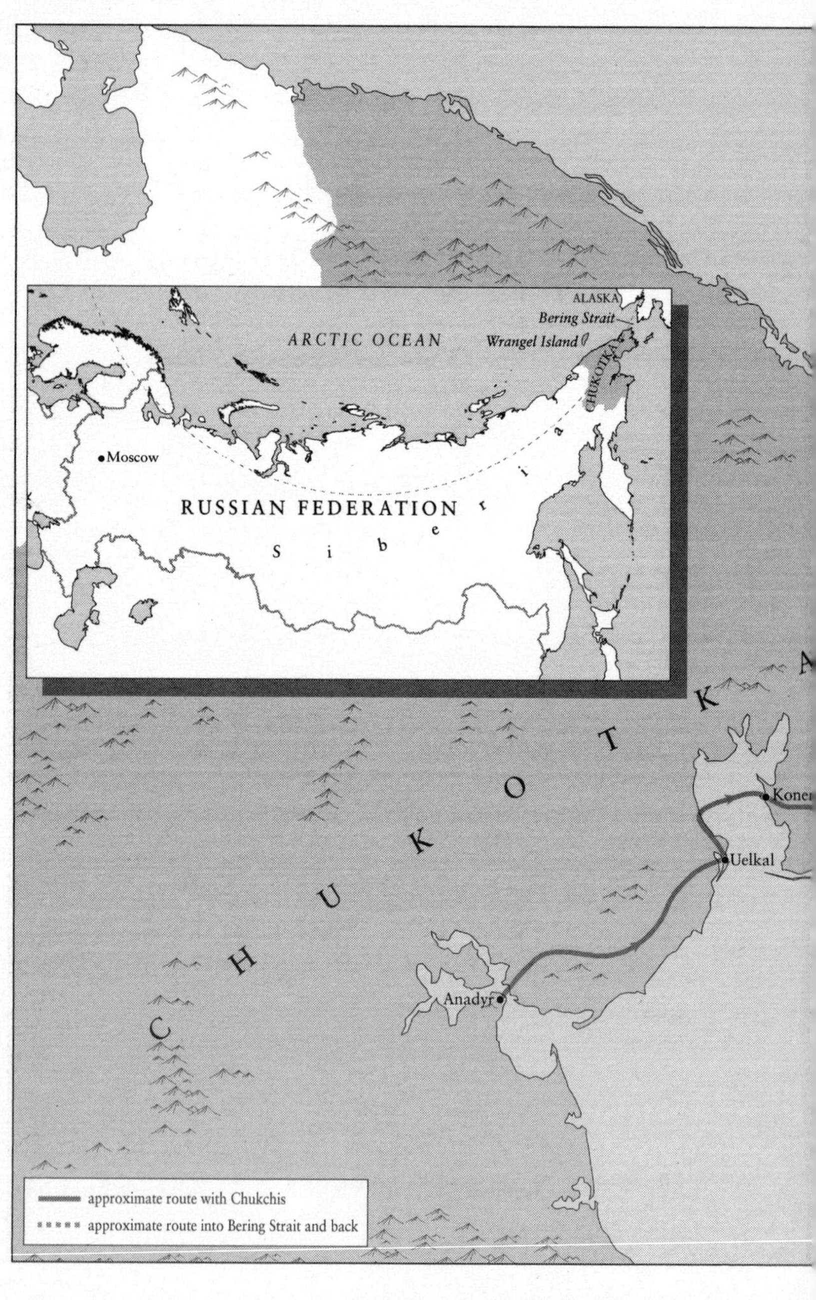
ALASKA
Bering Strait
ARCTIC OCEAN
Wrangel Island
CHUKOTKA
Moscow
RUSSIAN FEDERATION
S i b e r i a
C H U K O T K A
Kone
Uelkal
Anadyr
approximate route with Chukchis
approximate route into Bering Strait and back

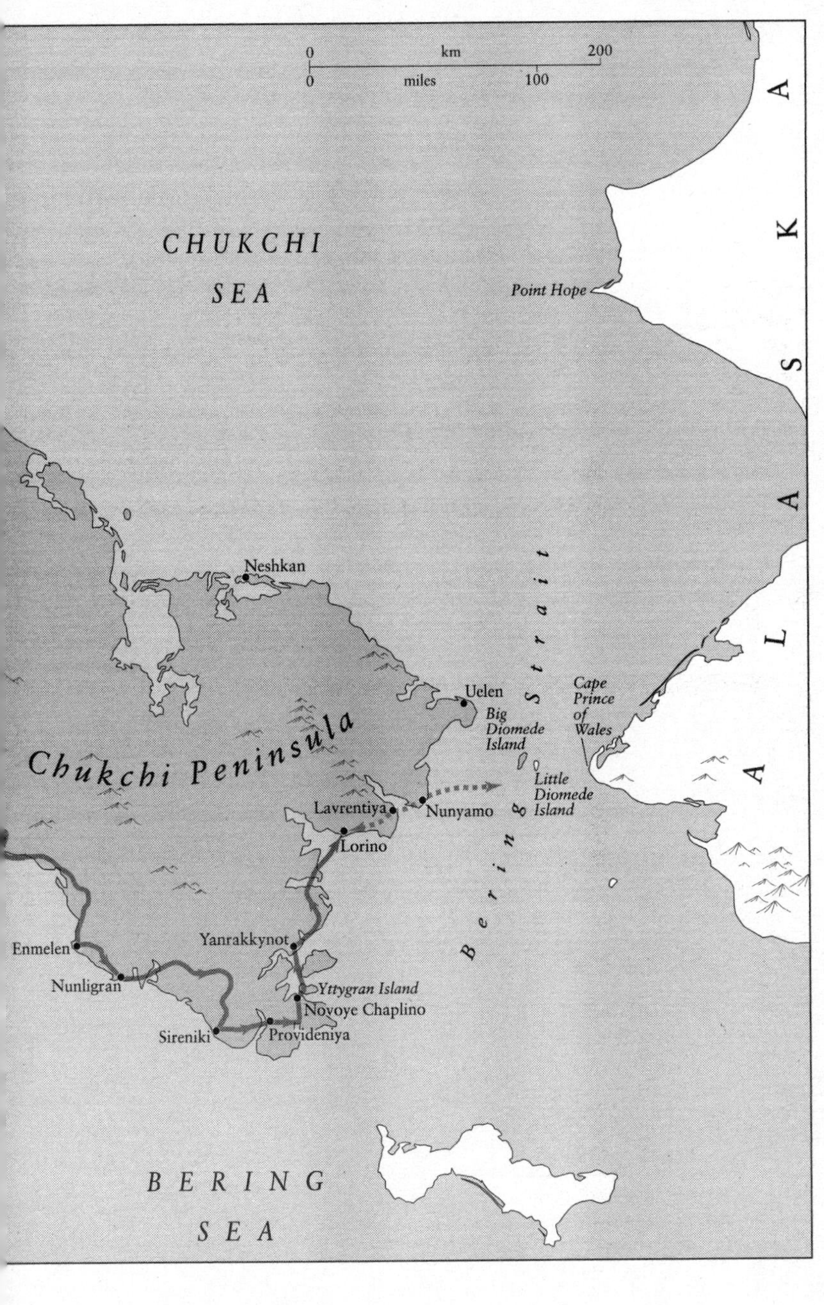

0
km
200
0
miles
100
CHUKCHI
SEA
Point Hope
A
K
S
A
L
A
Neshkan
Uelen
Big
Diomede
Island
Cape
Prince
of
Wales
Little
Diomede
Island
Bering Strait
Chukchi Peninsula
Lavrentiya
Nunyamo
Lorino
Yanrakkynot
Enmelen
Nunligran
Yttygran Island
Novoye Chaplino
Sireniki
Provideniya
BERING
SEA

I

When I think of Siberia I smile. That's not to say Siberia turned out to be a happy land of skipping children and promenading lovers, but if you're picturing that ridiculous old stereotype – a nasty, frozen-stiff, windblown hell, snow snagging occasionally on ruins but otherwise tumbling for miles – well, that's about right.

However, Siberia is a land of survivors as well as the Gulags, and survivors speak to us of possibility. A place of despair becomes the terrain of what might be. Even the smallest act becomes a feat, a fight-back. So when I think of Siberia I don't think of the unfortunate weather or my expedition as it fell to bits but the inspiration I found out there, a certain kind of rare beauty and strength. And I think of a night when I might have died – a night that stands out, even on this particular trip.

A cold silence had passed over my dog team. I couldn't see much in the starlight, but I knew the sounds of the ten dogs – the weight of their breathing, the click of their paws on the ice – and I sensed that something was very wrong. I threw the sledge anchor into the ground, but it was already too late. I saw my two lead dogs disappear; the two animals I trusted with my life had dropped from sight. And now I knew why the team had gone quiet. It was the moment that we all recognize instinctively, that moment when we know we've bitten off more than we can chew, when we have risked all and been caught out. The dogs had made a mistake, and they knew – as much as dogs can know about these things – that they might die. They were heading over a precipice.

Exactly how far the fall was, I'd soon find out – already the second row of dogs had followed the first off the cliff. The third would go too, then the fourth, their feet scrabbling in the air as they tumbled into the void.

Soon enough it would be my turn.

What happened next took only a few seconds, but time seemed to slow, giving me all the space in the world in which to contemplate our unhappy fate. As the sledge launched off the ledge and I flew through the darkness to what might be my end, I even managed a wry smile at the irony of it.

I was being taken to my death by hardened professionals. At minus forty, these dogs' only shelter was the snow; their food was frozen walrus; their water was the ice which they gnawed as they ran. Yet were they so different from us, these creatures? We are, after all, pack animals.

Each of my dogs was doing his utmost to make a go of things, as we humans do within our own tribes. You'll have seen them before: in your workplace, the alpha male who struts in the boardroom, the plodder happy in the corner of the office; or at home, the boy striving to get a half-decent mark at maths, his mum trying to be a better friend.

The ground rules were always the same: whether we lived our lives ponderously or in haste, whether as stalkers or grazers, in silence or in song, life was warfare. It was a sequence of skirmishes, advances and retreats, as we each sought to improve our chances of survival.

And if you really want to know how we humans go about the business of surviving, where better than Siberia? And what greater expression of man's ingenuity than the relationship we've forged with the dog? 'Man's best friend,' we are fond of saying. Well, in the Russian Far East he is sometimes man's only friend. There the two species can be seen working with geometrical perfection: man contributing his brain and tool-making hands, dogs their senses and physical stamina.

That is how it was that winter: my dog team, like a diamond-tipped lance, piercing the northernmost tundra. Nothing was quite able to stop us. We came to decayed settlements and communities steeped in alcohol, and the dogs passed through them, unscathed. They remained undiminished, without, it seemed, even a scratch. These animals succeeded in the harshest land humans had ever successfully colonized, while in less demanding parts of the very same planet we humans in our own packs have such mixed fortunes – so many disappointments and broken dreams.

Ten colleagues, then, each doing their bit tonight to deliver me through terrain that offered so little. Except that the dog leading this particular foray had made one elementary mistake and we were about to face the consequences.

It was upon us, the event that might mean our end. I wasn't much aware of the pain at first, just that I'd taken the first impact and that there would be more. I was close behind the rear dogs, and the 300-kg sledge had smashed me into the snow with what felt like the force of a train. But the sledge was still upright, and I sensed we were speeding up, not slowing. Skating down a crumpled bed of ice, perhaps. Snow was striking my face, flying past as we careened left, then right, creating what seemed like a funnel of light through the dark. But there was always the one comforting thought: if I was to die, it would be alongside my dogs.

That night there was something so exquisitely beautiful in their unity of purpose, something beautiful even in them flying, as one, into the abyss.

II

Even as a child I'd wondered at those with a capacity to survive. They stepped from burning planes, they hauled themselves from swamps, they walked in from the cold. I knew quite a lot about the latter because of Grandad's book about British polar explorers. A slim volume, it lay unnoticed at first among his Victorian editions of *Punch*. I remember first setting eyes on it as my grandfather, a man with a fondness for Fox's Glacier Mints and who had only one arm, was doing his best to ease it from where it lay trapped between the solid, leather-bound ranks. The cover was the toothpaste blue of a crevasse and smelt of Grandad's pipe tobacco; the spine was splintered and the pages inside had the palid, exhausted quality of old skin, as if the book itself had been recovered like a corpse from a blizzard. As it turned out, the book had been published during the Second World War to remind readers of the virtues of duty and sacrifice, although even aged six I noticed that rather a lot of these polar explorers had got nowhere near the Pole. Many had botched their plans and some didn't seem to have planned very much at all.

My favourite story was of Sir John Franklin, a Victorian of great distinction who got into trouble – or so it seemed – whenever he led his men beyond the Arctic Circle. Once, he was reduced to eating *tripe de roche*, which, I learnt, was a type of lichen. I pictured it as an omelette, only grey and with the texture of sea sponge. Franklin's men suffered, and then suffered some more, as they silently ate their *tripe de roche* and tried to escape the iron grip of the cold. On they staggered into a wall of icy wind. They ate their moccasins. They even ate bones chucked away by people who had been desperate themselves. And the great thing was, they didn't die! At least, not at first. Then one of their number, a native guide called Michel, decided he couldn't stand it any more. He got out his gun. But it wasn't suicide he was thinking of, it was his next meal. And while trying to solve the problem of where that might come from, his eyes alighted on a companion. I pictured the scene: a man with a face black with frost who was sick of eating spongy omelette and now had a really terrific idea that suddenly made him altogether perkier. He licked his lips and then he began stalking his friend as you might a passing deer. He aimed, fired, dragged the corpse to a convenient spot and then made a lovely roaring fire. When he had roasted him until he was just right, he ate him up.

'All of him?' my friends asked in the school playground.

'All except the left foot,' I said. But the truth was that I was doubtful about the details, and anyway, no one quite knew what he had eaten and what he had carefully put aside for later. The deed was done in secret, away from the other survivors, and they weren't keen on telling the world what really happened because cannibalism wasn't what Victorian expeditions were meant to resort to.

'What happened next?'

'The other survivors decided to shoot him,' I said, grimly, 'before he became hungry again . . .'

Franklin survived that trip, but things didn't really work out that well for him. When next he sailed into the Arctic it was with the latest equipment and 129 men in order to chart 'the Northwest Passage'. They all died.

There were other tales of the north: of thermometers exploding as the temperatures plummeted, of people whose fingers became brittle

Franklin's Arctic Experience: Background Info

John Franklin (1786–1847) joined the navy aged fourteen and accompanied Matthew Flinders on his exploratory voyages around Australia. He served at the Battles of Trafalgar (1805) and New Orleans (1814). He commanded the *Trent* on Captain David Buchan's Arctic expedition of 1818, which aimed to investigate the possibility of a Northwest Passage (direct from Europe through the Arctic waters of the Americas to Asia) and also to reach the North Pole. It was turned back by ice.

The following year, however, Franklin was given command of an overland expedition (1819–22) from the western shore of Hudson Bay to the Arctic Ocean, hoping to join up with Edward Parry and complete the passage by boat. It was on this expedition, with Native American guides who proved less than reliable, that Franklin embarked on what turned out to be his famous epic ordeal of survival.

The following is a paraphrased version of the account given by John Barrow, Secretary of the Admiralty and the person largely responsible for the bout of naval expeditions (the navy lying idle after the end of the Napoleonic Wars) in search of a Northwest Passage:

> The expedition members were desperately awaiting relief supplies to be sent along to them by George Back. Franklin split up from his companions – Dr John Richardson, Robert Hood and John Hepburn – and soon several of his Indian guides asked to join Richardson's camp, where firewood and *tripe de roche* were to be obtained. However, of the Indians, only one, Michel, arrived.
>
> At first Michel had proved a most useful Iroquois: he brought them a hare and a partridge. 'This unexpected supply,' wrote Dr Richardson, 'was received by us with a deep sense of gratitude to the Almighty, and we looked upon Michel as the instrument he had chosen to preserve all our lives.' Then he became sulky and refused to gather *tripe de roche*. He returned one day with meat from a 'wolf', which he claimed to have killed with an antler. They began to suspect that it was the remains of another guide. Michel now 'evinced a diabolical state of mind'. Hood was the next to die: Richardson heard a gunshot and found 'poor Hood lying lifeless at the fire-side, a ball having apparently entered his forehead'. He was at first 'horror-struck with the idea that, in a fit of despondency, [Hood] had hurried himself into the presence of his Almighty Judge, by an act of his own hands; but the conduct of Michel soon gave rise to other thoughts'. Besides, on closer examination, he realized he had been looking at an exit wound. Hood had been shot in the back of the head.
>
> Michel tried not to leave the two officers alone to confer over their suspicions, but when he did depart camp – perhaps to retrieve more meat – Hepburn and Richardson shared their thoughts. Something had to be done. Hepburn was the man who did it, putting a bullet through Michel's head as he approached. Already starving, they walked six days through snow, existing off the lichens and the buffalo cloak of 'poor Mr Hood' until they rejoined Franklin, who was also

> starving. He and the three remaining men of the expedition had been surviving off discarded bones, which they hardly had the strength to pound, and some old deer skins. Two died before a rescue party of Indians arrived a week later.
>
> A second overland expedition (1825–7), with the same aim of investigating the viability of a Northwest Passage, added new knowledge of about 2,000 km of the northwestern rim of the North American coastline, and although it encountered hostile Eskimos, returned with only two fatalities.
>
> Barrow's narrative was written at the time of the final (and, as it happened, fatal) expedition 'under the command of the gallant veteran, Sir John Franklin, whom, with his brave officers and men, may God preserve'. Having departed with the *Terror* and *Erebus* on 19 May 1845, they had last been seen by whalers in Baffin Bay that July.
>
> Their fate was not reliably confirmed until fourteen years later, when a search mission dispatched by Franklin's wife, Lady Jane, and led by Francis Leopold McClintock, reached King William Island and found the first skeletons. A note revealed that Franklin was among the first to die – conceivably of natural causes – on 11 June 1847. This, Franklin's final, ill-fated expedition, and the numerous subsequent relief expeditions, helped prove the existence of the Northwest Passage and did much to chart the Arctic waterways of Alaska and Canada.

and black with the cold and then broke off, like sticks of charcoal. But to me as a child the cruellest of all cold was to be found in Siberia, the heartland of nowhere. There, during the long, grinding winter, even the everyday acts of ordinary people become acts of heroism.

We had done Siberia at school. 'When the Bolsheviks overran Russia and needed somewhere out of the way in which to imprison the Tsar and his family, Lenin's first thought was of the empty lands to the east,' the teacher began rather impressively – all cribbed, we later discovered, from a book. Stalin too had noticed Siberia there on the map. It was an unproductive land but the one thing it had always done really well, even before the time of the communists, was inflict suffering. So he also sentenced people to go there, and off they went to join the others.

It was one evening after bathtime that I saw what I took to be my very first Siberian prisoner. I'd been allowed down for half an hour to watch the television, and I sat on the sofa in my pyjamas as he made his escape with a dog. His clothing was coming away, for in Siberia the cold seemed to feed on weak things, remorselessly chewing them apart. I watched as he struggled to make a fire, gathering kindling with fingers as stiff as bird talons. Finally, with a slow, swollen, quivering hand he managed to strike a match. He was going to live! The dog watched his master with a new light of hope in his eyes.

And then – I still remember the horror of it – a treacherous spark leapt from the match. It ignited the remaining matches, which, tied in a neat bundle, exploded in his mittens. He dropped the bundle in the snow. Even in the howling wind you could hear the hiss of the matches being extinguished by the tundra, and with the dying of the flame, so died his hope of life.

But the man had an inspiration. He had heard somewhere that if all else fails you might survive the wind a few hours longer by dressing yourself in a dog's skin. The prospect of what might happen next was too terrible for a child to contemplate. And yet I had to know. I looked at our own dog, a corgi called Toffee who was stretched out on the Afghan rug, and she looked back at me.

What exactly did happen, I don't know for sure – I was driven protesting up to bed. But I wasn't going to sleep until someone told me the outcome, and so my sister Katie was dispatched to my bedroom to reassure me. It was all right, she said. The man and dog survived somehow.

'How?'

'They just did. Now go to sleep.'

I didn't sleep. Under the bedclothes I thought of the bitterness of a place that had forced a man to think of sacrificing his friend. I was reminded of my grandfather leafing through the book of British polar explorers and surrounding me with the reassuring warm fug of the thick blue clouds of his pipe tobacco. But from time to time I would also glance up – that missing arm.

'Lost in the Great War,' the grown-ups had whispered, and I pictured the missing limb still out there somewhere, left behind when Grandad was gathered up from no-man's-land by the stretcher-bearers. And it seemed to me that Siberia must be a place much like no-man's-land: the Gulags suggested the fear, barbed wire, loneliness and mud of the Western Front.

A cross-examination of my sister over breakfast revealed that both man and dog had indeed survived, and although the details she provided didn't stand up all that well to scrutiny, the story was one of underlying comfort. It served much like a fairy tale: the moral was that, however bleak life was, if approached in the right way things might turn out all right.

The tale of the frozen man and his loyal dog hinted at another reason for hope. The northernmost segment of Siberia was home to the Eskimos and their huskies – and also the Chukchis, who in the photos appeared to be more of a reindeer-herding sort of native. Although further reading revealed that not all was rosy for these people – the elderly were rather expected to slip off the back of their sledge and die, and what's more, in hard times the dogs were eaten and the women had to haul the sledges in their place – you didn't see them shivering, only smiling. The screaming cold of the north need not, they reminded us, result in a story of despair; it might be a lesson in how to live.

It seemed only a matter of time before I sought out those who made a home of such a desolate place, the greatest no-man's-land of all: the tundra, that empty stage on which even the dimmest pulse of life was extraordinary.

III

But I was just one more child with dreams. I forgot about Siberia. Years went by. I went to university. I trekked across the Amazon. I became a writer. Then one day, on a lone expedition through the lowlands of West Papua, I found myself sheltering at an abandoned mission station. Amid the heat, the sweat bees and the leeches, I was gathering strength to make contact with the Obini, a hitherto unknown indigenous group about to be set upon by a band of over-enthusiastic missionaries. It was a lonely place for a twenty-four-year-old with huge ambitions but hopelessly out of his depth. A week or so went by as I tried to assess whether I should trust my guides, who were from the Momwina, a little nation that even a fervent brand of American protestants had failed either to clothe or disarm. Adding to my disquiet, the friendliest Momwina offered his girlfriend to me. She was a grass-skirted maiden with long, dusty eyelashes and a neat belly who dallied in the porch, though to no avail. In the mission house I'd discovered a shelf of eight books, including a paperback, partly torn up and digested by forest wasps, of *The First Circle* by Solzhenitsyn. Once again I found myself walking the permafrost of Siberia; I could hear the leather crack, feel the wind that scythed down the weakest in the bread queue.

I remembered the man in rags I had seen on the telly as a child – the prisoner with the dog. Was I absolutely sure he'd escaped from a Gulag? Wasn't this a Jack London story? If not, where did the dog come from? Perhaps he was a camp guard: as Stalin's paranoia deepened, he would sometimes decide, at the stroke of a pen, to purge the guards as well.

When I did proceed from the mission station through the dripping forests to the Obini, I soon found myself in trouble. The Obini had initially seemed a likeable bunch; they shyly accepted my presents of salt, even gently taking my hand and leading me across a fast river and into the heart of their camp. But there I found myself before a humourless-looking man who was perched up on a platform, braced for action and with his bow drawn.

It transpired that the Obini had been at war with the Momwina – or so the Momwina now claimed. But whatever the truth of that, the Obini certainly wished to join battle now. They began what you might loosely call a war dance. I fled along with the Momwina, leaving behind a little pile of hastily deposited gifts. Then it was back through the unmapped forests, which took two days, even running all the way.

Finally, I was back at the mission house. I slumped to the floor and began to take stock, as you might after a bad car crash. I sat staring at the contents of my survival kit spread out on the floorboards, knowing that these boy-scout tricks – the spare compass, waterproof matches, fishing hooks, distress flares, notebook and pencil – might not be enough next time. Then and there, I tore off a piece of paper and began writing out a list of guidelines. 'Remember the Importance of Having a Way Out' seemed a good start.

As I lay against the wall, an image kept recurring, tugging at my sleeve: that of a half-frozen man making his way with a dog despite the worst that the world could throw at him. I wondered why he had survived. Indeed, I was beginning to wonder how any of us get by at times – the businessman with the failing career, the mother at her wits' end, sunk beneath the weight of depression and hardly able to drag herself out of bed. However, it was hard to discern anything much, surrounded by all the confusion and complexity of the tropical forest. And in that respect, I decided, the jungle wasn't so different from home: the everyday clutter of our lives stopped us from seeing clearly. So what is it that you, me – any of us – find in ourselves to keep going in times of despair?

It took me two weeks to find a way out of the forest. The only payment I could offer the Momwina was my stack of razor blades, and even the Momwina knew they weren't genuine Wilkinson Sword but fakes from China. Nonetheless, all this gave me time to dwell on my earlier thought, that the Arctic offered something special: a perspective on how to go about the business of coping with disappointment, not to say downright ruin. The tundra was patterned by the deeds of those who refused to lie down and die; those who knew, in their agony, how to reach out and grasp at life.

My own life, meanwhile, went by fast. There were many more adventures – and equally, there were many more misadventures. I was chased, I was left to die, I was shot at. I began to look beyond those guidelines for emergencies in my survival kit. I emptied a drawer in my desk, and into it went any tales of survival I came across. I collected newspaper cuttings, I scribbled words I'd overheard. Being an adventurer, I had a professional interest in not dying, of course, but haven't we all? So I gathered up any clues from deserts, jungles, planes and buses. And gradually, I felt more and more of a yearning for some quality that seemed inherent in the bleak simplicity of the tundra, that frozen expanse that asked a lot of humans – too much, very often. 'If you gaze into the abyss, the abyss also gazes into you,' said Nietzsche. But if you got it right, the Arctic also offered a lens: there, the essentials of how to persevere in life and not yield were clear to see.

IV

Dogs. They, I told myself, were the key. I read up on the subject and learnt that of all those Arctic peoples who kept dogs – the Eskimos, the Samoyeds, the Mahlemuits and so forth – it was the Chukchis of Siberia who had what seemed to me to be the greatest sledge dog. And there was a good reason why: their homeland was a nightmare, like a blasted heath but worse. It offered precious little hope without them.

Chukotka, the land of the Chukchis, was that unfortunate chunk of the Russian Far East sticking out east towards America, cut off from the remainder of Siberia by mountains and from the rest of the world by icy seas. It had a balmy climate – in Siberian terms – with temperatures dipping to only minus thirty or forty. It was the wind, though, that was the killer. The Chukchi Peninsula, it was said, boasted not a single tree.

'Even the ordinary Siberians feel sorry for *those* Siberians!' chortled a Russian I met in a café when I asked his opinion. He'd emigrated from Moscow to Holland Park 'at short notice', he said mysteriously, and, much to the excitement of the waitress, paid for his cappuccino from a thick roll of fifty-pound notes.

'You know something else?' he went on. 'Out there, they talk about the rest of Russia as "the mainland", as if they were living on an island!'

'I must remember that!' I laughed. 'That's funny.'

But he wasn't laughing.

'Nine time zones from Moscow, Benedik,' he said. 'You sure this godforsaken place is where you want to get to?'

'It's *because* it's godforsaken that I'm going there,' I said. I would have told him more about how much more rewarding it must be to emerge safely from a Hades of tormented souls than from a luxuriant paradise, but he wasn't listening.

'Nine time zones from Moscow,' the Russian repeated slowly to himself. 'Shit.'

The library books were more optimistic – or rather, they were at first. I read how the earliest Chukchis had kept only the odd dog or two for guarding their livestock. Chukchis being reindeer-herding nomads, hungry dogs only spelt trouble. However, the Chukchis nearest the far eastern coast learnt from the Eskimos how to harvest food from the waters with kayaks and harpoons; they began seeking ways to negotiate the vast swathes of tundra which separated them from their inland, reindeer-herding cousins. They looked to their dogs.

Bitches were kept tethered while on heat to ensure an effective breeding programme, and rather than selecting for size and strength as the shore-dwelling Eskimos had always done, dogs were chosen for obedience and endurance. They ran at only moderate speed – but for long distances. They were small – and therefore easy for families to maintain – and each dog was of an amiable disposition, ideal for working as part of a larger team.

How I loved reading about these dog heroes who made a people great. 'They were of the fox kind,' reported Captain Cook, passing through the Bering Strait, 'and of different colours with long soft hair like wool.' Over generations, the Chukchis worked on their dogs as Grand Prix mechanics might change the oil mix and tweak the chassis of their cars, and they came up with a breed uniquely efficient in the tundra. Unlike Eskimo dogs, which had been engineered to perform an array of duties from short-distance freight-hauling to shoreline hunting, the Chukchi dog was a highly specialized transportation tool – over long distance more reliable and over the worst terrain more capable than anything man has yet to devise. The dog became central to every aspect of Chukchi life. The shamans even spoke of them guarding the spirit world.

I read on: the Russians began to encroach, and the sledge dogs found themselves key operatives in a guerrilla war. With reindeer cavalry in support, they thwarted intruders for three hundred years. Dogs could scamper up a precipice, whip across deep snows, charge through the blackest night. They were a match even for the brilliant and bloody Cossack. Of all the peoples in all the Arctic, the Chukchis alone remained undefeated. Directly or indirectly, their dogs ensured that they alone were masters of this land.

None of this particularly impressed the communists when their time came. The party embarked on a breeding programme to produce an official Soviet dog, an animal designed to represent the collective struggle of the proletariat as opposed to that creature from the Stone Age. It would be called the 'Leningrad factory breed' and it would be an amalgamation of Chukchi strains with larger, rangier and altogether more impressive-looking dogs. Frankly, the final product sounded like something off an assembly line, like a Lada.

Long before the break-up of the Soviet Union, the original Chukchi sledge dog – that small, friendly, indefatigable character – was presumed extinct. But then one day I was waiting in line at the Gate cinema when I was queue-barged by a Russian. 'Thank God for that bloody dog,' he said, when we got talking about Chukotka. 'The villages are bloody running short of everything.' He then gave me a very long list of shortages, beginning with fuel and ending with small parts for the snowmobile. That's how I discovered that in northernmost Chukotka, unlike anywhere else on our planet, whole communities were once more dependent on the dog. The day I heard this – standing in line for an evidently slightly disappointing French movie in Notting Hill – was the day my mind was made up. I wanted to be there, in the worst place in all of Siberia, more than anywhere else in the world.

My vision was of journeying with dogs alone across the Bering Strait. I'd launch out into a no-man's-land, that space between the Old World and the New, travelling across the winter ice until I hit either water or America – and then I'd come back. Out there I would be beyond rescue. That was crucial: no radio communication, no satellite tricks, no outside help. Only that way would I know how I stood with the furthest end of Siberia. Such was my dream – and we all have a duty to our dreams, do we not? I'd attempt it, even at the risk of ending up like poor John Franklin, eating sponge-textured lichen while lost to the wastes.

V

As my ideas began to coalesce, I tried to make the bleakness of the Arctic seem real by picturing my frozen peas sitting stiff in the packet in my freezer. I'd be eating and sleeping in a land five times colder than that. Speeding along with my dog team, my eyes might freeze over.

For the expedition I bought a lightweight plastic file – 'guaranteed indestructible' – that might accommodate my collection of notes on survivors, and I assembled yet more notes which might come in handy on this venture: 'FRANKLIN'S ARCTIC EXPERIENCE: BACKGROUND INFO,' began one. Another page was headed simply 'CHUKOTKA AND GOVERNOR ROMAN ABRAMOVICH: A QUICK OUTLINE'. Another: 'WHY SCOTT DIED AND AMUNDSEN LIVED: NOTES TO SELF'.

I did my best to recall the experience I'd already had of life below zero, walking with Kazak herders at minus twenty-five at the foot of the Altai range. I'd been comfortable enough wearing a coat fashioned from the pelt of a bear, but when the breeze quickened, the air tore at my flesh. The weaker cows dropped to their knees, and the Kazaks jumped down from their horses and cut the throats of the stragglers – in the Altai, such an act was a kindness. I watched the blood gush down the cows' necks in crimson beads and freeze before it reached the snow, slowing like wax running down a candle.

The message was simple. Left without food or water you might last weeks in the rainforest – I knew this from personal experience. In a hot desert you might last days – I knew that too. But in the wind-seared, ice-locked Arctic you'd last hours at best, and if you fell through the ice into the sea, you might have a heart seizure and be dead in thirty seconds. Unfortunately, a day trip to Cambridge – specifically to Professor Peter Wadhams at the Scott Polar Research

Institute – revealed that the sea ice had been increasingly fluid of late. Indeed, the satellite record indicated that the Bering Strait hadn't frozen over for twelve years.

I rang my contact in Russia, Ivan, a smiley, young, bearded individual from St Petersburg with thick eyebrows flourishing wildly on him like an outcrop of thrift on a cliff ledge. We agreed he should at least ask the authorities for permission for me to travel to Chukotka. I was optimistic; he was one of those rare, innocent, tender-souled little characters that people instinctively want to help.

'Tell him to f**k off!' a man had screamed at my friend from behind his desk.

'Perhaps he didn't mean it,' I said when Ivan reported back.

'He did.'

'Well, perhaps we should try to talk to someone nearer the top. This person sounds like lowlife.'

'It was the Governor of Chukotka himself.'

'Well, that's the end of that,' I thought. And who knows, perhaps it was for the best.

But suddenly an election was approaching, the governor floundering amid lurid allegations of corruption and a man called Roman Abramovich looking certain to get the post. Wealthy beyond the normal meaning of the word, and still aged only thirty-four, he seemed to think that, whatever I was really planning to do out there, in the larger scheme of things I was harmless.

Chukotka and Governor Roman Abramovich: A Quick Outline

In Soviet times, teachers and other administrators were offered three times the Moscow salaries to come to the remote region. By the year 2000, it was said, officially, that what had now become the 'Chukotka Autonomous District' had exports worth $14,000 a year – but even this modest achievement was better than the full picture. When Roman Abramovich, the second richest of the Russian oligarchs, won the governorship in a landslide victory, he discovered that debts exceeded the annual budget by four times.

Roman Abramovich: Of Jewish background he was born in Saratov, on the Volga, in October 1966, losing his mother when he was 18 months old. His father was killed in a construction accident when Roman was four, and he was raised (within Komi, the harsh Russian northwest) in modest circumstances by his uncle and grandparents.

Although he gradually accumulated wealth through a variety of enterprises, Abramovich achieved the majority of his early success thanks to the patronage of oil magnate (and Russia's first billionaire) Boris Berezovsky, who introduced him to Boris Yeltsin's inner circle. His big opportunity, however, came with the privatization of state companies in the mid-1990s. Under Vladimir Putin's regime Berezovsky fell out of favour, allowing Abramovich to take over various of his assets. In due course he become the majority shareholder in Sibneft, the immense oil company, and also a major shareholder in RUSAL, the world's second-largest aluminium producer.

In 1999, he was elected to the State Duma (lower parliament) as the representative for Chukotka and founded 'Pole of Hope', a charity to help the poor; a year later, as Governor, he committed himself to continuing his considerable personal and state support of the needy.

Chukotka: Geographically speaking, Chukotka lies within the Russian Far East. Although the East Siberian Sea extends along almost the entire north coast of Chukotka, Russians commonly take Siberia to be only that area located east of the Ural mountains and extending approximately 3,000 km to the Lena river. Chukotka itself, extending another 3,000 km further east, is generally lumped in with this vast region when it comes to discussions of history and ethnography.

Ecologically, Chukotka consists of alpine and low-bush tundra. Trees, including larch, pine, birch, poplar and willow, occur only in scattered locations in the valleys of major rivers. The whole of the Chukchi Peninsula itself, the easternmost region of Russia, is north of the treeline. 'The Country,' wrote Captain Cook, who charted much of the Bering Strait and was one of the first Europeans through it, 'appeared to be exceedingly barren, yielding neither Tree nor shrub that we could see.' Yet the Bering Sea is extraordinarily rich, providing more than half of America's seafood catch and a third of Russia's. The diversity of habitats across the broad continental shelf leads to a rich marine biodiversity: there are more than 450 species of fish, crustacean and mollusc. This results in huge sea bird populations – including ten million murres (guillemots) and auklets – totalling around 200 species in total.

Ivan had somehow made phone contact with the Chukchi Peninsula and a whaler called Gena: 'Said to be reliable. He talks about a thing called "new ice" – it's the temporary stuff that sometimes forms overnight. Might not have been picked up by the satellites. He says that, if you were the type to risk these things, it might provide a temporary surface to the other side. Not that the Chukchis have ever thought it sensible to try, of course.'

VI

Looking back at the reconnoitring trip, I see it as the thickening of clouds before a storm. Or perhaps I should just say that the desolation I was expecting to find extended well beyond the tundra itself.

But time enough for that: now at last we were flying over the far side of Siberia, the land I'd come so far to see. Below me was spread a fawn country apparently naked of higher life forms; I stared at this rock and dirtscape – it might have been the view from a spacecraft passing over a hostile planet.

'Soon time for the winter,' said Ivan portentously as he woke from a doze. Looking around I saw that not all the ice had quite melted yet – and it wouldn't now, even though it was 21 August and still the height of summer back home. The clock had already begun counting down to the onset of the winter that my journey required.

Even as we banked into Anadyr, I could see pitifully few signs of man having made an impression. Viewed from above, Chukotka was an unhappy mess of desert, marsh and tidal flats – occasional freeze-thawed hexagons, purple flares of algae in some black pools – but not a road, not a footpath in sight. Does no one venture out? I wondered. Even in the summer? The plane circled, and then circled again, as if it were a frightened bird reluctant to land.

As this empty terrain revolved below us, I tried to imagine myself down there with my dog team, calling to them, making headway. Then I cast around, thinking of Captain Cook, the Chukchis, trying to imagine *anyone* down there.

Upon landing, soldiers boarded the plane and examined our documents. I was quickly led off with Ivan to the grim airport block. 'Don't write anything nasty about us,' a young, pasty-skinned offi-

Captain James Cook's Encounter with the Chukchis

Cook entered the Bering Strait to investigate the Pacific end of the Northwest Passage on his third and final voyage in August 1778. There, he came across the Chukchis: 'We perceived on the North shore an Indian Village, and some people whom the sight of the Ships seemed to have thrown into some confusion or fear, as we could see some running inland with burdens on their backs . . . As we drew near, three of them came down towards the shore and were so polite as to take off their Caps and make us a low bow: we returned the Compliment but this did not inspire them with sufficient confidence to wait our landing.' However, by 'signs and actions' he got them to stop and receive 'some trifles I presented them with and in return they gave me two fox skins and a couple of sea horse [walrus] teeth . . . By degrees a sort of traffick between us commenced . . . but nothing we had to offer them would induce them to part with a Spear or Bow, which they held in constant readiness never once quitting them, excepting one time, four or five laid them down while they gave us a Song and a Dance . . .' – and even then they were placed so that they could 'lay hold of them in an instant and for greater security desired us to sit down'.

cial said, handing my passport back. 'We're not all horrible.'

I liked him for his wry humour and wished I could have stayed to exchange a few comments with this man, my first inhabitant of the Russian Far East. However, as I extended my hand, I noticed that from his mouth issued breath that was heavily laden with vodka. 'Another time, perhaps,' I thought.

Ten minutes later the taxi driver was dipping into his own stash of vodka. We sat passing the bottle around as the ferry carried us over the bay. It was still only 10 a.m.

'You've arrived in such good weather,' he said, directing his red eyes over the dull chill skies. Beluga whales and their young were parting the waves of the bay, and I watched as their thick white flesh slipped in and out of the choppy waters. Sergei, the fixer assigned to us by a Mr Raityrgin, our official point-of-contact, said, 'So, you're here to cross the Bering Strait . . .'

'We'll see,' I said.

He swigged from the bottle, winced and passed it on. Then, with

Ivan translating, he told the matter-of-fact tale of the most recent attempt. 'This one looked more promising than most,' he said. 'It was an amphibious vehicle driven from Salzburg. I thought to myself, "Well, maybe this one won't sink."'

'From Salzburg? In Austria? Are you sure?'

'Sure I'm sure. Got all the way here, across Siberia, but was soon in trouble in the Strait.'

'Any casualties?'

'The last man to leave was the team leader. Escaped through the roof, like any good captain.'

I got out of the van to evade the vodka, and stood in the cold wind. 'Cold in August,' I said.

'June and July are the warmest months,' Sergei said, pursuing me with the bottle. 'People even sunbathe.'

I tried to picture the sunbathers: a short row of people blue from the cold and wearing bikinis, fur hats and woollen mittens.

'But their hearts are in it less and less. They struggle on, those left here. You know – those left since the Soviet days. Russians, Ukrainians. The ones who can't afford to leave. They're stuck with the Chukchis and Eskimos.'

Of the Chukchis and Eskimos, there was no sign so far. But then again, there weren't many humans of any sort in sight. The driver spoke of 'half' the population having gone – the exact figure being difficult to determine because Chukchis kept moving in from outlying areas to fill the vacated apartments.

The taxi took us through a town of utilitarian flats banked up on a hill and in need of more than a paint job. Behind were two bulbous cooling towers, and although evidently still in action, they had the look of something from a great, lost empire. They stood stained and solitary, like lone pillars protruding from the ruins of ancient Greece.

The flat to which we'd been assigned was owned by Tatiana Zeenoviyeva, a large, handsome lady with good skin and soft hands and smelling of a soap scented with something slightly odd – vanilla, perhaps. She began talking to Ivan as if they had known each other for years, just like the officials at the airport. 'Everywhere it's always the same,' I thought. 'People just open up for Ivan.' Only now did I understand that this quality in him, the power he had even to disarm professional soldiers, made him potentially very valuable to me.

'In the Soviet days, life was good,' Tatiana was saying, as she packed up her things to vacate the flat. 'You knew how much money you were getting, you could plan.' She nudged her daughter, a sleepy, long-limbed teenager who'd curled herself into an armchair like a cat. 'Nowadays, you are lucky if you get any money,' she said, as her daughter opened one eye and stretched out her arms. Tatiana's husband Vitali worked at the power station. 'The workers there haven't seen any money for five months. Ordinary people suffer. The times suit crafty people, those who are nasty or pushy. It's dog eat dog.'

'Dog eat dog,' I thought. I pictured the dogs I'd be with one day, a disciplined squad of them running ahead. Until now, I'd chosen to think of them as tough but noble athletes. They would, after all, be leading me through hell; I'd die without them. But now I wondered if I'd be confronted by creatures governed by all that was worst in humans: savage, callous instinct.

Ivan and I set out on a walk through Anadyr. Any movement here – an opened door, a face glancing from a window – was unusual enough to draw your eye to it. We carried on stalking about the town, feeling as if we were tracing survivors of a catastrophe.

Small boats lay around in the middle of the street, along with scrap metal. There were unfinished roadworks and a peeling, faded mural of Lenin. And around everything clustered an air of wilful abandonment.

'My god,' I thought. 'One day I'll be out in that tundra and think back to this place as civilization.'

Naturally, I was watching for any dogs, but the first was a stray, scuttling up the main road with the guilty look of an urban fox in a back alley. The next was a woolly, submissive old mutt that was stretched out as if it were a summer's day – which it was, of course, but not the sort of day you'd think favoured lounging about. 'Could this be a retired sledge dog?' I wondered at first. On closer inspection, it was a sort of lesser golden retriever, probably an abandoned pet; certainly, its coat had gone to seed. But it had been loved by someone once, and when I stopped to say hello, it blinked its dark friendly eyes and thumped its tail contentedly.

We did eventually come across some humans. There were stout, older Slavic ladies marching briskly through the wind with polythene bags of shopping; and there were men, always in the act of repairing things. They stood on ladders and assessed the fallen cladding; they dug into broken roads, they poked at cracked pipes.

But who were all these people, drawn out here like me? Either idealists, I supposed, people ready and willing to serve the schools and hospitals at the furthest frontier of the former Soviet empire, or else misfits, the flotsam of the USSR, people who'd seen a chance out here and had now been left high and dry.

The cinema looked a brighter sort of building – a brighter shade of grey. 'Only one person came yesterday – a small boy,' Rosa the old caretaker said, adjusting her many layers of jumpers. 'He paid 25 roubles.'

I nodded sympathetically, though I was beginning to wonder how much use actual money was in Chukotka.

We walked on, past a clutch of pretty girls adorned with copious eye make-up, vermilion nail varnish and dyed hair stacked on their heads like a crop of sun-bleached straw. 'Dressed like the Moscow prostitutes,' observed Ivan.

'But who knows?' I thought. Maybe they *were* prostitutes. And who was I to criticize? Who knew what lengths any one of us would go to in order to get by out here? Well, we would see . . .

We searched out Sergei Raityrgin, head of sport and outdoor activities and our government contact. An impressive athlete of a man, he looked at me, the frail issue of a temperate little island of dog-lovers, and most likely saw a hopeless case. He informed me that he'd organized dog races for something called the Hope Challenge on either side of the Strait, and as I laid out my own hopeful challenge, diminished it with a series of blunt interjections that he'd learnt (I liked to imagine) while mixing with moustached and suspiciously muscular female East German shot-putters at the Olympics: '*Ein moment!*' '*Nein! Nein!*' Meanwhile, a bevy of secretaries took notes, each of them beautifully mannered, welcoming and, it gradually emerged, divorced.

Raityrgin pointed to the early failures of Dmitry Shparo, a distinguished Russian explorer who'd attempted the journey on skis. 'By the way, when the time comes for your rescue you must hide from the American Coast Guard,' Raityrgin said, as the bottle-blonde secretaries sat with their bits of paper, scribbling it all down. 'That's what Shparo did. The coastguard wanted to charge $250,000 on his last failed attempt, but luckily he managed to radio the Russians and be saved by them instead.'

Shparo did get to America in the end, partly traversing the waters on a little block of ice. Departing from a northern promontory on the Russian side, he was taken 300 km northeast by currents, ending up at Point Hope, Alaska. Accompanying him were his son and an exciting array of gadgets linking him to headquarters. Faxes were received as he bobbed across; he made phone calls; helicopter pilots stood by. His chunk of ice had, in effect, been converted into an office.

As for my own expedition, the more insistent I was, the more varied and extreme were Raityrgin's objections. Finally, he said a crossing over ice was '100 per cent impossible. Forget it. What chance do you have? Shparo tried four times, and when he did land in Alaska it was way north of the Strait – even with all the help in the world.'

Before I could press further, Raityrgin swept us off to a restaurant with his colleagues and secretaries. After the first toast, he gallantly led them to the dance floor, swinging them in waltzes, the music provided by an obese drummer who sat on stage framed by a strip of irregularly flashing orange lights. For my part, I waltzed non-stop with the delightful Tanya, until it transpired she was married to the man presently seething with anger at our table, who'd already introduced himself as an instructor of aikido and other martial arts. He remained silent most of the remainder of the evening, and when he did speak it was to say just two words to his wife: 'Ты блядь!' ('You whore!')

It was lucky everyone was on their best behaviour. At the neighbouring table was Roman Abramovich with his entourage. They were unlike anyone else in the room. What was it about them? Their youth and vigour? Their quietness? Discipline, I decided. Here, in a modest suit too tight around the shoulders, his face somehow hushed, his blue eyes those of a sensitive child, was one of the richest men alive; no one of his age had ever had such wealth. But there was no carousing, no drinking. His people were gathered quietly around him, sober, attentive to each other and, like a cohort of nursery bees, tending to him; but they were always careful not to attract attention – they might have passed for a tight-knit bunch of postgraduate students.

'No one disturbs him,' I thought, 'nor is he disturbed by Siberia.' Carefully, Abramovich had sealed himself off from the dangers to be found circling here.

Ivan and I slipped away but found ourselves drawn to a restaurant run by a waitress called Natasha – although the word 'restaurant' gives quite the wrong idea, as does the word 'waitress'. We arrived in time to see the police breaking up a fight among the women. An ambulance was called, and by now my opinion of this town was such that I was thinking, 'Wow, Anadyr actually has an ambulance?'

Five minutes later, the lights were turned back down again and the furniture was being repaired. Natasha was lining up vodkas for herself at the bar, and Volodyr, a sad-faced poet, was back at his keyboard. He felt moved to play the Beatles song 'Let It Be', though he didn't know any more than those three words, and everything was as normal once more, but for the repair man hammering away.

'My husband is a jealous man,' Natasha said, leaning into both Ivan and me. She wore an army jacket, black tights and not much of a skirt, and seemed to give out a great deal of heat. 'He's a teacher,' she continued. 'His life is not compatible with bars.' She planted her eyes on mine and for a while wouldn't take them off again.

I looked around at the young faces here and compared them to Natasha's. She must have had pale, buttery Slavic skin once too, but Anadyr had worked to transform it into unwieldy putty. 'So . . . this is the capital of Chukotka,' I thought. 'This is my launch pad into the most hostile environment that man has made a home of.' I stood there amid the smoke, the bulbous men getting to their feet to make glorious toasts to brotherhood, others producing chocolates and plastic roses and making tearful declarations of love to their sweethearts, but mostly people losing themselves – Ivan now suddenly among them – the whole huddle swaying together, like survivors washed by heavy seas, wailing the words 'Let it be, let it be . . .' as if calling out a last prayer. And for the first time I had a sense of unease – that we might not be inspired by Siberia but instead be corrupted by it.

Thus ended, at around four in the morning, my first day in Siberia.

Ivan and I bided our time, awaiting our plane – delayed for no clear reason – north to the Bering Strait for our rendezvous with Gena, the Chukchi whaler who I now hoped might be my guide. Sometimes we ate at a restaurant called Pizza – it didn't actually sell pizzas – otherwise, it was back to Natasha's. We'd order supper and she'd thump it down in front of us – plates of burnt chicken, nasty crude lumps of it. 'Sorry,' she'd say. 'I'm not feeling well.'

'But where's the steak?' Ivan would ask.

'And the *pelmeni*?'

'What do you expect?' Natasha would say. 'I'm drunk.' Then she'd stagger off to continue her duties and Volodyr would arrive with his keyboard. 'I don't ever bring my girlfriend,' he'd tell strangers. 'She's a ballerina, you know.' And they would nod, saying they'd look forward to meeting her very much, but no one ever did.

Nights came and went like this – Volodyr at his Casio singing, 'Let it be, Let it be . . .'; occasionally in the background there was the sound of someone dropping a glass.

And sometimes, as if through the smoke of battle, I'd again catch sight of Abramovich with his lonesome blue orphan eyes. I'd wonder how he endured here, how he grew stronger, not weaker. The same Siberia that brought so many men and women untold misery, lowering them to their knees, gave this man untold wealth. He seemed to understand the secret.

VII

All of a sudden, our plane to Lavrentiya seemed likely to go. 'There may be a return flight in four days,' said Sergei, our fixer. 'Or not,' he added, making more of an effort to be realistic. 'You have your tickets and *presente* ready?'

'A *presenty*?'

'A *presente* for the airline,' he said. He explained the system: the airline kept back tickets, saying the flight was full. This had the benefit of forcing the most desperate passengers to give them a *presente*. It wasn't a Russian word, Ivan explained helpfully, 'but it's one that's well understood'.

With a *presente* of $50, we were soon made more than welcome. We scrambled on board with our boxes. There was no safety belt for my seat – 'stolen' said the bloke in the leather jacket who served as the flight attendant. Then he took his seat, surrendering himself, like us, to the vagaries of ancient Soviet aeronautical power.

The plane set off along an extremely long runway – excessively long, you might think, until you thought a bit more and recalled that until recently this had been the front line against America. Tanks, ballistic missiles, anything you might need to begin and end the Third World War might have to be landed here, and probably had been.

Once airborne, we headed north up the coast, the route I'd be following in the winter. The gravel beaches, grey cliffs and bilberry-heath tundra – all this would be plastered over with snow and ice. Gliding over it, Gena and a mate of his would lead my dog team for 1,000 km, as our little party threaded its way from Anadyr all the way to their settlement near Lavrentiya, and then I'd be on my own, heading out into the Strait now to our right.

I looked more carefully: further still to the right, there was what would be my navigation points, the two Diomede Islands split by the international border, where the Russians and Americans had pulled faces at each other during the Cold War. Further east, just out of sight, was Alaska. Between here – Eurasia – and there – the Americas – the waters of the Bering Sea were flecked even now with wedges of ice.

On landing at Lavrentiya there were more security checks, but we were kept on a loose leash – after all, where would we go? Even prisoners sentenced to twenty-five years' hard labour in Siberia rarely chose to escape. I looked at the dull hills, spread like an unappetizing, stale, crusty loaf. In the foreground stood a band of decaying office blocks. Between them were a few greenhouses, perched, somewhat improbably, high up on top of old iron sheds to catch maximum light. 'Not one garden, not one field,' I thought to myself. It was taking time to sink in. This wasn't a land for Europeans or any other great people of the plough. We would be uneasy here, as long as we refused to roam like the Chukchis and Eskimos, living off animals plucked from the sea and land.

Ivan was soon in conversation with the soldiers who stood on the runway, wiping their running noses.

'You like it here?' I asked Igor, a second lieutenant.

'We are happy to be here. We wouldn't come otherwise.'

'You have a choice?'

'We can put in a request. But we are proud to be here. This frontier is sacred to Russia. It's our duty to defend it.'

'Sacred!' I thought, taking another good look at Lavrentiya. 'Are you joking?' It looked like leftovers, bits of something no one else wanted. And always lying in wait behind, that relentless, disquieting tundra, military aerials sprouting from the ground instead of trees. Maybe it hadn't failed Russia, but Russia had definitely failed it.

'Would you prefer a posting in Chechnya?' I asked. It wasn't such a stupid question, given our surroundings. He was ready to fight for Lavrentiya, official population now down to 1,333, and still decreasing.

'The war? Of course not. But if asked, it would be an honour to go.'

'An honour to go.' I stared at him, wanting to understand. Let me underline how remarkable this young officer was: I'd had to slip a $100 bill to the Russian mafia just to get my cameras from the airport to my hotel in Moscow; half the Russian officials I'd dealt with so far smelt of alcohol; and in Red Square a soldier of Igor's age with no legs and with no pension worth speaking of had been moved on by the police for begging from us, although all he'd said to me was one word: 'Afghanistan.' Now here was Igor, a twenty-five-year-old prepared if necessary to fight and maybe die to defend Lavrentiya.

'Could you tell me what you know about the ice in winter, out there in the Strait?' I asked.

'The ice?' Igor said. He turned to Ivan. 'He wants a description of the ice?'

Ivan smiled sympathetically, while Igor began summoning up images of the ice moving about, packing tight, swirling, spinning and undoing. 'You can hear it sometimes,' he said, and I imagined a groan. The Bering Strait that the officer described was a nasty, actively malignant destination even in summer, where storms could whip up the waves or fogs descend and seem to flatten the sea as if with a silent, still hand. 'Believe me, you do *not* want to go out there, if that's what you are thinking.' He turned to Ivan. 'Does he understand any of this? Tell him.'

Ivan told me, and then we went to the administration block to find out more about those who still herded reindeer or worked the waters for fish, seals, whales and walruses. In a little room labelled 'Agricultural Department', there were two Chukchis, one called Sergei, who immediately disappeared on an errand, and another who blinked a lot and called himself Vladimir. He wore huge thick glasses with weighty Soviet frames that covered his face like a mask. He was stabbing his wide seaman's forefingers at a computer keyboard, whacking out Russian in a very large font. His focal length appeared to be ten centimetres, because that was the distance of his eyes from the screen, even with the spectacles.

'If you really want everyone's opinion about the ice, the best chance is to stay until September,' Vladimir said, getting to his feet. 'There's a native assembly coming up.' He tweaked the geraniums eking out an existence in an old milk pot.

'How often do they meet?' asked Ivan.

'It's the second time ever.' With one finger Vladimir pressed his thick spectacles to his face. Heavily, the lenses rose a short way up his nose. 'We've got to decide what to do.'

'He means about the winter,' I thought. The people of Chukotka were bracing themselves for the coming season, just like me.

'Each year it's worse. We've been forgotten by Moscow.'

Vladimir followed us out into the corridor. Beside us stood an orange tree, the first tree I had seen. It was flourishing, benefiting from the Mediterranean climate the Russians have given the natives in exchange for the tundra – as long as they stay indoors. To the Chukchis living out in their skin tents long ago, the Russian settlements, with their steaming, dripping pipes lacing the houses, circulating energy from the coal boiler at the heart of the system, must have seemed like the handiwork of people who held the future of both nature and man in their hands.

Sergei, the second Chukchi, arrived back. '*Presente!*' he exclaimed. He handed over two onions. He hadn't been on an errand; he had gone off to fetch us a gift. That simple act, the giving of two home-grown onions, was as profound as anything I had seen here. I was being handed a rare bit of cultivated life, a hatchling nurtured in spite of a hostile world. This moved me. It was as if I had been lost in the Sahara and a passing Tuareg had jumped down from his camel to hand me a leathern bottle of water.

Later, Ivan and I went to the local museum – to be honest, not expecting much. Lavrentiya was still recovering from last winter, and on our way we were sidestepping mud, shattered panes and tiles yanked away by forces that would be back again soon. Ducking inside the building, we found ourselves face to face with the owner.

'A FOREIGNER!' she cried out to Ivan. 'AND HE'S VISITING!'

Her name was Valentia, and she guided us round in an almost inexcusably loud voice, as if she was still outside in the wind. 'LOOK AROUND!' she bellowed, then stopped me to proclaim how she had built up the museum over five years. 'WHY DO IT? FOR THE SAKE OF ALL THESE GREAT PEOPLE OF THE TUNDRA!' She pointed out her treasures: her mammoth skull, her Eskimo and Chukchi bone carvings with their little slots for accommodating daily offerings; scrapers and other domestic implements; a drum skin fashioned from the lining of a walrus stomach; a windcheater of walrus intestines; harpoons with detachable heads whose design was still employed today. I ran my thumb over a hollow sepia bone; I lifted it up and smelt it; I tapped and listened, hoping to catch sight or sound of the lives that had bequeathed us these relics. And where were the master spirits who governed these lives, the Chukchi's all-seeing raven who patrolled the skies, the killer whale who surveyed the seas? What of

The Chukchi: A Potted History

The reindeer-herding ancestors of the Chukchi, Koryak and Even arrived in the region after the Eskimo and probably in the first or second century AD.

The Russian term 'Chukchi' comes from the Chukchi word '*Chauchu*', meaning 'rich in reindeer', which was formerly used by Chukchis to distinguish themselves from the Anquallyt, 'sea people', those of their population who had settled on the coast to exploit the sea's rich resources. The Strait is a major transit route both for migrating birds and sea mammals: the bowhead or Greenland whale, grey whale, seals – including the bearded, common, ringed and ribbon seal – and also the Pacific walrus.

The predominant present-day indigenous people of the region, the Chukchis call themselves *Lyg'oravetl'an* – 'real people' – and are closely related linguistically and ethnically to the Koryaks of northern Kamchatka. Their origin is unclear, but they are presumed to be from present-day Mongolia or China. As they advanced, the Eskimos were left with only a tiny fringe of land along the Bering seacoast, Chukchi coastal communities developing fast once they had adopted the Eskimos' specialized sea-hunting technology (see p. 35). As well as devising the leather open boat, the angyapik, the Eskimos had developed the kayak, or closed leather canoe, and a new piece of technology, the harpoon toggle, which enabled them to hunt whales.

However, it was only with the arrival of the gun from Europe that food became plentiful for both Eskimos and Chukchis, and dog teams expanded from half a dozen to a dozen or more. Captain Cook was among those who recorded that dogs were being eaten by the Chukchis: 'Several lay dead about them that had been killed that morning.'

The Chukchis of the tundra practised reindeer pastoralism; this was documented when the Russian Cossacks first encountered the Chukchis in 1641. Dezhnev, the Russian explorer, reached Chukotka by ship in 1648. Steadily increasing incursions from Russia led to increased hostility from the Chukchis, less cultural interchange and the Chukchis becoming more isolated. When the Cossacks withdrew, the Chukchis expanded their territory, and although they withstood Russian attempts at subjugation into the nineteenth century, Russian trappers and hunters did manage to make inroads into Chukchi territory, bringing with them trading opportunities with Alaska – and also influenza, small pox and alcoholism. There was an influx of traders and trappers too, notably from the Hudson's Bay Company, to the east in Canada. The wild reindeer, once widespread, has now given way to the domesticated animal and is all but extinct.

The Russian government annexed the peninsula in 1789, but by then they'd long since abandoned the idea of direct rule. In 1837, the government more or less gave up with these people, signing a treaty giving the Chukchis independence within the Russian empire.

The arrival of commercial whalers in the mid-nineteenth century had a severe impact on the whaling settlements and, in 1905, the completion of the trans-Siberian railway brought further outside control. However, it was the Bolshevik Revolution of 1917 that brought about wholesale social change. In 1924, a Committee of Assistance of Peoples of the North was set up, and from 1929 reindeer herds were forcibly collectivized and the Chukchis' traditional patterns of nomadism eroded by the establishment of settlements providing education programmes, hospitals and the accompanying communist ideology. Now, party officials were overseeing each Chukchi village to ensure compliance with the Soviet modernization programme. The *kulaks* or village heads, often the best dog breeders – having a large dog team was a matter of great prestige – were weeded out, with the shamans, to encourage the disintegration of Chukchi culture.

From the 1940s, the Soviets began to introduce large-scale industrial projects, bringing with them ethnic Russians, Ukrainians, Estonians and others. Reindeer herds declined and many herders settled in coastal villages, where the minority Eskimo population, the Yupik, were often forcibly moved, and many took jobs in the oil, coal and manufacturing industries. By the 1980s, the indigenous population was a mere 10 per cent of the total. In 1991, with the fall of the Soviet Union, the Chukchi joined twenty-five other native Siberian peoples to form the Association of the Peoples of the North; the region devolved to become the Chukotka Autonomous Region, subject to the Russian Federation.

After the Cold War, an American–Soviet agreement signed in 1989 allowed visa-free access across the Bering Strait. While this has brought welcome trade opportunities to the Chukchis, it is of more significance to the Yupik, who may again visit relatives on the other side of the Strait and possibly seek political alliances with the larger Inuit community in Alaska, Canada and Greenland.

the Eskimo shamans who journeyed to higher and lower worlds and negotiated for the sick or asked spirits to pacify the forces of the seas and winds? What of the ancestors who could be summoned by the lonely and who offered a guiding hand to children in fear?

I hoped to understand better what anthropologist Hugh Brody meant when he said that Eskimo parents were inclined to trust their young to know what they needed, respecting the 'elder who lives in the core of the child'. But here there was no sign of the respected elder – or the shaman who might journey protected by his cloak of amulets to do battle with the demons of invisible worlds. Once, the overlapping peoples of the tundra believed in a cosmos inhabited by spirits of the wind, sea and stone, a universe of physical and spiritual dimensions intertwined; now this cosmos lay shattered about me. There remained just these few fragments assembled by a Russian called Valentia. 'ON TO THE NEXT ROOM!' she yelled as she led the way.

By the end of the tour I wanted to start again – not to look at old bones polished by the caring fingers of the Chukchis or a mammoth's skull the size of an armchair but to hear Valentia. She loved the tundra for the occasional glimpse of beauty it presented to her. She was another of those remarkable people who helped remind me why I was here.

Then a delegation in uniform thumped at the door. I recognized the officer in charge: Igor. 'Sir,' he said, with a formality lacking on our encounter on the runway, 'an order has come from high command that there is a military manoeuvre and no foreigner can venture out.' He turned to Ivan. 'Does he understand?'

The Eskimo

The sea people in Chukotka referred to as Eskimos, but elsewhere increasingly as Inuit, originated in East Asia and belonged to the last wave of peoples to migrate across the Bering Strait from the Chukchi Peninsula. The Eskimos followed in the steps of the penultimate people to cross the waters, the Athabaskans, who were forest-dwelling hunter-gatherers and fishermen whose dogs were used not to pull sledges but to carry pouches. Although hardly evident now in the Siberian Arctic, where the Chukchis came to dominate, the Eskimos spread from western Alaska through to Canada and Greenland, becoming one of the most widely dispersed indigenous peoples in the world.

The word 'Eskimo' is possibly derived from a native word meaning 'Eaters of raw meat' or a word related to snowshoes; however, the few remaining Eskimos in Siberia (in time relocated by the Soviets to just two settlements, Novoye Chaplino and Sireniki) call themselves Yupigyt or Yupik, meaning 'authentic people'. They belong to the same language group as those Eskimos on St Lawrence Island and the Seward Peninsula on the other side of the Strait.

The origins of the Eskimos are only now, with DNA analysis, becoming clear. It is likely that proto-Eskimos subsisted as reindeer hunters in the Chukchi Peninsula before expanding – alongside ancestors of the Aleuts – in a third and final phase of human migration to the Americas between 4,000 and 5,000 years ago. These two related peoples became the first to populate the Arctic coast of the New World, their spread across the Strait made possible by the retreat of the last North American glaciers but also by key advances in sea-hunting technology.

Elements of what we define as their culture – skin-covered kayaks, specialized harpoons for seal, walrus and later whale – emerged on the Bering Sea at this time. Their descendants, including the Siberian remnants of the population, the Yupik, did not keep deer; meat and fat from fish and sea mammals provided nearly all their sustenance and were supplemented by seaweed and berries in summer. Their sea-hunting culture was based on the bone- or stone-tipped harpoon (tied to a seal-skin float), club and spears; whale-bone clappers were slapped on the water to imitate killer whales and drive the seals to land.

Summer dwellings were rectangular tents constructed from walrus skins laid over a frame of whale bones and wood poles that sloped down to the rear wall; they were anchored with bones and rocks and had seal-skin windows. The winter home was the *nynglyu* ('igloo'), a semi-subterranean ice dugout or a construction covered in earthen sods. There were no snow igloos, unlike other Eskimo groups; their dogs were kept only for limited sledge hauling. The Eskimos traded with Chukchis, providing them with fish and seal skin (waterproof but brittle if not wet); the Chukchis provided reindeer skins for jackets, hoods, etc.

The Yupik were composed of patriarchal clans. Boat crews tended to be men from the same clan or lineage; marriage partners had to be from a different clan. Each clan had a unique myth concerning its origin, and clan members were buried in the same place. Products of the hunt and foraging were shared equally.

We both nodded. Igor shrugged rather apologetically and turned away. His platoon shuffled off behind him.

'THERE'S NO MILITARY MANOEUVRE,' Valentia exclaimed.

'They don't trust us to go off down the road to Lorino, where Gena lives,' Ivan said. 'I'll see if I can get him to come here.'

Valentia didn't want us to leave. She was flicking through her photo collection. 'HERE IS NIKOLAI,' she cried. 'A DOG TRAINER. THE VERY BEST.'

I looked at him. 'Rather a stern face,' I thought. 'Very controlled, very exacting. On top of things.'

'DEAD,' Valentia said.

Ivan said, 'She says this guy's dogs suddenly bolted after a sable. They went over a cliff. They all died. Every one of them.'

'Must have got overexcited . . .' I said. 'The dogs.'

'THAT'S WHAT CHUKOTKA DOGS ARE LIKE . . .' Valentia bawled. 'IT'S THEIR STRONG BLOOD. CAN'T STOP THEMSELVES.'

I discovered more about the Chukotka dog's inability to stop itself that evening, when I met my first one. Just a puppy, it had ransacked our accommodation. Sergei, our fixer, had bought the pup from a stranger.

'It's a *presente*,' he said. 'My friend will love it.'

'Are you sure?' I said. It had broken out of Sergei's shoulder bag and was working on breaking out of the room. Everything seemed to have been destroyed or spoiled, and the whole room reeked of oily faeces, which it had scattered liberally under the beds.

'Don't know what I'll feed it on when we run out of walrus,' said Sergei, referring to the meat he'd been given along with the dog. We turned to examine it, but the pile had gone.

'My friend's a Canadian,' Sergei said. 'It's a surprise.'

'It will be,' I wrote in my diary later. 'At night the pup shows no distress at being removed from its mother, as a normal puppy might. It is playful, as you'd expect, but independent and defiant, even as a newborn.'

The next day, Gena arrived from Lorino, along with the other Chukchi he thought might be right for the job. Gena – full name Gennadi Inankuejas – had an easy manner and a face filled with silver teeth. 'Perhaps a little smooth, perhaps not,' I thought. It was my job to work out the motives, as well as the capabilities, of this guide into whose hands I would place my life.

Tagging behind was Alexei Ottoi, who was quiet, thin and someone whom I instinctively felt I might trust. I could see two things immediately: that he was a listener, altogether less showy and vibrant than Gena, but also that he had had little sleep lately. His eyes looked grey and haunted: he was wrung out.

Gena noticed me looking at Alexei as I weighed up whether he'd been on the booze. 'We didn't go to bed last night,' he explained. 'We were out whaling.'

First, I got Ivan to quiz Gena about crossing the Strait. He nodded steadily as he listened to the plan, his lips gathered slightly, a hint of a smile at the very notion of it.

'Dangerous,' he commented, 'though the ice might hold in a very cold winter.' I pictured the thin mantle lying over the sea, capping the troubled waters below. He motioned to me how the ice was in a normal year, slowly shifting his hand sideways through the air to indicate not one sheet but innumerable plates sliding. In this, as in his speech, he was very deliberate, his words balanced, full of thought and careful rhythm. 'If you get a storm, though, and a lot of luck, yes, it is possible.' In this context, I understood, a storm was good. You'd need winds to bunch up the floating ice and a snap of cold to encourage 'new ice' to spread over any water – a continuous sheet that might last a day.

I began to realize he was speaking slowly not only to be precise but because he wanted to communicate directly with me, not through a translator. He was trying to include me. This was good: he'd be a leader but also a team player.

'This fresh ice is not a solid thing: it bends as you travel along, and you ride it like a wave, water rising up underneath you.'

'Wouldn't it be a good idea to take a boat, in case you have to cross a gap in the ice?'

'Of course you take a boat!' Gena looked at me, assessing this ignorance I'd suddenly betrayed. 'It would be madness without,' he said slowly, his eyes now sharp, measuring me, weighing me up just as I had been measuring and weighing him. 'We take boats everywhere. They're light, made out of seal skin. They sit across the back of the sledge, like this,' and he did a neat sketch. Not the spidery, Palaeolithic scribble that his great-grandfather might have managed but the product of someone schooled by my kind – 'educated', we'd say. Indeed, my guess was that he was a top pupil; he had an architect's precise, quick eye for form. 'Stops the sledge from sinking,' he concluded.

I studied Gena as he jotted numbers across the paper, quickly calculating dates and supplies. I'd hoped to learn from Chukchi culture, but finding this Chukchi so well educated by Russians was, I suddenly found, enormously encouraging. He knew and had worked the sea and ice, but that experience he framed and articulated as a westerner. His claims couldn't be dismissed readily by outsiders, people like Raityrgin or respected polar scientists like Professor Wadhams who amassed piles of data on their seas.

He outlined two possible routes: a northern one, where the gap was narrowest, up towards Uelen; and a southern route, just south of the two Diomede Islands. The latter was the one I should go for.

'The one not chosen by Dmitry Shparo,' I thought. Did Gena *really* know what he was doing? Maybe this was all just bravado.

'The important thing is not to get wet. For the dogs it's not important – their fur dries out quickly. But for humans, it's very dangerous.'

'That word "dangerous" again,' I thought. 'Second time he's used it.'

He said the ideal crossing time would be around 25 March.

'It sounds very late to me,' I said.

Gena was smiling. 'Most people would say it's ridiculously early.'

But it was Alexei I wanted to listen to now. I needed to hear from someone else that it was all right out there. I'd been watching him as Gena carried out his calculations. He had unflinching bird-like eyes, creased white skin encircling them as it does those of a macaw. A dry face, wrinkles spreading like dusty Martian streams over his cheeks. A scar ran like a further rivulet down the side of his long nose; smaller scars caused by hooks and gutting knives criss-crossed his fingers. I pondered on those fisherman's scars and at the incidents that had brought them about in a man who last night had been in an open boat, harpooning whales by hand. Surely Alexei was strong enough not to be swayed by the smooth power that spread through the room from Gena.

'Alexei, how far out have you been?' I asked. Ivan translated.

'Not as far as you want to go!'

His was a strangely low-pitched, husky voice for such a narrow frame. He told me he himself had dogs and that there were now sixty teams in Lorino, a number that was growing all the time. 'Again,' I thought, 'you get the feeling these people are building themselves up for the coming onslaught, storing, recruiting help from wherever they can, which is no longer the Soviet Union but instead their own tattered past.'

Alexei interrupted my thoughts. 'Have you had experience of the north?' We all knew what he meant: living in a place where you might die if, for example, your stove broke.

Both men looked reassured when I said I'd stayed out in minus twenty-five degrees – and not with westerners but with Kazak herders.

'Herders?'

'Reindeer herders, perhaps,' Alexei said to Gena. 'Ordinary, honest people like us.'

In this comment I thought I detected a distrust of outsiders, a distaste even. Distaste for the way you and I think, the way we act, the way we shape other, smaller people's lives.

'The wind here,' Gena said, 'that's the issue. There's wind from the north, wind from the south.'

'Colder than the Pole,' Alexei murmered.

I said that I'd been told that, ten or so years ago, winds were northerly but now they were from the south, which meant less ice in the Bering Strait because winds pushed it up, wasn't that right?

They shrugged. It didn't matter what the cause was.

'You *will* be coming?' said Gena abruptly. 'Definitely? We need to begin preparing the dog meat.'

'Harpoon some walruses,' Alexei said quietly. 'They are out along the beaches now. Need to take a few.'

It was against my instincts to choose a guide so quickly. I took weeks or months choosing companions to cross rainforests and deserts – and those particular environments I knew about. I knew nothing of the tundra. I thanked the men and acknowledged that we'd need to arrange for them to plant depots of raw walrus in the settlements along the coast between Anadyr and up here at the Bering Strait. But I was saved from committing myself right then because the door swung open and Sergei burst in.

'Good news!' he announced breathlessly. 'There's a man here from Dmitry Shparo's expedition.'

Gena looked unenthusiastic.

Sergei looked from Ivan to me and back again. 'Shparo's a Hero of the Soviet Union!'

A smile passed slowly and relentlessly across Gena's face. He was out in the Bering Strait much of the year. No one called him a hero, and nor was he asking to be. But it can't have been easy sitting there listening to Sergei get excited about Shparo. The poor old Chukchis, they seemed to owe the Russians everything. They were educated by Russians, lived in Russian houses, ate Russian food. The Russians even documented their past for them, because they'd lost their history when their shamans were eliminated. Did they have a folk costume, hanging on the back of a door somewhere? If so, the needle it was sewn with was brought to them by the Russians. Even the nail it hung from came from the Russians. And the bitterness of it all was that these Russians who'd given them liberty from the tundra had also detached them from it. The Chukchis had lost all that gave them their independence – and they were expected to be grateful.

Sergei was still standing there, waiting for my enthusiastic response. But I was busy observing this clash of two worlds that was occurring right in front of me: settled man versus the nomad, the cultivator versus the pastoralist and hunter-gatherer; between our individualist culture that placed emphasis on 'rational', proven facts and a culture that valued a passed down, collective lore and trusted to the spirits and some unspoken age-old understanding: the voices in the wind, the smell of the ice, the tug of the currents, the taste of the salt.

No one had spoken yet.

'He's not,' Gena said slowly, into the silence, 'a Hero of the Soviet Union. He just has the Order of Lenin.'

Sergei was taken aback, but only for a second. 'Well, he also has the very much coveted Order of the Red Banner of Labour.'

This sentence didn't seem to have the desired effect; it produced yet more weighty silence.

'Benedict, he can tell you *everything*,' Sergei suddenly blurted out.

Alexei coughed. 'And then you can be rescued by helicopter, just like him,' he muttered.

VIII

One meeting had been around a table, drinking tea with men who'd been out stalking whales at dawn. The next was with a man in combat gear, standing in front of a map marked with a strange, thick black line that extended from Moscow all the way across Asia to Anadyr, as if it was a lifeline thrown into the abyss.

Sergei Yapishka had all the swagger of a young army captain but (and there was something disturbing about this) also a geekish quality, made manifest by his rose-tinted glasses and the three or four hairs sprouting unplucked from his chin. He began by cataloguing Shparo's attempts, which began back in 1996 and ended with the crossing in 1998 with his son Matvey. Yapishka had coordinated the expedition from the Russian side. '*Every* element of the operation was coordinated,' he said triumphantly. He even had someone standing by the rescue helicopter to make sure the pilot didn't run it early, clocking up extra flying time to earn more cash.

I told him what I'd garnered so far from the Chukchis.

'If you try on 25 March , you'll just get drowned,' he said flatly.

'These people should know, if anyone does,' I said, feeling the Chukchis deserved to have someone stand up for them.

'My faith is in facts,' he said. 'The natives claim their grandfathers crossed over on the ice. Bullshit. They never crossed. It's fantasy.' He pointed at the map with a hunting knife.

Ivan turned to me and said in English, 'I hate it, the way they talk.'

'They?'

'These modern "explorers". They know shit about what it's like out there. What about the little guys and their huskies?'

Ivan did this sometimes, suddenly revealing an angrier vein that apparently ran through him. God knows, no one welcomes conversation with the arrogant, but Ivan – from whom charm issued forth so easily – would occasionally take me by surprise, confronting people who, he felt, went about spoiling things. And quite right too, but so much rage so quickly, and always on behalf of what he called the harmless, 'natural' people, would set me pondering on what else lay beneath the skin of this sweet, sheltered, urban, beetle-like man with formidable powers of persuasion. Perhaps he was just one more town kid who sentimentalized the countryside, or perhaps one of those tender, soft-hearted individuals who need more beauty in the world than the rest of us. Whatever it was, he seemed to take it very personally when he saw the innocent quashed, the wings of lovely creatures broken. It mattered not whether he was able to measure the value of such a loss: all his geniality would be gone and he would kick out.

'I know, I know,' I said, 'but let's see.' I turned back to Yapishka, and Ivan dutifully masked his frustration and translated as his job required.

'These people put their lives on the line daily,' I said. 'These few like Gena who still have dogs, they breathe, taste and smell this environment every day.' I was defending people I didn't know, but I felt it was unkind to ride roughshod over local sentiments, right or wrong. Also, it was unwise: Gena was probably a good man, but if not, he was still one of the few people capable of rescuing you when your helicopter fell to bits.

Yapishka was playing with his knife, smoothing his fingers down the blade. 'I've flown over there,' he said, 'seen the ice for myself. Everywhere mid-Strait is impossible.'

'The locals say . . .'

'I accept the locals can go quite far with their tricks. And there's a 70 per cent possibility if you go the northern route, although you can never tell.'

He meant there was a 70 per cent chance if you floated over on a chunk of ice, accompanied by technology like Shparo. But that wasn't what I was here to do. I had come to learn from the Arctic, not from home. And that meant launching out alone into it with dogs.

Yapishka was still talking. 'First, your support team will have to be based here in Lavrentiya with the choppers – with plenty of benzine.'

'I won't have a support team,' I said. But it was no use.

'Second, you need a lot of food, in case you get stuck. And keep it light, so you don't sink. Dmitry calculated eleven days – and was on the ice for twenty. Third, careful of bears. Dmitry met a lot, but they weren't hungry. Fourth, once you are over the borderline, you have to rely on US rescue. The Russians can't cross. So you need someone in Alaska to coordinate this. And when you are being rescued, you have to be on one side or the other of the border zone.'

There was more – much, much more – concluding with what Yapishka announced was the key to success: taking 'a satellite phone WITH FAX FEATURES'. Dmitry actually took two satellite phones, Yapishka confided, 'and they gave him info from Russia, Japan, Alaska, etc.', he said. 'That's the way he conquered the Bering Strait,' he ended proudly, but it seemed to me that Shparo had been conquered before he left Moscow.

Exploration of the Strait

Danish navigator Vitus Bering (1681–1741) sailed in the service of the Russian navy, in a sense discovering America for Europe by going *east* in the same way that Columbus did going west. Peter the Great commissioned him to investigate the American coast and see as to the feasibility of a Northeast Passage (i.e. north of the Eurasian continent) to China. He's often credited with discovering Alaska and that the American continent was not connected to Russia. (Actually, in the same way Columbus was repeating the discovery by Vikings, Bering was duplicating much of the work of Semyon Dezhnev [c. 1605–73], a Russian navigator who in 1648 for the first time traced the north-easternmost shores of the Eurasian continent, sailing through the Bering Strait and establishing that the American continent was not part of the same land mass. However, his report lay buried until the eighteenth century.) Bering travelled overland through Siberia, constructed ships in Kamchatka, and in 1728 explored the far eastern coast of Siberia, encountering the two islands in the Strait on St Diomede's day and naming them accordingly. On a return expedition with two ships (and accompanied by the naturalist Georg Wilhelm Steller) he sighted America in the summer of 1741; however, Bering's ship was caught by a storm and wrecked on the island later named after him. Racked by scurvy, he died (with nineteen of his crew) while forced to overwinter in a shelter made of driftwood. A few survivors made a boat from the wreckage of their ship, the *St Peter*, and in

August 1742 reached Kamchatka to relate their story of the discovery of Alaska.

In the summer of 1778, James Cook explored the Bering Strait with the ships *Discovery* and *Resolution* while charged by George III to seek the Northwest Passage. Making use of the Danish navigator's maps, and a more accurate chronometer, he traced much of Alaska's coast, naming Prince William Sound and on the Eurasian side noting, among other things, that the Chukchis by now had iron for their spears and blue trade beads from the Russians. He rounded the Chukchi Peninsula, before being forced back by ice.

I went for a walk with Ivan in the wind, an exhausting wind that came from the four quarters in turn.

Ivan couldn't hold back his feelings any longer. 'Arrogant shit,' he said.

I could see Ivan's point of view, but for all the high-handed talk and intrusive gadgets, I had also been shaken by the Russian's systematic analysis of the 'facts'. Perhaps the Chukchis were indeed being overly optimistic; perhaps they spoke out of wounded pride. Even the few skills that we invaders had left them with were dismissed nowadays.

'Well, Shparo is a professional and has achieved great feats. And even his sidekick can't be dismissed out of hand.'

'These f**king adventurers from Moscow with their satellite phones and helicopters talk as if they know everything. You must forget them and trust the Chukchis.'

'Not so fast,' I thought. True, I'd come here to learn from indigenous people, but all the weight of outside opinion (not to mention scientific evidence) was against them. It was infuriating, but strategizing was what we westerners did best; our watchword was advancement. To us, challenging the elements was good.

Ivan knows I'm torn. 'Why are you worrying?' he says as we walk.

He wants me to be on the side of the 'little guys', because Ivan is a nice enough chap and he feels for downtrodden characters like Gena and Alexei. 'And why else?' I wonder, adding up the bare facts. I sense Ivan's had a tough upbringing: he's hinted at children left behind, a wife and conscription into the brutal ranks of the Soviet army. It's left him with a resentment of authority; he has a suspicion of those who he thinks want to be seen as heroic (which might, I note to myself, make me a possible target if I do end up pressing on into the Bering Strait alone). The result? He sides with the Chukchis, about whom he knows nothing but who've lost everything to the outside world except a few dogs.

'Have faith,' Ivan prompts me. 'Take a risk with their huskies.'

Ivan stands waiting, wondering if I will nod my head and take on this adventure or whether I will shake my head and suggest that we go back to our homes in St Petersburg and London and forget the whole idea.

I'm tempted to commit myself to the Chukchis' assessment of the Bering Strait right there and then. Of course I am: I want more than anything to be with my own dogs out there on the brink, watching the ice, saying goodbye to Gena, hoping the elements will be kind to me. It's what I've come to do. And as it happens, I'm a bit like Ivan: I'm inclined to rail against people and organizations who try to push me about; I have a tendency to side with the 'little guys'.

But I hesitate. It's not unreasonable, I tell myself. The decision I make now may determine whether I'll be alive next summer. You'll think I'm exaggerating – and Ivan no doubt thought the same. 'He assumes I'll abandon my plan at the last minute if it seems dangerous,' I think to myself. 'He takes me for an easy-going, *laissez-faire* type of person, which is how I come across. But at times a maddeningly stubborn voice takes hold of me, driving me on and often landing me in trouble. Besides, I also happen to have experience of living alone months at a time with indigenous peoples of all sorts and I suspect that, however brave Gena is, not one Chukchi or Eskimo would have thought to head out alone on the ice with dogs, as I propose to do. 'Well, Ivan, you know that's the way I prefer to do my trips. No fancy stuff from home, no satellite phone . . .'

But we both know I'm stalling, buying time.

As we stand there in the wind, a thought floats into my mind: a zoologist told me that a bunch of stray reindeer turned up in Siberia not long ago – and they'd been tagged by Alaskans! They'd crossed the Strait, heaven knows how. I'd been encouraged when I heard this, but right now this story seemed to carry more weight than any fact produced by Yapishka. Those reindeer had made the crossing, and without the help of a single machine with fax facilities. Suddenly, I feel ashamed of my lack of faith in the Chukchi dogs and their masters, who surely must be more capable than an instinct-geared quadruped like a deer. So I nod my head and say yes, of course we should have faith in the Chukchis and not those Russians and others like me from the outside. And with that, I was committed.

Ivan nodded, watching me to see if I meant it, and, satisfied, smiled to himself as he turned and began walking away.

'Thank God for you, Ivan,' I thought. 'Quietly there in support, always charming everyone with your huge stock of magnetism. It can't be easy at times – you hiding all that strange inner fury, and me with my stupid schemes. What would I do without you?'

'Let's go and look at some huskies,' he said.

IX

We made our way to the end of the settlement, where the hills with their bristling antennae crept down to the crumpled wooden shacks by the sea. Along the shore lay scattered cabins and the rusty hulks of broken whaling boats with split seal-skin hulls and old metal vessels now offering daytime accommodation. And here, among the coils of rope, fish odours, scrap and oily timbers, at the foot of a home cut out of a discarded giant cylinder of iron, were clusters of sledge dogs. Silent, stationary, coats parted by the wind, there they were, domestic creatures of the ice, spread about the shallow slope.

They were in the midst of losing their winter coat, but under all the loose tufts of hair I could see they only had the build of a sturdy sort of border collie. With big feet and patterned variously black and brown, they were just as described by William Hooper, who was on-board a vessel up here searching for survivors of John Franklin's final expedition: small, long-haired, wiry, in 'many points resembling both the wolf and the fox'.

Waylaid While Searching for Franklin

After Cook, one of the next witnesses to the coastal Chukchi was Lieutenant William Hooper, aboard the *Plover*, a ship sent to find John Franklin, who had set out in the spring of 1845 'and of which no tidings had been received'.

Following the disappearance of the Franklin expedition – which turned out to be the death of him – it was determined that three expeditions should be sent out early in 1848 to 'different quarters of the frozen sea, for the purpose of seeking, and if necessary, relieving the missing voyagers'. Sir James Ross was dispatched to follow the expedition's route and investigate the Davis Strait; Sir John Richardson, who had accompanied Franklin on his overland expeditions, headed overland with Dr Rae into northern America; and a third expedition was composed of two ships, the *Herald* under Captain Kellett and HMS *Plover* under Commander Moore. Hooper describes how the *Plover* finally ventured into the Strait, having sailed down past South America, visited the Falklands, rounded Cape Horn and then journeyed up to northern climes; headwinds and strong currents drew them across the Bering Strait to where few had been since Cook (see Exploration of the Strait, pp. 43–4).

By the time the ship arrived to determine whether Franklin had safely emerged at the Bering Strait, it was getting towards late 1848. There was still no sign of Franklin, but 'after considerable running to and fro', narrates Lt Hooper, the Chukchis launched four boats – a 'people of whom less is known than any on the face of the habitable globe (if we except, perhaps, some of the tribes in the interior of Africa) . . . We had at first considerable doubts as to the sex of our visitants; all were clad in loose hooded overshirts of skin, to keep them dry, and being destitute of beards, might well be mistaken for the tender sex.' Using sign language, though, they got on to a good footing. A fiddle was produced for the Chukchis' amusement, 'and in return we were regaled by the monotonous beating of a species of drum . . .' Soon, on 25 October, the decision was made to overwinter.

The Chukchis proved amiable and honest, though they were confused when they visited on a Sunday to be told that bartering that day was prohibited: 'one day in seven was set aside for rest and relaxation'. The visitors were invited to their *yarangas*, the Chukchis' dome-shaped tents of walrus and reindeer skin. At one gathering, the British sailors showed off the power of their magnet, causing needles to dance to music and throwing 'the natives into amazement at our superior mode of conjuring'. More villagers crowded in. A native then took his turn, 'seating himself in the space before us, performed a number of fantastic contortions of face and figure', and all to the sound of one of those 'deafening and large' drums of theirs.

As for the dogs, some 'favoured few' of the Chukchis, Hooper noted, had big fast dogs imported from the Russians – these were conceivably the 'rather large' dogs that Cook described – 'but the native dogs will outlive cold and hunger'.

The dogs look up at us and some step forward to the limit of their chains. But they remain quiet. These animals instinctively safeguard their energy; you can see it burning only in the lustre in their eyes, some of which are a ghostly sapphire blue. These eyes are alert, watchful. But the dogs are patient, very patient. They are waiting for their master to return or perhaps for the return of the ice.

Ivan bends to talk to the dogs. I'm wondering if petting these working animals is such a good idea, but each dog he greets licks his hand. I squat down to talk to a dog whose black coat has the blue sheen of a crow. 'So,' I say aloud, 'creatures just like you will be my only ally out here.' The dog nuzzles my hand. 'Just as you are the only ally the Chukchis have left.'

A man strode up. He introduced himself as a Russian by the name of Evgeni. His hands were large and heavy, but the skin was dry and flaky, as if like a snake he was about to shed it. 'Admiring my dog food?' he said. He was referring to the mound of whale fat in a wood pen. 'Better if it sits a while. Has more vitamins.'

'Right,' I said, though I was a little doubtful.

'Know how I know that?'

'Nope.'

'Nor do I! No one does. We ask the Chukchis, and they think back and see if they can remember from the old days. They've grown soft, most of them – the Chukchis, I mean. Got used to heated homes. Forgotten too much. And you know the funniest thing? Now even we Russians are rounding up strays to see if they will fit into dog teams. Can you imagine? Grabbing the pets richer families abandoned when they left.'

'Is that so,' I said. 'Times do seem bad.'

'And getting worse. People see no future. They are looking back, way, way back. To before we arrived here. What's more, the Russians are becoming hunter-gatherers now – hey, just look at me!' He waved at the dogs. The dogs' eyes followed his thick, dry hands.

There was no sense of shame. I could see Evgeni respected the Chukchis; it was just regrettable that for all of them things had come to this.

'Tell me about your dogs,' I said.

He said that all his males had been castrated, except one. 'The other dogs don't like him.'

'What? Because he hasn't been castrated? It's envy?'

'That's exactly what it is. They'd fight him, given the chance.'

He'd chosen this male to breed from because of his long legs and gentle temperament. 'It's disastrous if you turn up at someone's house and your dogs argue with theirs. Always been that way.'

'The reason why Ivan hadn't been bitten,' I thought.

'You use females?'

'The females are not as strong but have stamina – more than the males. Some dogs are good for going uphill, others are stronger on the flat. I have to balance the team. The youngest members are two years old – only just old enough.' He waved those hands of his at an older dog that was sitting chained to a post by herself. 'Nine years old,' he said to her, 'aren't you?' She pricked her ears and gave a thump of her tail. 'She still likes to run along with the young when the teams set off. But she's happy to be retired. We use her for light jobs.' He passed a hand forcefully over her head. 'Why don't you come hunt with me in the winter, if you're here?' Was he talking to the dog or me? I wondered. The dogs were looking at Evgeni: they'd recognized the word 'охотиться' ('hunt'). 'We'll go out on to the ice with the dogs, nab some seals.'

'Ah, but I'll have my own team. I'm hoping to cross the Bering Strait.'

'Interesting!' Evgeni looked at me anew, his eyes watery now in the wind.

'He's wondering if I'm up to it,' I thought. He asked Ivan something I couldn't understand and smiled politely at the answer. Meanwhile, the dogs were still looking to Evgeni, still waiting, hoping that there was going to be a hunt right now, even in the summer. In that gaze of the dogs, all twelve of them looking into the eyes of their master, I saw what a task I had ahead of me. I would not only have to learn to trust a team of dogs but they would have to trust me, even to the point of forgetting the man who had raised and trained them.

I must have looked a bit pensive because, as we shook hands in parting, Evgeni said, 'Take heart, Benedict. Our dogs may not have nice teeth like American dogs. But do you trust the Americans better for having straightened-out teeth and big smiles?'

'Well . . .'

'Of course you don't! And the Chukchi dog is loyal. He has a good heart.'

'Loyal to whom?' I was still wondering as the time came for us to go to the airport in Anadyr. There was a gale hurling rain at us, and along with it came large white swirling flakes of snow. Even in the bay the waters seethed, the waves kicked. An hour earlier the very same water had been flat.

'It's begun,' a passenger said. 'Winter.'

'We'll be freezing in a fortnight or so,' said someone else, 'and it'll stay like that until mid-May at best. Eight months.'

We fought our way aboard the plane. The stewardess served us red wine that highlighted the colour of her drunken, bloodshot eyes. 'Do you want meat or egg?' she asked.

'Egg, please.'

'Sorry, we do not have.'

'But you just said –'

'I am just practise English language.'

She disappeared to learn another phrase.

Between encounters with the stewardess, I thought back over the preceding days. Already, on this brief recce, my expedition had been in some way menaced by the Russian Far East; it seemed destined to go the way of so many grander projects. And not just those of Franklin or, indeed, Bering, another pioneer who met an icy death out here. At school I'd learnt of the zeal of the communists and their plan to scatter coal dust over Siberia to absorb solar radiation and change the climate to a temperate one. Where was this plan now? Where now the fearful Gulags?

Even the crew of the plane, just touching down for an hour in Chukotka, seemed to have been tarnished by this land.

'Are you smoking?' the stewardess said, plonking herself down in the seat next to mine. Now I see the stained teeth, the lipstick flakes around the mouth, the patchy nose powder.

I drew a cartoon of her struggling valiantly onward, just like so many good citizens of Chukotka. It would decorate that indestructible but unsightly plastic file labelled 'SURVIVORS' now housing the quotes and jottings that I'd assembled over two decades; these, above all else, should accompany me on my return to Siberia.

'My expedition will be like that,' I thought. 'Siberia will damage it, but I will come away in some sense richer.'

Gulags

The word 'Gulag' is actually an acronym, standing for *Glavnoe Upravlenie Lagerei*, or Main Camp Administration. The tradition of deporting 'politicals' to Siberia had its origins in Tsarist times, but in 1917 Lenin declared that anyone deemed a 'class enemy' should be categorized as worse than an ordinary criminal. Trotsky reinvented the idea of the concentration camp (introduced by the British in the Boer War), and a system of exiling undesirables was more fully implemented by Stalin in the late 1920s.

The Gulags were not death camps *per se*; those considered dangerous in Stalinist times were more likely simply to be shot. Nor were they comparable to the Nazi camps in that they were not designed for any particular category of person. You didn't, for example, have to be a gypsy or Jew. These were simply forced-labour camps for undesirables, and they included criminals of all types.

In 1952, the International League for the Rights of Man documented the existence of more than four hundred such camps in central and eastern Europe. Total death estimates vary from 1.6 million to many times that.

The Gulags began to be closed in 1956, when Khrushchev denounced Stalin's cult of personality in his famous 'secret speech' three years after his death; it took four years to empty them.

A note I made in February 2001, when my plane was diverted to Magadan en route to Anadyr:

> 'Magadan' – the word sends much the same shiver down the Russian spine as Auschwitz does to others. The prisoners were unloaded here at the docks and set to work on the road running north. Some say a million died out here. The bones are visible along the road in the summer, along with seas of shoes, but many died before arrival. The guards used to open cells and spray water on the prisoners. They died in seconds and were lifted out as a block.
>
> Many say that twice as many people died as in the Holocaust. The shock isn't the memorial that now stands on the hillside in Magadan, but that this is the only really substantial memorial in Russia.

Triumph over the odds

Or not. The reality was that I was reliant on a wounded people. Gena was no doubt a fine whaler and perhaps a very great adventurer, but did the Siberians as a whole really have the strength to prepare me? An image surfaced of Natasha standing in ruins at the bar in Anadyr.

For the moment I must have faith in the Chukchis. They had endured, despite everything. So I should try to look forward with optimism – indeed, preparations were already under way. The walrus meat was being placed in depots, and an old lady in Neshkan, northwest of the Bering Strait, had promised to stitch together reindeer skins for my Arctic clothing. She'd selected a jovial Russian hunter of approximately my dimensions who would act as the tailor's dummy in my absence.

As for the Bering Strait itself, to stand a chance of crossing the ice it seemed I had to pray for a very severe winter. A strange thing to be wanting in a land where even in summer you must hide from the wind.

As I drifted off to sleep, my last thoughts were of crossing the bay to the airport that morning. By the time the ferry approached shore, there was a gale blowing. Women had to be helped off first, as if we were sinking. One at a time we made the jump to the quay, over the swirling water. Then I turned around, conscious of someone's eyes on me. I met the gaze not of a person but of a dog. He sat high up on a metal hatch, watching us all with his lead-blue eyes. And I held on to that image until I arrived home – a portrait not of the corrosive elements of Chukotka but of a Chukotka dog standing firm.

X

As summer in England gave way to autumn, the carpet in my front room was covered with an assortment of the latest polar gear, which I could use if my reindeer skins and other local accessories never materialized. There were outer jackets and inner jackets, there were boots favoured by lumberjacks 'guaranteed to 40 degrees of frost', petrol stoves, snow shovels and – my favourite – snowshoes like tennis rackets which were devotedly worked by Canadians from hide and white ash. In line with the current thinking of those running teams in the Iditarod dog race through Alaska, there were little pots of vaseline and antibiotics for the dog pads; 1,500 little boots were fashioned to protect the feet of three teams over the course of the trek. Into this room, too, came polar adventurers, disciplined men who talked of strategies for if disaster struck. One kindly veteran crafted a pair of wooden ice spikes – to help me crawl from the water in the two minutes I might have before I succumbed.

And all the while the Chukchis were out there preparing just as I was, except that they were slipping into a winter routine they'd known since birth. As the temperature dipped to minus ten, they'd be exchanging their woollen hats for those of fox or hare, and when it dipped to minus twenty-five, they would take out their hats of deer or even wolf fur. I imagined Gena and Alexei shoring up their walrus-meat supplies and sewing their dog harnesses, the women stitching my reindeer suit, and outside, the shoreline waters thickening as they froze. Ice would be extending its fingers out into the bay and then into the Strait. These fingers would meet others. They'd join, rise up. They would be creaking; they would be moaning and squeaking. And at last, the white sheet of Siberian winter complete, the dogs would be baying as their masters attached them, one by one, to the sledge.

Suddenly, there's a phone call. 'Gena's dropping out,' Ivan said, breaking the news down the line from Moscow. 'He's really sorry. An international whaling conference – a big chance for the Chukchis. He can't let his people down.'

'But that leaves only Alexei!'

'He won't come either. Not without Gena.'

'But . . .'

'Gena says not to worry. You'll be using Alexei's dog team. Alexei will still teach you the commands and names and all that. But two other men – Yasha and Tolia – will guide you from Anadyr to the Bering Strait. They are good men. They don't drink.'

I was to be guided by men I hadn't chosen myself. I tried to think back to when I might have done this before – in the Chalbi of Kenya? The Mongolian steppe perhaps? What about the lowlands of Borneo? No, never. And now I was going to do it in the Arctic, of all places.

But there was another pressing issue. People say you should be careful what you wish for; it seemed I hadn't been careful enough.

'Temperatures in eastern Russia have fallen below minus fifty degrees Celsius as Siberia confronts is worst winter in living memory,' announced the television newsreader. 'Dozens of people have died in the past weeks. Many more have suffered terrible injuries from frostbite.'

Days later the weather charts for eastern Siberia were still indicating minus fifty, not the minus thirty I was equipped for. Some villages had disappeared, lost in heavy snow as the wind came in from the south; some were locked in ice as the wind swung in from the north.

I felt stupid for having hoped for something I didn't understand. Like a child in a fairy tale who plays with magic, casually summoning up forces he has no power to control, I had brought forth this destruction – for what? My idiotic notion of travelling over the ice alone. And yet I couldn't help but think that now there'd be a real chance that the Strait would freeze over and deliver me to America.

On the last night before setting off, I take one final look at my luggage before going to bed: my diary along with all the background notes and, above all, my decorated plastic file containing my stash of material on survivors; lying beside the holdalls full of clothing are the magnificent wooden snowshoes, cameras with Arctic cables and a satellite phone which the BBC have asked me to take, though everyone knows I have no intention of taking it all the way. I've also been issued with a transmitter with which to send a daily signal as to my position. That won't be going with me into the Bering Strait either. Last of all, there's the survival kit that has always accompanied me on expeditions. I unzip it and check everything off: the spare compass, small stove, petrol, plastic whistle, waterproof matches . . . And that crumpled bit of paper, the one dating from New Guinea. It was now discoloured by the ochre sands of the Kalahari, buffed by the winds of the steppe and stained by Amazon fungi. It was even dappled with

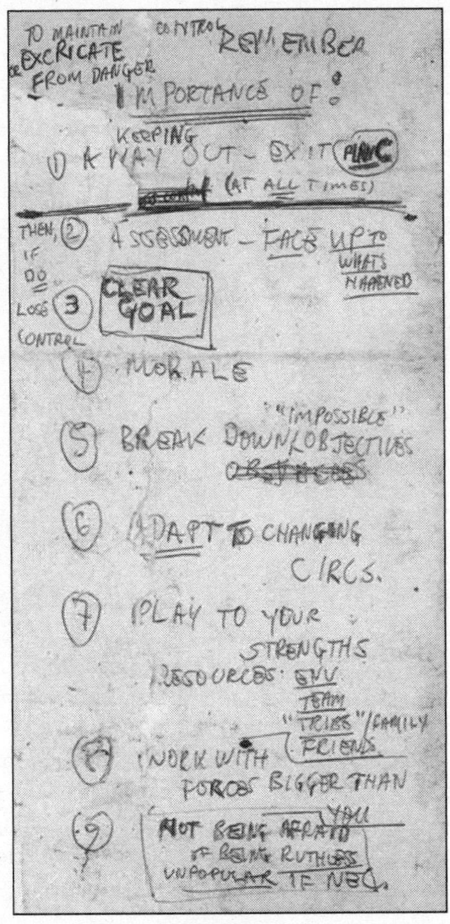

XI

Was it the strain of what promised to be a difficult time? Was it the realization, on seeing the nine holdalls of Arctic gear, that he was lumbered with another man's dangerous ambition? Or was it Siberia itself, the way the cold of the tundra had a way of boring like a shipworm, probing for weakness in a character? Whatever the cause, a weakness is there to be found in all of us and it began revealing itself in Ivan even in Moscow.

A full week we had waited for the weather to clear for our flight, seven days in the hotel sitting with our holdalls and those snowshoes which were so impressive. 'Enough!' we thought. We would take a ride into town. Accompanied by John Hesling, the film producer who'd be lending us a hand for a few days, we headed for the Chesterfield, 'Moscow's hottest nightspot'. And there, somewhere in the two-metre space between the bar and dance floor, Ivan abandoned himself to drink; his dancing became wilder and wilder; he seemed relieved to just let go. John and I had to intercede, apologizing to the Russians he veered into. Girls were holding back their increasingly irate boyfriends as Ivan spiralled, pirouetted. His eyes were euphoric now as he was carried further and further away by some kind of demon. We later discovered him outside, trying to get into a car. Was he trying to break in or just catch a ride?

'He's going to get beaten up by someone at this rate,' I said.

'Maybe by the police,' John said. Ivan lurched off through the snow, now applying himself to getting inside a plush apartment. He pushed aside a woman who was inserting her door keys.

'Let's just go,' I said. We flagged down a car. The driver looked unhappy when it became clear we were bringing along Ivan – presently spread in the snow – but I opened the door, and with John at the other end, chucked him in.

When we finally landed at Anadyr it was into a formidable headwind, snow whipping past the windows, rapping on the fuselage. 'Ten days' delay,' I thought, 'waiting for weather as good as this.'

'Broke in half in the sky,' a passenger said, referring to last week's helicopter crash. 'Eleven people died in that one. It was just the usual low maintenance problem. Same as the submarine, the *Kursk*.'

We stared out of the window through the flying snow to the other fifteen helicopters that used to service Chukotka. Picked apart for spares, they lay in a row along the runway like carrion, corpses placed there by a gamekeeper as a warning to others.

'Let me see,' continued the passenger. 'That leaves just four helicopters now.'

While waiting for the return of our documents, we bumped into Victor, the helicopter pilot often to be found stalking the empty corridors of the airport. A tall, delicate creature who was at a loose end following the demise of the Soviet helicopter fleet, he stood about in his favourite tight leather trousers, one leg hanging limply, like a wounded heron hoping to be tossed a scrap to eat. We all knew he'd never fly again.

'Your pilot must have been drunk,' said Victor.

'No, no,' I corrected him. 'They definitely said the delay was due to the weather.'

'I've seen planes landing here every day. It was drink. Believe me, I'm a pilot.'

I laughed. 'In which case, they were drunk for more than a week!'

But Victor simply nodded. 'Yes, that's a fair explanation.'

No need now to take a ferry over the bay to Anadyr – you could drive. Land and water were united, frozen to a metre's depth, and over the top spread a continuous pelt of fresh snow. Our van cut across the ice, trundling along behind a hefty coal lorry. Occasionally, I spotted figures huddled over fishing holes. I asked the driver to stop, and we watched someone's catch being hauled up, extracted from the comfort of the depths. Hoisted into the air, the fish flapped and flipped on the end of the line as if overjoyed, now suddenly relishing the chance of a visit to our world. Five seconds later the merciless breeze had claimed him; he was stiffening, his flesh freezing solid before our eyes. I watched, appalled. There had never been a more graphic illustration for me of the danger of being exposed to the Arctic: that poor fish, one moment breathing and five heartbeats later a slither of ice.

The streets of Anadyr were padded with fresh and also ancient-seeming snow. Dusty old boulders of it were banked against the apartments; it hung from roofs in thick crusty swathes. Children in hats were out enjoying what counted as a warm day – minus fifteen – and meat had been hung in bags from windows to keep it nicely frozen.

But Anadyr was showing its age, sitting grey and grubby amongst the snow, and so that very first day I insisted we went to Natasha's bar. 'It's important to me,' I said. I wanted to know that Natasha had survived, sustained by whatever it was that kept her going. More to the point, I wanted to know that anyone else unsuited to Siberia might, in the long run, be all right.

The new minder allocated us by Raityrgin took some persuading to come along.

'I never go there,' he said.

'Natasha's bar?'

'That dump, yes. I never go there. After an incident . . .'

When we did drag him there, I found everything very changed. 'Sacked her,' the owner said, steering us to a table. 'I was losing too much money.'

'Poor old Natasha,' I said.

He looked at me sharply. 'Natasha couldn't remember who had paid, who not, and what for,' he said.

I looked at the empty bar, the owner who resembled the man satirised on the label of НОВЫЙ РУССКИЙ (New Russian) vodka – a bloated 'New Russian' in very tight swimming trunks, draped with a gold crucifix and other glittering ornaments and wielding a mobile phone – and felt gloomy.

'Hey! You a friend of hers? I've got to be able to live too, you know!'

'Victor the bouncer,' Ivan asked. 'What happened to him?'

'Fired. An alcoholic.'

'Petr?'

'Fired too.'

'Vladimir, the third bouncer?' Ivan said. 'What about him? Hardly drinks at all.'

'Not in my restaurant he doesn't! Not any more. Fired.'

But Anadyr had plenty of people wanting to celebrate or forget, and soon they thumped their vodka on our table, inviting themselves to join us. There seemed to be nothing we could do about it, as more arrived.

'The average Russian consumes a whole bottle every other day,' John commented, counting the array of bottles in front of us. 'That's a WHO figure.'

We should have left right then. We'd had warning enough. But my friend Yana then swirled in with her cousin Olga and hung up her furs, and when next I saw Ivan he was among a bunch of Russian soldiers and already looking undone. Our minder too had been transformed. From someone who had been, at the outset, rather too formal, if anything, now his tie was half-hitched and he looked like a racketeer. But my attention was on Ivan. Again I had a sense of losing him, and over the next hour I watched as he drifted away, casting himself off.

'Time we left,' John said, coaxing him to the door, but the evening ended in further disarray, Ivan breaking down a bedroom door in pursuit of Olga, John locking himself in a room which was inhabited, as it turned out, by a seedy white cat, and with me thinking again and again this one thought: 'We need to get on with the journey right away.'

But the winds rose up again and we kicked our heels, day after day, as we waited until it was possible to take a cargo plane to fetch the dogs.

'Will things get any worse?' I asked myself.

'Oh yes, much worse,' would be the answer. But not just yet.

XII

'They're wondering what's up,' said Yasha, shouting down the phone line from Lavrentiya. It seemed that our sledge dogs were waiting, curled up beside the runway. 'They know they'll be doing something different.'

'But are they all right?' I asked anxiously. Ivan translated, shouting the question back down the line.

'All right? Is this Britisher a fool? Of course they are all right!'

'But it's probably minus seventy in the wind,' I thought. 'They have no kennel, no nothing.'

As for Anadyr, I began to understand that it no longer offered the protection to humans that it once had. The tundra was making deep inroads, and, just as with the tropical forests I'd seen, where nature had a way of discerning one weak tree in a thousand, the same was true in the Arctic: like an unfit species, the weak of Anadyr were being discovered.

Natasha's bar was the first to fail. The evening it was to close down we went along to say goodbye, standing beside Volodyr as he played his last note on the Casio. The two fat kitchen ladies leant on the bar, watching. And then the moment came: Volodyr solemnly unplugged the keyboard from the wall. It was as if that keyboard were a life-support machine and we were standing by a hospital bed. We gathered our coats, exchanged grim smiles and left quietly.

The golden retriever – that friendly old chap who thumped his tail to greet me on my arrival in the summer – had disappeared. And reappeared – or one suspiciously like him – as a fur hat at the bric-a-brac stall in the market. All around us the less able were sinking as if through the ice, whole institutions closing down as if they were limbs succumbing to frostbite. But still the Siberians fought on. Once, out in a snowstorm getting some practice in, I found shoppers there with me in white-out conditions. Peering through my goggles I could make out old ladies trudging by, their plastic bags shattering, made brittle by the cold. Elsewhere, I discovered a tanner secretly curing polar-bear hides – he discouraged visits from the hunting inspector's dog by propping a massive dead wolf by his door. And Uri the Kazak, who invited us round to his flat, opened his window and, his speech slurred with drink, invited us to aim the barrel of his rifle at his neighbours. 'What could be the harm?' he said, fixing us with his one remaining eye. Then he lined up the telescopic sight on the citizens of Anadyr as they sat having supper, chatting, watching telly.

Such women, such men, unfailingly hopeful, yet seeing tragic possibilities everywhere. Still they fought. Who couldn't love these exiles for refusing to surrender their stoic belief in their motherland and the impossible? As for me, I began to think of the Chukchis and their detachments of dogs as the cavalry. It was a question of hanging on, waiting to be rescued.

XIII

The call finally came from the airport. No one had got into Lavrentiya for three weeks, so a mass of other passengers hitched a ride in our cargo plane. Out of the snow and up the tail ramp we clambered, hauling dog crates which had been lovingly fashioned by Victor the helicopter pilot, only to find ourselves sitting either side of a coffin. It was a roughly hewn plywood box, military issue, marked 'ФРАХТ 200' ('FREIGHT 200').

'Killed in Chechnya,' we agreed.

Though there was precious little room, what with our bulky Arctic clothing – it was minus thirty-two even on-board – I tried to give the dead soldier some space. Other passengers were doing the same; it seemed the least we could do. This was someone who had succeeded in breaking out of Siberia, and now, as if reminding him he'd been under a life sentence, the outside world had punished him and sent him back.

Our plane lurched into the sky and onward up the coast towards the Bering Strait. As far as the eye could see the land and sea were caked over; open water had been my prime concern, but below was a heart-warming, glorious, strong, continuous mass of ice extending for the twenty-five or so kilometres I could see to the east. Just occasionally, freshly healed scars ran across the white skin, and there were patches of raven-black water where the ice had been freshly torn open by the winds. It was better than I had dared hope.

On our final approach into Lavrentiya we were buffeted by winds laden with snow, and after touchdown the plane skidded on its lacerated tyres through the icescape for what seemed a full five minutes. The pilot kicked open the cabin door. 'You haven't long,' he yelled above the engine noise. 'Half an hour, max.'

We step outside. We stand a moment in our Arctic clobber: balaclavas, neoprene face masks, hoods; our vision is obscured, the sounds of Lavrentiya muffled and distant. However, around us a throng is eagerly looking on. They are wondering what this plane, the first for so long, is going to deliver. No eyes are visible beneath the hats, only scarves frozen by their owners' breath into stiff white face masks.

There's no time to see who claims the coffin. We need to get to the dogs. We march briskly through the crowd, readying ourselves for the first view of them.

No sign. Nor are we sure, among all the oncoming, swathed Chukchis, who might be Yasha, Tolia and the all-important owner of my future dog team, Alexei. In fact, it's difficult to take in much at all. In the gusts, the wind chill must be minus sixty or even eighty.

Ivan is directed to two men. They are short, wide people. Even in their jackets, motley furs and padded Russian army overalls, each seems to be a squat concentration of force, relaxed but held ready, like a fist.

Behind them I spy dogs lying about, curled up in thigh-deep snow. It's not clear if they are our dogs, but my excitement grows anyway. They lie attached to sledges, pegged out in what must be two or three separate teams. Amid the bustle around the airport they are passive, occasionally showing through the snow like the folds of an abandoned old carpet.

The two men come over to shake hands. I can't see their eyes through the pale blur of slanting snow, just their square outline as they stomp up to us with a stiff, clockwork gait. The larger Chukchi is evidently the boss. 'YASHA!' he shouts through the screeching wind.

These first impressions are important, and I wonder what they are thinking of me, standing there limply in my flashy, synthetic red attire. For my part, even through all my Arctic cladding I can see how at home they are out in the blisteringly cold wind. They are relaxed at minus sixty, for heaven's sake. Tolia is smaller and has a glass eye – an unfortunate shooting incident, he tells me later – but the way he shakes my hand, clamping oversized fingers fast around my right gauntlet, shows he's not exactly frail.

But of course I'm wondering where Alexei is.

'He hasn't come,' Ivan shouts, pitching his voice into the wind.

'Say again?' I say. But it's not the wind preventing me hearing, it's the shock of what he is saying. Alexei is the man who alone knows the dogs I'm to handle. Who knows their faults, their qualities. Their names. The man whom they trust. 'I misheard, Ivan. Tell me I misheard . . .'

'Alexei hasn't come,' Ivan repeats. 'It's the weather. Apparently he's stuck in snow – or perhaps just trying to keep his family going. Either way, he's not coming.'

I'm trying to take in the implications of this. I look at the sledge beside me. On it, great mounds of meat, frozen in this outdoor freezer. Chunks of walrus, lengths of seal. Flippers stiff, like propeller blades. All waiting to be driven away by the dogs. But how?

Even through the whistling snow Yasha sees that I'm stunned. 'Tell him it's OK, Ivan. We can probably teach him the commands.'

'Probably?'

'Definitely. Tell him that definitely we can teach them.'

Ivan says, 'Never mind about this for now. We must hurry up on to the plane.'

'The dogs,' is all I can say. 'Which are my dogs?'

'Пошли!' Tolia says to me. 'Come!' He wades off through the snow, but not far. It seems they are entombed somewhere right behind me. I've been virtually standing on them.

I see Alexei's dogs for the first time – or their outlines. It's hard to make out what is a clump of snow and what is a dog. I walk along the line of paired-up dogs and establish that there are ten – ten snow heaps which rise and fall as the dogs breathe.

'Must hurry,' John says. The weather seems to be worsening, and even on the way here we were worried the pilot might be risking it.

The dog I must see right away, though, is the leader. The dog who one day might lead me to my death – or safely away. And it is now that I lay my eyes on a huge creature curled up in the front row. He has a bright coat, the clean white of an Arctic wolf, and even at a glance I can see that he's by far the biggest here. Whereas the other front dog – fawn coat, small but thick-set, scarred muzzle – hasn't, I notice, even opened his eyes; he remains resolutely curled up. A moment later the large dog, who I'm going to have to get to know and love and who'll have to get to know and love me, abruptly raises his head and snarls.

I step back – not a good move to appear submissive to my team leader, but I had my health to think about. This dog isn't quite the size of a German shepherd, but could, at a guess, kill any German shepherd I'd met.

Something else was on my mind: I'd been waiting for my dogs as someone might wait for reinforcements during a siege. But seeing these dogs sitting cosily in this wind was enough to make me feel queasy. So much of what I'd hoped for over so many years was now lying spread out in front of me. Leaving aside the matter of being three weeks behind schedule, how would I ever get them on my side without their names or commands?

It was time to get the dogs on-board. 'This is going to be fun . . .' murmured John.

Once alerted to the idea of impending movement, the dogs became frenetic. They were so excited they didn't know what to do with themselves. There was no barking, just a whining howl, and as they danced around, it became more and more shrill. We watched the unfolding mayhem as Yasha and Tolia lined up the first dog team with the wide cargo door in the tail of the plane. Half a dozen other Chukchis were suddenly around us, blocking any miscreants from leading an escape. These men waded in, yanking the dogs back, adjusting them here and there in the team as if they were parts of a machine.

But this is only *my* dog team I'm talking about. The other two teams both ran straight on-board. I couldn't hear the orders that Yasha and Tolia gave; I just saw the dogs disappearing without hesitation or deviation out of the tundra and into the dark, forbidding, oily belly of a decayed Soviet transport plane.

The sledges, more walruses and more equipment were loaded, the dogs themselves conducted into the crates made by Victor. Ivan and I dashed to get my reindeer-skin outfit. It had arrived the previous day on the first flight out of Neshkan for a whole month, unexpectedly tossed my way in a now strangely kind act of fate.

The engines were already screaming as we clambered up the tailgate, with twenty-five new hitch-hikers close behind us. These proved to be Chukchi schoolgirl athletes. All swathed in their Arctic furs, they looked like they were dressed for a glamorous night out. Finally, a bewildered and obese Canadian Red Cross official, here to distribute provisions to the malnourished, wheezed aboard. These passengers barely had time to find space for their feet between the lumps of walrus before we were lurching off again.

I'd almost been sick on the way here as the plane yawed in the crosswinds, but now we had to endure the putrid flesh of walrus. Soon, however, this was of little concern, for as the plane accelerated across the snows, hurling itself forward, Victor's beautiful dog crates concertinaed. The girls, hitherto silent in their furs, suddenly betrayed their Chukchi origins and launched into the task of saving the dogs. They were hammering their boots against the crates, punching out splintered slats, flinging dogs clear of danger. At last order was restored, the girls calmly hitching their pretty leather coat belts around the crates to reinforce them.

I went about the sorry job of finding out how many dogs were done for, their backs broken perhaps, their paws and noses pincered. But on closer inspection the whole lot were unharmed – indeed, they were already lying half-asleep. 'They accept everything,' I thought, 'as if each new experience is just one more blizzard.'

This was so remarkable that I kept reliving the near-disaster in my mind, how the dogs had not shown fear but total trust – not one dog had squealed in pain, not one dog had yelped in fear. These were disciplined soldiers, not like the wayward Greenland dogs of the Eskimos, large beasts bred for hauling raw meat over sea ice and which the polar explorers had marshalled with whips.

Above the din of the engines I try to engage Yasha in conversation. Then Tolia. It's no good. They are very nice about it but don't see the point. 'Good to meet you too,' is all they say. They have come to do a job and are content just to be with their dogs. I rather like that in them – Yasha, a huge chunk of muscle and a flat, readable face, Tolia with his eager, take-me-as-you-find-me eye and that other false one, a glass sphere that stares ahead in permanent shock. 'I don't think they'll plot and scheme,' I write in my diary. 'I think they'll be loyal, satisfied enough with just a good day's work.' Soon they are snoozing; they sink down and end up spreadeagled among their dogs.

After a while we find ourselves flying over trees. Trees! I'm already saying to myself, 'Oh God, the pilot's drunk,' when he flings open the cabin door. 'Too much wind in Anadyr,' he shouts. 'We're heading to Markovo.' Looking at my map I find Markovo to be 400 km inland.

We land in a corner of Siberia surrounded by calm. It is disquieting to be without wind. In these conditions, it seems, minus thirty-five can actually be extremely pleasant.

As the tailgate descends, one dog runs for freedom. 'Don't worry,' says Yasha, and sure enough, although he runs for all he's worth down the runway, he stops when he finds he is alone. Then he runs back and lingers by the undercarriage, waiting for his mates to come out.

'His whole existence,' I say to myself, 'lies within that bunch of dogs. It's as if he has nothing without them.'

'He's from *your* team,' Ivan says, looking on.

'At least he has spirit,' I say. I notice that already I'm protective. I haven't even looked properly at the dogs, but I know my destiny is wrapped up with theirs. The cavalry have arrived – my reinforcements, my rescue party. At last I can build the force I need for my purpose here, and this realization, the unbounded relief of it, lends me a new energy. Time to see what the dogs can offer me and show the dogs what I can offer them.

XIV

'Think of it as an agreement,' I thought to myself. A contract. They carry me through the Arctic, and in return I give them – well, what, apart from food? Leadership and security seemed to be the answer. And this, surely, was a very good deal – and not just for these ten sledge dogs. The arrangement had worked well for dogs all around the globe. Sticking with us, they had an alliance with the most powerful species on the planet. We alone could imagine a future, we alone could shape it.

The relationship must have started uneasily. The wolf was a predator of early man's herds. Yet it was to the wolf that the human turned when he first thought to look for assistance from other species. Not the horse, not the camel, not the ox, not the elephant.

Something favoured the development of a bond between these enemies. Both species, wolf and man, functioned in family groups; they knew the value of co-operation; they organized themselves around a leader; they devoted much energy to rearing young, maintaining a close relationship even in adulthood. Sharing this same social structure gave both species the ability to recognize in the other qualities that could be used to their mutual advantage.

In time, as man spread yet further afield, dogs provided effective support on hunting trips; later, as he began to colonize the harshest climes of all, it was to the dog that man turned once again, this time as a means of transport. A small, flexible unit of intelligent power, the dog's greatest talent was to be able to read the needs of man. No other creature, not even our nearest animal relative the chimp, had learnt to interpret our needs so effectively.

Later, when man aspired to reach the ends of the earth, it was dogs that took him to the North Pole, while at the South Pole it was the

Dogs Across the World

Dogs are a member of the family Canidae, which includes foxes, the African wild dog, wolves, jackals and the coyote. Some archaeological evidence suggests that early, 'proto' dogs diverged from wolves around 100,000 years ago. In the last few years, however, DNA evidence studied by Peter Savolainen and colleagues has pointed strongly to an origin of the true domestic dog at just 15,000 years ago – and all in one location (possibly from only three female wolves) in East Asia. The question remains, however, how? It was one thing for Palaeolithic man to decide a wolf might be useful for guarding, hunting and herding, another to get this predator to swap sides. A tethered wolf might still be a valuable guard for these bands of hunting-gathering nomads, but wolves do not bark and are notoriously unbiddable, even if adopted at birth. Nor is there fossil evidence of wolves having been kept by man.

Suppose, however, certain wolves did find a way of living in proximity to man. Take, for example, a subordinate male, chased from the pack and unable to find a mate. For these individuals, unable to plunder herds as others did through co-operating with members of the pack, considerable advantage was to be had from following man and scavenging from leftover foods. Those individuals less cautious of man and more acquiescent to him might benefit more than those who were afraid. The tamer these individuals were, the more conditions favoured their survival, thus reinforcing this trait.

Perhaps different species of wolves were domesticated in different locations and died out. Indeed, perhaps an uneasy association with proto-dogs at one level or another existed 60,000 years ago, as man spread rapidly through Asia, the north and Europe. Man's discovery of fire had offered climate control, his skins and insulating shelters allowing him to spread yet further north, and with the proto-dog now trusted to run down prey that he speared, man was also a formidable hunter.

We know for certain that when the time came for man to colonize the Americas 12–14,000 years ago and he crossed the land bridge that then existed between Siberia and Alaska, the dog came along too. Around this time something had happened that cemented the relationship for ever: man began to establish more permanent settlements. Now there were resources to ween pups and select for desired characteristics; now the dog could join in duties guarding livestock, sometimes against the dogs' very own ancestor, the wolf.

The Natufian people, hunters and gatherers, offer us the earliest reliably dated evidence of being the first to keep domesticated dogs. The close bond between man and dog is evident in burials at Ain Mallaha in present-day northern Israel that date back 12,000 years. One grave contains an oldish man cradling a young dog with his left hand.

Once across the Bering Strait, no further domestication took place, a mark of how quickly man moved south through the Americas. The dog remains found in the Americas pre-dating the arrival of Europeans are more closely related to Eurasian grey wolves and Eurasian dogs than to the local North American grey wolf; that is, dogs throughout the world are descendants of Old World wolves. And by 10,000 years ago, this animal seems to have been almost everywhere: a rock painting in Iraq shows people hunting deer alongside dogs with curly tails; in Algeria, dogs, along with a spear-carrying human, are depicted surrounding a bovine creature. However, they were not in sub-Saharan Africa until around 500 AD, suggesting man hadn't been back to Africa since they were domesticated. Already man and dog were inseparable.

explorer who recognized the value of dogs who returned safely – and the explorer who didn't that died. One of the first signs that told Scott he was defeated was the footprints of Amundsen's colleagues – 'the clear trace of dogs' paws – many dogs,' he recorded on 16 January 1912. 'This told us the whole story.'

The tracks did indeed tell the whole story – that man could do great things but was a weakling when exposed and without allies. Which was a shame in my case, because I'd come here armed with my file of survivors on an expedition which would take me to the very brink – and I'd been counting on a lot of help from my own allies, these dogs. And in at least one regard, all dogs were very vulnerable themselves. The process of natural selection that had seen the emergence of the modern dog had, when you thought about it, brought into being a creature that was less and less like an adult wolf and more and more like a baby one. The modern dog even looked like a wolf pup. Most breeds had tails curling over their heads, like baby wolves; they barked, another characteristic more typical of the juvenile wolf; they tended to have floppy ears, again like infant wolves; they licked your hands as pups did the faces of their mothers and aunts among wild packs, hoping they would disgorge their food. It came down to this: in order to work alongside man, these wolves had had to surrender the fear and aggression that were their armaments in the wild.

No wonder the Chukchi dog is said to be fearful of the Arctic wolf: he is a version of them, but one rendered helpless. My dogs had been bred for stamina and would be strong – formidably strong – but like all dogs they would also be as needy as wolf pups.

Yasha and Tolia drove the dog teams off the plane in a glorious sweeping curve to the edge of the airstrip so they might bed themselves into the soft snow for the night. Now the lines of staked-out dogs formed a neat semi-circle. All except mine. My dogs have to be escorted to the vicinity – 'frogmarched' would be a better word for it.

All the way, Yasha and Tolia are trying different commands. They whistle, they coo like doves, they grunt. They are ignored.

'You see that?' I said to Ivan. 'They don't even obey the Chukchis, and they've been handling mutts like these all their lives.'

'The dogs don't even look up!' John said, marvelling at the sight.

Yasha was quietly amused. 'They're waiting for Alexei,' he said marching up to us. 'It doesn't matter what command we give!'

I go over to the dogs. There's the occasional ear cocked as I near them, but nothing else – until I get to the front row, and then the large white lead dog stands to block me from getting near the other, smaller one.

I couldn't help feel a sense of disappointment, inspecting – as best I could – the second lead dog. He looked weather-beaten, his coat covered with chunks of ice that moved with him like the plates of an armadillo and his muzzle so disappointingly cross-hatched with those blackened scars. This suggested, I thought, a dog that was not so much a leader as one at the bottom of the pack.

As I moved closer, he took shelter under the big white dog, as if ashamed. 'God knows,' I thought, 'I don't know much about dogs, but it doesn't seem to me to be a particularly good sign that I've a downtrodden dog in my front row.'

That said, the crow-black dog in the third row was, if anything, even more pitifully subordinate. 'Pull yourself together,' I wanted to say. His running mate was not yet fully grown, but even he had no problem in usurping the black dog's place in the snow, which looked no better than his patch of snow anyway.

I got out my notebook. 'For the moment, I'll put down your name as Blot,' I said.

'Trouble is,' I then wrote, 'he's not the only dud. The rest of them look like they are out of a dog pound. The big, flashy white lead dog, who has a beautiful mask of a face and runs as lightly as a show dog, must be the alpha male. As for the others, we have a labrador, a border collie, a creature with a wolf's long narrow muzzle and slanting eyes, and to cap it all, a dog like a runt St Bernard but without a tail' – bringing to mind the dogs of the Edwardian explorers who got frostbite because their owners felt the need to bob their tails.

I took more notes. The dogs remained calm as I stepped over them, heads down, eyes attentive. 'Basil,' I wrote, naming the irrepressible, very young, reddish dog after a glove-puppet fox on children's TV. 'Under age?'

All in all, the team was a sorry sight. I looked them up and down once more and groaned. But of course, what owner in their right mind would give their prize dogs to a novice?

Yasha joined me. 'So, Benya, what do you think of your dogs?'

What I thought was that I had been given a bunch of third-raters. The other two teams were twelve strong, instead of ten, and were composed of light-limbed dogs, richly undercoated in wool, their outer coat a fine display of mottled brown and smoky black hues; sometimes these fox-wolves had golden eyes and sometimes icy pale, just like the dogs I'd seen in the summer. They matched precisely the Chukchi sledge dog breed that I'd feared extinct as a teenager. 'They never appear so heavy as to suggest a freighting animal nor so light as to suggest a sprint-racing animal,' read the official criteria of the Siberian husky breed, which had used the Chukchi sledge dog as their original breeding stock. The description fitted Yasha's dogs to a T. Were his team members each 'with moderate bone, ease and freedom of movement'? Yes, indeed they were. 'No higher than 23.5 inches'? Absolutely not. And was each dog 'moderately compact, with well-furred body, erect ears and brush tail – the balance of power, speed and endurance reflected in his proportions and form, his well-developed muscles not carrying excess weight'? Yes, yes, yes, in every case.

These were not descriptions that sat happily with my dogs, which ranged from the sleek to the stumpy, from the bulky to the dainty. My dogs had an array of just the characteristics a breeder might be trying to breed out. I tried to think of something positive to say to Yasha. 'They are so . . .' After a while, I gave up.

'Some of your dogs,' said John gingerly, 'well, they don't seem as uniform as Yasha's and Tolia's.'

'As capable' would have been more to the point, but it seemed unappreciative. I cast a mournful eye again over Yasha's dogs, laid out in neat pairs. And mine, higgledy-piggledy.

'You know,' Yasha said, 'the weakest-looking dog could be the one that saves your life.'

I looked at Blot. It seemed unlikely.

'When will they start listening to me?' I asked, eyeing the front dogs – the reticent fawn character and the powerful animal who scared me.

'Who knows!' Yasha said. I could see he couldn't help himself smiling. 'We would never go anywhere with someone else's team!'

'It's not that funny actually,' I said to myself. But it was attractive, this lightness of spirit in the Chukchis, and at the moment it was more important than the dodgy appearance of my dogs, who had, I had to keep reminding myself, thought nothing of spending three weeks lodged in the killer wind beside a runway. Has any one of us ever met a dog capable of that?

Yasha and Ivan leave, and I pause for a moment alone with the team. 'Maybe we should just forget the Bering Strait,' I tell the dogs. I'm already preparing myself for having to lower my sights. It does seem improbable that I'll ever be alone in the Arctic with this lot. 'But we'll at least give it a go, me and the ten of you,' I say aloud. 'Won't we?'

Not a single dog looks up.

XV

Extract from my diary, 25 February 2001:
Markovo – hundreds of years ago a base for the invasive Cossacks. We were billeted in the hospital, in various wards, along with the pregnant, lame, jaundiced and forlorn. The building has such a lean that you have to sleep upslope to stop the blood going to your head. Cement comes off the exterior of the building, plaster from the interior. There's little in the shops by way of essentials but there's a quantity of inessentials – Markovo is a shoppers' heaven if you fancy loo paper and plastic vases.

It's not till midday the second day – still stuck in Markovo, still among trees – that we find that the helicopter pilot Victor is somehow here with us. He's accompanying us for no reason that anyone can quite remember.

'We should feed the dogs,' I suggested. 'Where are Tolia and Yasha?'

'Partying,' Victor says.

'No, seriously. Where are they?'

'Partying.'

We found Tolia. Then, in another part of town, Yasha. Tolia was still slightly drunk. 'He doesn't want to talk to the camera in case it shows,' said Ivan, explaining why Tolia kept ducking out of my viewfinder.

'Cheeesus,' John said. 'You need to watch that.'

'He'll be all right,' I said. 'It's a blip – he wouldn't look so guilty otherwise.'

We go to feed the sledge teams at the airport – and find the dogs sunk down into the ice, which has melted around them, creating neat little pockets, each moulded to their own shape and favoured position. There they lie, totally uninspired and undaunted by their travels and their arrival in a land of giant vegetation – the birches with silver trunks shorn clean by the wind, the firs that blocked out the light and fenced in the air. Nor do they acknowledge our approach by looking up, as you'd expect a dog to do. It seems that even the wagging of a tail is a needless depletion of that scarce resource, energy.

The morning was still and warm – minus twenty-two – and we discussed our plans right there on the runway. 'Yasha's explaining,' said Ivan, translating, 'that we are short of meat. Waiting for us in Lavrentiya, they've been using up the walrus supplies. They are talking of cutting down your training. From a month down to, er . . . five days.'

'Five days? Five days? Aaaaargh! No, no, Ivan. Even a month was ridiculously short. For heaven's sake, we don't even know their names.'

'I cannot let my dogs die,' Yasha said quietly. 'They feed my family; they are my livelihood.'

'Of course not, of course not,' I said, knowing I'd been insensitive. 'But it doesn't help my situation,' I thought.

Yasha brought some dog food from the plane: walruses that looked like old, bloated human corpses. Now the dogs sprung into action; it was as if their power supply had been turned back on. They were on their feet and howling.

Red-eyed and reeking of drink he might have been, but Tolia began hacking the walruses up without a pause, proficient axe blows cutting into the solid, marbled granite, fibrous flesh as easy as Stilton, each chunk having exactly the same dimensions.

Fired up by the alcohol, he chatters away enthusiastically in Russian as we breathe in the fetid, fishy, ugly smell of walrus. I recognize the word 'vitamins'. 'It's what stops me getting scurvy,' I realize he's saying. It seems that this walrus flesh is for humans as well.

Now it's the dogs' meal time, though, and Tolia fills three sacks, one for each team. 'It's important that *you* feed your dogs, not us,' says Yasha.

I can see that: the way to a dog's heart is through his stomach. But the dogs are not the creatures they were ten minutes ago. Even the other two teams were no longer ordered squads of well-drilled soldiers. The whole lot are a rabble. Whichever dogs were once allocated

Markovo: The Birthplace of the Siberian Husky

Markovo is, arguably, the spot where the Siberian husky emerged as a breed. A century ago, Markovo was still one of the Chukchi trading settlements along the Anadyr river where they bought and sold their dogs. And it was here, according to Michael Jennings' *The New Complete Siberian Husky*, that a Russian fur trader, William Goosak, came across the breed. He returned to Alaska with nine dogs in the summer of 1908, the first year of an imaginative competition, the All Alaska Sweepstakes, a gruelling long-distance race which would be completed using dog teams. He proposed to run them the next year. At first no one took these docile, compact little dogs seriously; the large, stubborn but mighty Malamutes had won the first year, and Goosak's dogs appeared more fox than wolf. But he almost won – and would have done if the driver, Thurstrup, hadn't messed up his tactics. This made those with an interest in this ground-breaking new sport sit up, and another man, Fox Maule Ramsay, returned to Markovo Fair to select seventy of the best dogs. He duly swept the board at the 1910 race, his teams coming first, second and third. It was proposed that these dogs be used for Roald Amundsen's 1914 attempt on the North Pole, and when this was cancelled following the outbreak of war, they were raced the following year by the Norwegian Leonhard Seppala. He then went on to win the race with ease the following years as well. The event was discontinued in 1917, partly because there was so little close competition for him.

The little sledge dogs from Siberia were soon to gain wider recognition, however. In 1925, diphtheria threatened the population of Nome, on the Alaskan side of the Strait. Somehow the diphtheria serum had to be delivered 1,053 km from Nenana, the end of the railway line from Anchorage. Seppala got his dogs into action, with the lead dog Togo – now stuffed and on display in a museum in Vermont – travelling 544 km, by far the longest leg in a series of relays. The serum arrived in only five and a half days, a feat commemorated today by the annual Iditarod race. Unfortunately, the wrong dog, Balto, went down in history: a dog rejected from the main team, he nonetheless had the good fortune to lead the final short 80-km leg and was immortalized by the press. He is now cherished daily by pilgrims who visit his statue in Central Park.

The Siberian husky, as breeders recognize it, is founded on these early dogs imported into Alaska and those imported directly into New England by the Arctic trader Olaf Swenson, who selected Chukchi dogs from the Arctic coast in 1929; possessing an exclusive fur-trading agreement with the Soviets, he was, it's said, the last contact the Chukchis had with the outside world in the communist era.

the role of team leader, no dog now cares. Each is straining to be first to sink his canines into the meat.

Yasha shoves a sack of frozen walrus into my hands. 'Never, ever hand it to them – they'll take your fingers as well. And I'm not joking.'

As he speaks, the flashy white alpha male lunges at the end of his leash; his teeth snap sharply together like a mantrap.

'Near miss,' says John.

'And keep talking to the dogs. They've got to get to know you – your voice, your smell.'

I chuck the flesh to the dogs, one at a time, trying to be scrupulously fair. 'One for you, Blot. Another for you, Flashy White . . . Basil, a piece for you.'

'And don't use your everyday gloves,' Yasha says, but by the time I understand the Russian it's too late. My gauntlets are stinking of walrus, a smell that apparently never quite comes out.

The next day the dogs are loaded aboard again. My team duly causes mayhem. Victor walks delicately aboard in his polished leather trousers and the girl gymnasts follow in their gorgeous furs. Finally, the overweight health worker gasps his way to his seat, and we are away.

At Anadyr airport a strong wind sweeps loose snow over our feet. The cold is such that it is dangerous to touch the metal of the dog harnesses without gloves. And we still have to get the dogs from the airport across the bay to town.

Yasha reassures me. My dogs, being so far from home, are sure to follow the other teams' scent. 'Besides, Ivan will ride your sledge along with you to help slow you down.'

'Slow me down?'

'And as a safety measure, I'll hitch Fatty to your team.'

'Fatty?'

'Fatty. He's one of my lead dogs. Great character, he is.'

Novices and their Dogs

The Arctic explorer Fridtjof Nansen's first solo dog drive, with only half a dozen dogs attached to his Samoyed (Nenets) sledge, was not a triumph. Fruitlessly yelling, 'Pr-r-rr, Pr-r-rr!' as he'd been instructed, he found himself dragged ignominiously over the ice. 'I tugged, swore, and tried everything I could think of, but all to no purpose.' When he tried lashing them with a whip, 'they jumped to both sides and only tore on the faster . . . I inwardly congratulated myself that my feats had been unobserved,' he wrote. But unfortunately he had been: a witness afterwards recorded being startled by Nansen uttering words 'not to be expected of an educated man'.

Forty years earlier, in 1860, Isaac Hayes – who had served on an expedition by Elisha Kane in search of Franklin – was introduced to the Eskimo dogs of Greenland. These creatures, his dog handler Jensen explained, had to be controlled by a seal-hide whip that could reach the length of the team. Jensen was kind enough to give a demonstration. 'You see dat beast?' he said. 'I takes a piece out of his ear.' Hayes watched diligently. 'Crack went the whip, the hard sinew wound round the tip of the ear and snipped it off as nicely as with a knife.' When he took the dogs out on his own to give it a go, the dogs were soon running amok, Hayes having to disable his sledge and thrash the dogs to try and restore his command. 'I think they shall remember the lesson,' he commented afterwards, 'and so shall I.'

I had a sense of impending doom. Apart from Yasha, ahead was only whiteness, what Fridtjof Nansen called 'the eternal death-stillness of the ice'. And I seemed to remember that the great Nansen hadn't exactly fared well on his first sledge journey.

'Oh God,' I whispered.

Ivan and I clambered aboard our sledge, the dogs ahead of me prancing to the left and right, overexcited. I thought of Amundsen's words: 'Strange as it may seem, I can assert that these animals love the harness. Although they must know that it means hard work, they all show signs of the greatest rapture at the sight of it.' Too true, it seemed: the ten dogs were hysterical now at the prospect of action after such a long wait, and apparently on an escapade without Alexei, their master. They were egged on by Fatty, a mad-eyed, broad-shouldered individual who wanted to be up ahead with Yasha and his mates and who was working himself up into an ever greater frenzy.

We adjusted our face masks and gauntlets. John was standing up ahead, doing his best to hold down my front dogs; Tolia was alongside, ready on his own sledge, shouting that the iron claw attached by string to the sledge was an anchor. The baseball bat with the spike was for jabbing into the ice as a brake.

'Shouldn't we have further instructions?' I said to Ivan, shrieking above the baying dogs. 'What about the commands?'

'Your dogs won't listen anyway,' might have been the answer. Or it might not, because before anyone could say the words, Yasha was off and Fatty refused to be held back any longer.

I can't recall what happened to John. All I remember was the loss of control. We blasted off as if we were cosmonauts accelerating into space, heading into the sublime whiteness with no control over the source of propulsion. The dogs were unstoppable. We breached the perimeter fence and other layers of airport security. We thumped in and out of ditches, under fences, dodging oncoming army trucks, skating off roads, bouncing off signposts, aerials and telegraph poles.

A precious, long-awaited moment, my first passage with dogs through the Arctic was, it transpired, dictated not by me but by this imbecile Fatty, a dog on a mission to get closer to his own ever-elusive dog tribe. Neither the brake pole nor the metal anchor were of any use; like ill-disciplined pirates who'd got hold of the grog, the dogs ran amok, and all the while the long-muzzled, slant-eyed wolf-dog, from his position in the second row, lunged at the alien dog Fatty, as if determined to toss him overboard.

Then calm. The airport was behind us, and we were carving a straight line across a smooth white world. The grace with which we slid in silence over the bay gave the impression that we were floating; again, there was that notion of having broken free of earthly bounds. It was wonderful, the ease with which we cut across nowhere, the pattering of the dogs' feet only disturbed by the occasional snarl from the wolf-dog as he dived again at Fatty.

Slowly, the sun sank through the clear sky and the only sounds now were the sounds of Tolia talking to his team – the cluckings and warblings of a bird – and Yasha barking the commands *takhté*, left, and *steeyr*, right. I tried these on my own team, and so did Ivan, and so did Tolia and Yasha while riding alongside us. My dogs were oblivious.

1 No gloves – a balmy day, minus 15°C: Yasha (left) and Tolia (right), with failing Soviet buildings behind them.

2(a) Anadyr, capital of Chukotka and seat of Governor Roman Abramovich.

2(b) Early days: Flashy White, the alpha male and guardian of team leader Top Dog, who, at rear, doesn't even acknowledge me (behind camera).

3(a) Me, trying to get 'Bumbling' Bernard's attention, while the true team leader watches from behind my back.

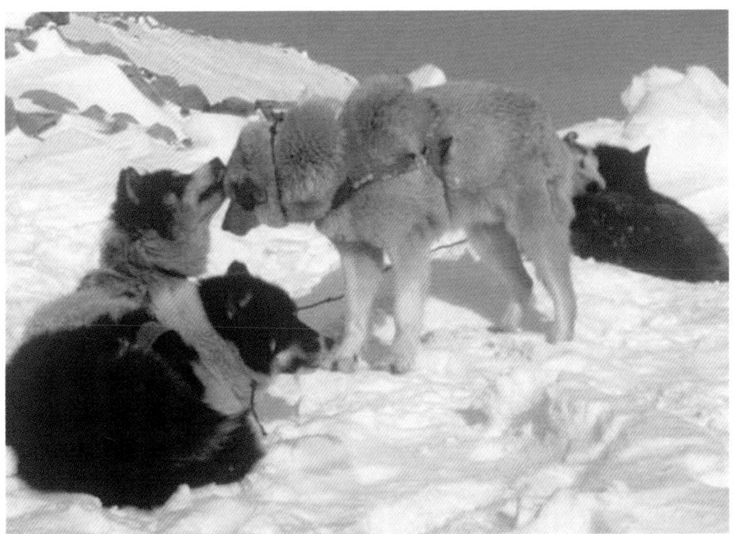

3(b) Top Dog, inspecting his team, succeeds in receiving Bernard's attention.

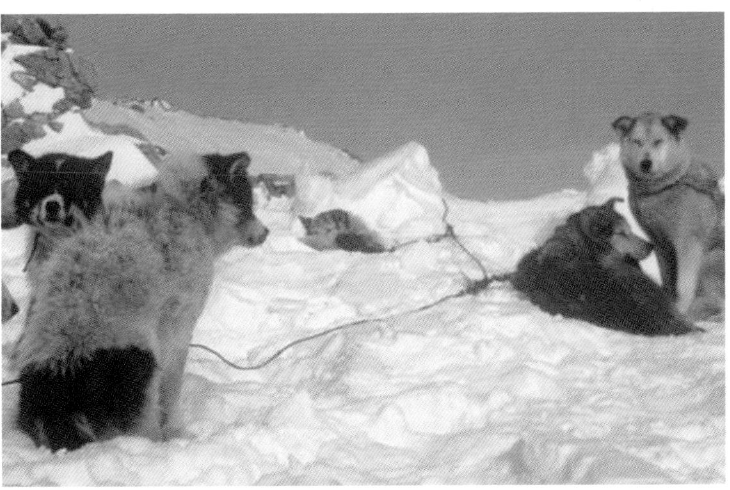

3(c) Allegiances: Jeremy tucks in close to Bernard; Frank hides behind an ice block from the feared Mad Jack (centre); Top Dog, sitting by the apprentice Basil, still eyes me (behind camera).

4(a) Top Dog, the team leader, supported here by Mad Jack (right), the only dog ever hopeful of an encounter with wolves.

4(b) Over sea ice: Yasha lays down a trail for the other teams to follow. Tolia, on right, with dogs trained to sniff for water, stays between my team and thin ice.

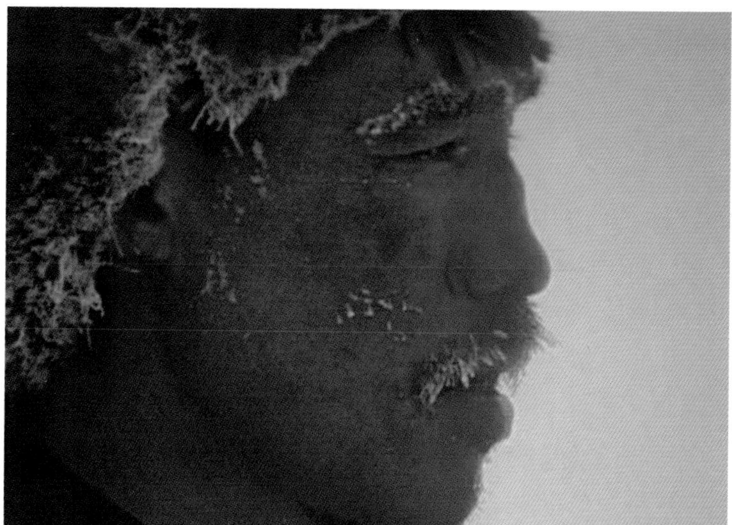

5(a) Tolia.

5(b) The constant winds which make the Chukchi Peninsula one of the least hospitable places man has settled in.

6(a) Raw walrus meat, awaiting consumption.

6(b) An abandoned outstation in the tundra.

7(a) Testing the courage of my dogs: Tolia's 'water-sniffing' team leads. The water opens up to the right – and almost immediately stiffens as it freezes over again.

7(b) The cliffs of Sireniki: snow from the Siberian interior blows into the Bering Sea, where the ice has been parted by the gale.

8(a) Novoye Chaplino: a building, not quite buried.

8(b) My dog team: no bedding, no shelter, and able to cope at minus 50°C.

But no matter – the dogs were settled in themselves now, content to be running; the movement seemed to exorcise a demon in them, answering some demand of their genes, some call of the wild. The wind picked up and we grew numb, but the dogs ran on without slackening their pace; at last I was experiencing the power that lay waiting within my team.

We drew to a halt at the far side of the bay, beside a flat owned by a former reindeer herder called Uri. Yasha staked out the dogs, right there on the icy edge of Anadyr. 'Today my dog Fatty was pulling yours along,' he said, stamping a sledge anchor into the ice. 'It'll kill him if he has to do that again many times. You must learn quickly.'

I nodded, although it seemed obvious to me that Fatty was a delinquent.

'Poor old Fatty,' said Ivan, looking at me accusingly.

I looked at Fatty. He belched.

'Did you see that?' I said to John.

'What?'

'He belched.'

'Dogs don't belch,' John said.

'Fatty did. He belched at me. I saw him.'

'The way to win them over,' said Yasha, 'is to be with them all day. Feed them, and as I said, talk to them. Cough with each one, so they know your sounds.'

But it was minus forty, so he waved me indoors for now. I glanced for the last time at the dogs, and only the eyes of young Basil looked back. As far as the rest were concerned, I was still irrelevant.

XVI

'So, what sort of equipment have you brought?' Yasha asked, knocking the snow off and stripping away his layers of garments, unpeeling, unzipping, unbuttoning, unfastening. Once more I felt like a spaceman: we'd entered Uri's flat through a double set of insulated doors, as if via an airlock, entering the mothership from the hostile vacuum.

'Just you wait!' I said. Proudly, John and I got out the huge snowshoes. 'There. Look!'

Yasha began shaking. He was trying not to laugh out loud. He called Tolia to come and have a look. Now, the two men were both shaking, using their hands to stifle their guffaws. They giggled and snorted like this for a while.

'What,' said Yasha, trying to pull himself together, 'what . . . else have you brought?'

Uneasily, we got out the sack of 1,500 dog boots.

The Chukchis were unable to hold back now. Tolia was laughing so much that water was seeping out from around his glass eye.

When the men had mopped up their tears, Yasha said, 'Maybe we'll take ten.'

Tolia glanced at him, wondering if he was being serious.

'In case a dog cuts a paw,' Yasha explained with a shrug. 'You never know.' They dug into the sack and plucked out just two each. I sensed they were only being kind.

We settled down to eat stew around the kitchen table. From time to time Yasha and Tolia chuckled together.

I tried to engage the two men in conversation, but it wasn't much use.

'We are not people who talk much,' Yasha said. 'Uri is different, because he's been in the town so much. He can talk on and on. He's brilliant at it!'

'You could tell me a *little* more, though . . .'

'OK. Well, I've kept dogs since I was a little boy. And they look after me as much as I look after them. And now that I've grown up, I have a wife and children. I hunt whales and seals to get us all something to eat. And there you are,' he said, wrapping the conversation up after only these few sentences. 'That's my life.' No further explanations needed.

He began pulling apart a torch of mine. 'Does this need fixing?' he asked.

'It does now,' I thought.

'I'll fix it if you like,' Yasha said kindly. For a second I watched him work. Everything looked so very breakable between his thick fingers.

'There's more to your life than that,' I persisted.

Yasha shrugged. 'I go out. I catch whales. I come back.'

'And you go fishing?' I suggested, encouraging him on.

'Me?' He turned to Ivan. 'What does he mean? Fishing is what Russians and women do.' He turned back to me. 'Men don't hunt fish, they hunt whales . . .'

'And then you sell the meat . . .' I said. I could see he wanted to get on with reassembling the torch.

'For money? I haven't seen proper money for a long time. I just swap things.'

Tolia wasn't much more forthcoming. 'Yasha is my teacher,' he said bashfully. 'I came out of the army and faced a bad future: no income, no food – that's how it is here.'

I nodded. I could see how it was.

'Under Yasha's guidance, I built up a dog team so that I could go out catching seals on the ice. Have something to eat for my wife and children.'

This was all I'd learn from the two Chukchis for the moment, so I went to the sitting room to examine my reindeer-skin furs. They weighed exactly fifteen kilos, and the carefully chosen Russian of my size on whom they were modelled must have put on a hell of a lot of weight before the final fitting because they kept falling to my feet.

But I slept well that night. These good, strong men, Yasha and Tolia, were on my side.

'Now,' I thought next morning, 'just how do people around here get ten dogs under control when it's blowing minus fifty?' By their collective silence, these ten Arctic citizens seemed to be ganging up on me; they just lay there in the snow, unwilling to share their knowledge.

'You must repeat the same reassuring words to them again and again,' said Yasha. As he spoke his breath billowed and then froze gently over his eyebrows. 'Keep saying, "Good doggy, good doggy," or whatever you British say. They will listen to you. They may seem to be sleeping, but they are observing you.'

While Yasha watched, I walked up and down the dog lines, politely saying good morning to each of my teammates in turn. When I turned to Yasha, I caught him shaking his head – either at me forced to walk like a clown in my excessive circus furs or because I was talking to these dogs as if they were pets.

'How long do they live?' I asked.

'They last fifteen years if not driven hard.'

It's what you might say of a battery, a Duracell in your bicycle lamp. Siberia always seemed to come down to expenditure of energy – how you stored it, how you spent it. It made me wonder if life for all of us was only ever about that one thing: calories. We went about gathering energy up wherever it was to be found; then it was a question of maintaining what energy we had and expending it at work or play.

'But the leaders live two years less than those at the back. It's stress, you see. They are the first to know about the wolves, the polar bears. You have to be a brave dog to be out there in front.'

He walked up to my two lead dogs, the beautiful white alpha male and the buff dog always in his shadow. The large dog rose to his feet, slowly tilting forward as he stretched. Yasha let him sniff his glove but didn't pat him. 'So, out in the tundra, we always call out to them to encourage them onward,' he said. 'You must do the same.'

'Your lead dogs, they make mistakes?'

Yasha went silent. I noticed this silence, even standing in the screeching wind.

'Once, I lost all my dogs,' he said.

The way he said it, I knew he didn't mean he'd mislaid them.

'They went off after a fox. Headed out over some thin ice. As it gave way, I managed to cut the dogs from me. I saved myself, but they drowned. I lost them . . .' He stopped. 'I lost all of my dogs.'

Yasha left me to get to know my dogs before we took them out for a run. I stroked each team member as best I could through my polar gauntlets and inner gloves. The dogs tolerated me, as a good dog might tolerate a teasing child. Only the youngster Basil seemed to appreciate the experience of being fondled. So I tried a different approach: I walked up and down the ranks, making each dog get out of my way. 'Above all, I must show I'm boss,' I thought. We all knew wilful dogs at home who tried to sneak on to the sofa, rearranging the family hierarchy in their favour. But as for their individual characters – which animal might one day be especially loyal to me or jealous of attention or stupid – the dogs betrayed nothing. Soon they were again just lying curled up in conspiratorial silence.

Time for their first serious run. Ivan lined up my dogs on the shore, carefully pointing them back east into the bay, and away from the open sea. However, even the bay had its hazards: Tolia said he'd be sticking to my right, to stop me 'straying towards any thin ice'.

'Ivan, I don't want Fatty leading my dogs again, thanks. Tell Yasha, "No Fatty."'

He called out to Yasha. 'He doesn't want Fatty.'

Yasha waved back, merrily. He couldn't hear: the dogs were howling, and the wolf-dog was screaming to get at Fatty. I'd already marked this animal as a potential troublemaker – Mad Jack was the name pencilled in for him.

But it was all right, Fatty was still with Yasha's team. Now, with Ivan and John holding my lead dogs, I sat on the sledge, preparing myself – positioning my throat guard and balaclava, pulling up my face mask, pulling down my goggles. Preparing for blast-off. Ahead, the water spread in a frozen rippled plain before us, contorted, bulging, buckled, full of pain and tension, the shadows of clouds strewn over it; at the far end of the bay the clouds themselves, oily grey smudges weighing heavily on the tundra.

We were just about to launch out when Yasha got up from his sledge. 'Wait!'

He unhitched Fatty and walked him to the front of my team.

'What's he doing? I said, "No Fatty."'

'I almost forgot!' shouted Yasha. He hitched him to the lead dog, Flashy White.

'NO THANKS! NO FATTY!' I called out.

'What?'

'NO FATTY!'

'Yes Fatty. I remembered him just in time.'

It was useless. Whether I liked it or not, Fatty was destined to come with me and bring about – I felt certain – disaster.

Yasha leapt on to his sledge and accelerated away. My dogs set off, led by Fatty and abetted by the highly strung Mad Jack, who was trying to get at him from the second row. Whatever I did, whatever I called, made no difference. My dogs knew that their master Alexei – yes, they probably even knew his name – was not present and Fatty took the initiative instead, giving chase to his own team and just occasionally veering to dodge the teeth of Mad Jack.

The dogs flew onward, and the sledge and I spun along behind, two powerless objects tossed and battered as we struck various hummocks of ice. Later, beyond the rusting cranes of Anadyr's quayside, the sun shone and the ice lit up around us; here the dogs might have settled into the run; I might have listened to the clatter of the dog claws, the hissing of the runners beneath me; I might have enjoyed the thought of the power that might one day be mine as the white pillowy hills sailed by. But there ahead, between thick untrammelled blue sky and white ice, was a lone man in furs fishing through a hole. Silhouetted against the dazzling icescape he looked like a cartoon Eskimo. He even had a primitive half-igloo to block off the wind and, I noticed, a small dog. This began yapping at us.

Was this a sensible thing to do, bark at a gang of approaching ruffians? With a display of unity I'd never before seen, and one that would have been commendable in other circumstances, my dogs pricked their ears and surged forward. Led by Fatty, the dogs acted as one to destroy the little pest.

I knew the danger. I felt it as we swerved from Yasha's trail and hit mounds of thin, warped ice; I felt it in the grip I was having to exert on the sledge just to stay on – the blood was not getting through to my fingers and they were going numb at the tips; and I felt it in the attitude of the dogs, their minds consumed by furious mob instinct. 'But what can I do?' I thought. 'Just jump from the sledge and abandon the dogs on my first day out?'

I dug into the ice with my anchor, stabbed with the wooden stave. It was little use. Fatty was offering just the sort of leadership I was unable to give.

I had already overtaken Tolia, who was meant to be guarding me from the weak ice, and was now passing Yasha.

We accelerated yet again. The little dog had thought better of defending his master and fled. Now there was nothing else in the world for these dogs, just the old primeval struggle: that of the hunter and the hunted.

We came to the Eskimo. I waved an apology as the front dogs knocked him down and the others ran him over. He looked up with a sad but resilient face, watching his day's catch disappear, the fishes snatched by each dog in turn, as if I was just another random blow of fate to be endured in the grim wastes of Siberia.

As for my own existence, it rested on the strength of the thin ice beneath; it had a turquoise lustre, I noticed, and occasionally offered up the sound of something cracking. My progress through the Arctic, my progress through life indeed, seemed about to end before it had got fully under way.

The dogs, however, were also uneasy about the weak ice right beneath them. They seemed to regain a sense of where they were. They looked around as if coming out of a trance and found they had no Alexei to turn to. A fight broke out between Fatty and Mad Jack, and we came to a halt.

Yasha drew up and stomped passed me. He thumped Fatty, hoicked him up in the air, cursed into his face and dropped him.

'You OK?' he said to me in English.

'Better head home,' I said. However, now we were a long, long way from anywhere. On the outward leg of this first run, the dogs had already clocked up twenty kilometres.

The dogs were calmer homeward-bound. Although I was thrown from the sledge once while dodging a coal lorry, the dogs were easily headed off by Tolia's team. They had had enough for one day.

XVII

'I know he is wild,' said Yasha, once we were indoors, 'but I like Fatty.'

I looked at Yasha. Once upon a time his dogs had almost killed him, yet he was happy to keep a faulty character in his operation. It didn't sound very sensible, but I admired Yasha all the more for his soft heart.

Feeling was returning to my fingers now and they started to sting. I began taking off my gloves – the gauntlets, middle gloves, inner gloves – to inspect the damage.

'I have to keep shouting at him to get him to concentrate,' Yasha continued.

Then he stopped. Tolia's eyes had alighted on my fingers. Yasha leant forward. Nearly all the tips, and the ball of one thumb, had pale, deadened ends, as if they'd been badly burnt. Personally, I was relieved: the damage was more extensive than what is often called 'frostnip', but I wouldn't lose anything.

Yasha must surely have been alarmed by the way the cold had damaged me so easily, making light work of someone so tall and lean. But he was good enough not to go on about it. 'This will hold us up for a week,' was all he said. 'And your fingers will be more susceptible to cold now.'

Tolia was still peering at my hands. And though he said nothing, later I noticed his eyes checking over my ears and cheeks, looking for any other damage.

It wasn't an ideal first day out, but Uri produced some vodka to cheer us up. 'Just a swig,' he said. 'No harm in that.' I noticed his face light up as he poured. By the second glass Yasha was telling us about how he lost his tooth while harpooning walruses. 'He forgot he was holding the line in his teeth!' Uri butted in, unable to wait for the punchline. 'And now, Yasha, you must tell them about that bear you met.'

'Which bear?' said Tolia. But his eyes were still on my hands. I felt like removing them from sight. Quite large and strong by the standards of home, they looked like a child's beside the blocks of brown knotted flesh that were Yasha's.

'I was out in the tundra,' Yasha began, 'and so was she! She stood up just ahead of my dog team, out of her snow hole. She had two large cubs. When they are with their young they are the worst – hell, they can be irritable, mother bears in the spring. And immediately she came at my dogs. The lead dogs swerved away, which swung my sledge right into her path! So I swiped my brake pole at her. She felt the wood, stopped a moment and thought about it. But next thing, her young started chasing us, so she decided to chase as well.

'Thank God, we came to a road! I managed to stop the dogs and look back. I saw the three bears silhouetted against the sunset. They were still running after us! And the dogs saw them too, loping along right on our tail. We all looked, horrified. The dogs and I pelted for Uelen, five kilometres away. They wouldn't stop till we were in the middle of the settlement! The next day, my hair was white and my voice was gone. I'd been shouting at the bear. I don't know what I shouted, but I'd certainly been shouting something!'

The bottle was empty, and looking at it, Uri said, 'Well, looks like the party's over.'

He turned in for the night, but Yasha, Ivan and Tolia sat in silence a while. Then Tolia said, 'Perhaps we should have given gifts to the spirits. Is that right?'

'We should have,' said Yasha, though he didn't look certain. 'Yes,' he then said with gathering conviction, 'that's definitely something we should have done.'

'Perhaps both sea and land spirits,' said Tolia.

'We'll give something before we set out.'

'Tobacco, a bit of tinned fish maybe . . .'

'Yes, someone must know the right procedure.'

But no one did.

XVIII

Things would be a struggle. I'd accepted that long ago, but I was struggling to maintain my vision of why I was here. We were weeks behind schedule, and now I couldn't even feed my dogs – the frostbite had reduced my fingers to two rather weak clamps. My chances of even reaching the Bering Strait before the summer melt, let alone 25 March, were slim.

I decided to slip away. A walk along the frozen beach would do me good. I stepped outside and immediately I felt the hairs in my nose stiffen as the moisture on them froze.

It was a sallow-skied day and the low hills to the north lay spread in a narrow spectrum of opaque and pallid colours. This was what the explorer Vilhjalmur Stefansson called the 'Friendly Arctic', and on a day like today you might be able to convince yourself it really was. The tundra was, in fact, a 'commonplace country', Stefansson announced after a five-year stint up here, quietly relegating the deaths of various members of the expedition to the Appendix.

Far away, the liquid blues of the bay ice were infused with the smouldering yellows of a polar-bear coat, and these paler tones gave way to an older, haggard landscape. Ice-capped rock jutted from the shoreline like broken teeth. Beyond, smeared thinly over the permafrost, were stubborn, stained snows that had been lodged here six months ago.

I walked down to the beach, where last summer surf had tumbled over the shingle; above, the low cliffs had been tufted with saxifrage; there had been lyme grass, cloudberries and forget-me-nots. Now, just the dead weight of snow; and where once I'd smelt the sea and heard it roar, now it lay down lifeless. Everything was held tight; time itself seemed frozen.

The Friendly Arctic, Vilhjalmur Stefansson's View in 1921

'To the members of our expedition the glamorous and heroic polar regions are gone and in their place is a friendly but a commonplace country . . . it is the mental attitude of the southerner that makes the North hostile. It is chiefly our unwillingness to change our minds which prevents the North from changing into a country to be used and lived in just like the rest of the world.' Inspired by Nansen's model, in which he had used his ship the *Fram* as a 'sort of floating boarding house', Stefansson went one step further, with none of Nansen's respect for the ferocity of the Arctic – which drove even the Eskimos to starvation at times – and concluded that '. . . a party of men could be as safe and comfortable without a ship as with it, that on any ice field you will find snow for a sanitary and excellent house, and that for adequate food and fuel there will be seals and polar bears'. Three members of the expedition died on Wrangel Island, just north of the Bering Strait; the remainder of the party was rescued after Captain Bartlett and his Eskimo companion Kataktovik and seven dogs went for help. The full, 'untold' story of how this occurred was revealed only in recent times by one of the young survivors, William Laird McKinlay, in his book *Karluk*.

Yet as I stood squinting into the light, the ice stretched out to the east as if offering a way forward. We all knew it to be treacherous, but it was also uplifting in its unsullied purity, a crystalline shelf proffered like a palm stretched out towards a new world. It suggested hope to me, as in prehistoric times the land bridge here had to the first peoples of the Americas.

I went to see my dogs. Basil lifted his head as I came up; the others watched from where they lay in their holes, looking up through their tails. I bent down to the shy fawn lead dog, and Flashy White as usual snarled. Was he protecting him? I wondered. Or was this jealousy? Yasha had warned me not to show favouritism – 'the other dogs will take it out on him'. I was only grateful the dogs were true to their breed in one way at least: they might not seem it, but all things considered they were a forgiving, docile little gang.

'There is not a trace of chivalry about these curs,' wrote Nansen of his Samoyed dogs. Job, for example, was 'torn in pieces by the other dogs'. In the daytime, someone was usually at hand to break up fights,

The Bering Bridge

The last across the Bering Strait were early Aleuts and Eskimos, who crossed to America by sea or winter ice 4–5,000 years ago. But long before this, a 1,600-km-wide land bridge connected the highlands of the Chukchi Peninsula with the uplands of Alaska, before it was swamped by the meltwaters of the last glaciation. The land bridge has a 70-million-year history and has been the route of important migrations of animals over that time. One such creature, the American mastodon, an elephantine creature with a straight trunk, plodded from its African homeland and into the Americas 15 million years ago. Back the other way came horses and camels, the horses dying out in their place of origin by the end of the last Ice Age, before the North American natives could harness their potential.

During the past 3 million years, the northern hemisphere has experienced a fluctuating climate, episodes of glaciation lowering the levels of the Chukchi and Bering Seas by a hundred metres and exposing the land bridge, and times of melt swamping it. Bison, lemmings, musk oxen, voles, deer and mammoths had all crossed through the so-called Beringia plain and settled in the Americas. Theoretically, people could have entered North America at repeated intervals between 40,000 and 13,000–10,500 years ago; artifacts suggest people lived on both sides at least 12,000 years ago, and present research suggests that the Bering bridge was inundated about 11,000 years ago. We can surmise that people, bison and horses were free to cross until that time; by then the mammoth was extinct and pollen samples indicate vegetation much like the present-day tundra, with sedge, dwarf birch and low-lying willow.

but at night, 'they seldom fail to tear and bite one of their comrades. Poor "Barabbas" is almost frightened out of his wits.'

He tried letting the dogs sleep on the ice again rather than on-board the *Fram*. 'The result was that another dog was torn to pieces during the night. It was Ulabrand, the old brown toothless fellow, that went this time.' But maybe Nansen was being unduly harsh about his dogs' lack of chivalry, for after Job's demise he noticed that Old Suggen was 'lying watching the corpse, so that no other dog could get to it'.

I stalked up and down the line of dogs, wondering why Alexei had

Explorers and their Dogs

The American Robert Peary, the man who is sometimes credited – though nowadays with less conviction – with being first to reach the North Pole on foot, launched his expedition from northern Greenland using local Eskimo dogs. Similarly, Nansen chose not to use the Chukchi sledge dog for his polar bid. Although he acknowledged that the dogs of eastern Siberia were said to be the strongest over distance, in the end he trusted to the dogs of the Nenets or Samoyed, a reindeer-herding people, dispatching a Latvian called Trontheim who'd been exiled to Siberia to obtain them. When Nansen at last met up with the thirty-four dogs to survive the trek from northwestern Siberia to the coastal rendezvous with the *Fram*, he was impressed by their strength on trial runs. However, the Siberian harness, a band around the dog's waist, was inferior to the Greenland Eskimo one, not as efficient at spreading the strain and also causing irritation to the scrotum. Such was Nansen's reputation that Scott also contacted Trontheim and asked him to obtain twenty-five for his first Antarctic venture. It was an extremely limited order: only nineteen survived to be put to use in Antarctica, these tied on a single trace pulling a train of five sledges. After the *Discovery* expedition, Scott brought the Samoyeds to England, and these became the foundation of the modern breed. The thirty-three dogs obtained for his final expedition were all mid-Siberian dogs (except two, called 'Esquimaux Peary' and 'Borup') and these were collected by Cecil Meares, who drove them across Siberia to Vladivostok with the help of the dog-driver Demetri Gerof.

Despite Amundsen being a protégé of Nansen, he, like Peary, chose Greenland Eskimo dogs, which he considered the most hardy, for his bid on the South Pole, bringing south no fewer than ninety-seven of them. His rival Scott's dogs had come from Nikolayevsk, in the southeast of Siberia; coming from a coastal town situated at only 54 degrees north meant they were unlikely to be as tough as either Amundsen's or Peary's animals.

The Samoyed (Bjelkier) may be used in small teams. It weighs three kilos more than the official Siberian husky breed: the male of the latter is 25 kg and 56 cm at the withers; the Samoyed is the same height but 28 kg. Today's Chukchi sledge dogs – which DNA analysis reveals are one of the oldest of all dog breeds – are perhaps a couple of centimetres shorter than the modern Siberian husky they gave rise to. Many explorers came to prefer the Samoyed over the Greenland and other Arctic dogs – such as the Chukchi dog and the powerfully built Alaskan Malamute (kept by the Mahlemuit, who used them to haul heavy loads) – because of their tried and tested ability on polar adventures.

designated particular individuals to the left, others to the right, and why some, like Mad Jack, were in the team at all. The other dogs bared their teeth at Mad Jack as I led him past, warning him off, understanding he was a bad apple. And, as if the dog that was like a lesser St Bernard wasn't ridiculous enough, dawdling along with his harness slack, the border collie alongside him on the fourth row was apparently inseparable, as inconsolable without him as Old Suggen and his late lamented friend Job.

It was enough to drive you to drink, which was the solution Uri kept advocating. The dogs too were driven to distraction, the strain of having no Alexei to watch over them beginning to tell. The dog resembling a labrador – or some such breed better suited for work as a gun dog in Hampshire than out here – took to biting through the central gang line (to which each dog was attached), thus separating the two all-important leaders from their team. However, I felt for this dog. He seemed a straightforward, honest chap – I named him Frank – and I too was better suited to Hampshire. He had frostbite on his rump, and as if the world wasn't bad enough for him, it was his lot to run alongside Mad Jack.

So many complications, so many machinations. Docile they might seem, but this was a little nation of politicking clansmen, each seeking their security in different allegiances, and in varying degrees, to master, to food, to companion. And where was the leader of this band? If Flashy White was such a great alpha dog, why was yesterday's debacle out there on the ice led by Fatty?

'They don't trust you,' Yasha had explained. 'When they do, they'll lead for you. They'll believe in you.'

'But they're *right* not to trust me,' I thought. Swenson, one of the first foreigners to realize the potential of Siberian huskies, had to work on his leader Bilkov for six months before he could get the dog to accept him as boss; until then he 'constantly took matters in his own hands'.

There was no time to waste, and over the next days Yasha drove the dogs for me as I screamed the commands from the back of the sledge – '*Takhté! Steeyyrr! Steeeyyyyrrr!!!!*' – to no avail. I felt increasing sympathy for Frank the labrador, the dog who looked like he wanted to get out of here.

'He's agitated. He needs security,' was all Yasha or Tolia could say when Frank again bit through the gang line. 'He knows the tundra will claim you all!' a passing Russian drinker chipped in, unhelpfully.

Yasha gave the dog a severe thumping, and afterwards Frank and I stood side by side, both feeling sorry for ourselves. And yet we would be leaving soon: given our diminished food supplies, we had no choice.

XIX

The dogs needed to develop more stamina. On training runs now they were managing 60 km around the bay. Sixty kilometres; 37.5 miles. No, these dogs of mine were not strays from a pound.

But I had no authority over them: they blithely followed either Tolia's or Yasha's dogs, whichever suited them better, while I forlornly screamed '*Steeeyyrr*' and '*Takhtě*'.

Each day I'd accompany the rabble into the haze lying beyond the cranes of Anadyr and seem to reach the nothingness at the far end of the ashen blue sky. Then we, Bumbling Bernard and the rest, would turn back, and Yasha would ask if I'd spotted the natural leader yet.

'To be honest, the second and third rows seem about as responsive as my front dogs.'

'It's in your hands. If you see a leader, even in the back rows, you must promote him.'

I said that the only dog I had a relationship with was the adolescent dog, Basil. 'He sometimes turns his head to listen to me.'

'Then bring him forward to the front,' Yasha said.

I thought, 'A lead dog who is a puppy?'

'They either have it or they haven't,' said Yasha. 'Like humans. See my lead dog? Sarah. A delicate little creature. But she is so strong, the strongest of the team! She is two years old, and still a virgin! Usually they start having sex at the age of seven months. But the boys are scared of her! And I am careful about beating her – she remembers. She is so complicated: I haven't worked her out yet.'

I looked at the ranks of males – chunky dogs, each of them prepared to follow this dainty bitch Sarah because she had a sort of charisma, a mix that we detect in the eyes of our leaders, far more than just intelligence, far more than just bravery. She trotted into the white desert, so brave, so petite, confident in her unique bond with her master.

I did try the young dog Basil as a leader, but not for long. He hung back, terrified by the whiteness, just as a child might be of the dark.

'Try another dog,' suggested Tolia.

'Which one?' I thought. 'Blot, for heaven's sake?' I walked up to the dogs. 'Frank,' I said, 'what about you?'

He looked up, worried to have been singled out.

'What about the big one without the tail?' said Tolia. 'You've got to hurry up and do *something*. We're out of time.'

'Bernard? A leader?' I said. 'He doesn't even bother pulling.'

'He doesn't pull?' said Yasha.

'Not at all?' said Tolia.

After some discussion, Ivan said, 'They say you're wrong. He *is* pulling.'

'No, he isn't,' I said.

Yasha laughed and shook his head. 'Oh, I see . . . Benya is joking!'

But I wasn't.

By 6 March, John had left, along with the lovely snowshoes. Yasha took me out with the dogs two or three times a day now, and we would watch the front dogs for signs of obedience. He would take my dogs out himself, and he too ended up disappearing longer than he had anticipated.

'As I say, they don't trust us,' he said back indoors. 'And as for that fat dog . . .'

'Bernard,' I said.

'Oh yes, "Benarrd" . . . Well, "Benarrd" doesn't pull!'

'Told you,' I said.

'But Alexei's put him in the team for some good reason,' Yasha said. He went silent while he had a think.

'Yes,' said Tolia. 'Must have.'

'To make up the numbers?' I said. It was an uncharitable suggestion, especially as it turned out I wasn't the only one with dog problems. I'd been watching Yasha's dogs, and his team wasn't the smooth operation I'd once thought. We all knew about Fatty, but Yasha also had to endure constant leadership struggles, a dog pining for home, and one particular individual who had learnt to tug the gang line. 'He knows it's the signal I use to start the dogs off!' said Yasha one bright morning, storming off into town to fetch his team back.

'Dogs are fools,' I thought. I meant they possessed a foolish honesty and devotion of the Shakespearean kind, the kind that reveals the faults of their rulers.

Yasha's cousins turned up to lend a hand: Liza and a fleshy teenager called Luda, both of whom had been banned from the house for leading the men astray. Sometimes I stood at minus forty just staring at these ladies – lining up the dogs, lunging at escapees – parcelled up in their furs and undaunted by anything. Bold, nimble, soft and yet formidable, they made themselves useful outmanoeuvring the dogs and outpacing the men, and always without fuss, without much effort even. How could Chukchi men live alongside women of such excellence and not want to be ruled by them?

As for finding a dog leader, there's only so much anyone can take. And perhaps Yasha knew this all along, because one morning out in the bay, with the wind cutting through to my cheekbones, a dog did choose to obey me. Not Flashy White, the alpha male, but his quiet running mate in the front row: the brown dog with a scarred muzzle that suggested he'd had to struggle all his life. Right before my eyes he veered left, as ordered, barging into the heavy flanks of Flashy White to get him to shift.

I slowed the dogs and called to the Chukchis.

I watched, Yasha watched, Luda and Liza watched while Ivan lined up the dogs and I repeated the exercise. '*Takhté!*' There was no doubt about it: he ducked under Flashy White's rope to steer him left; for a second time, the alpha male gave way to him.

It was at this precise moment, the moment of the true leader stepping forward to take up his post, that I understood how like ours dog society is. I'd taken the more powerfully built character to be team leader, but he'd been the alpha male of the pack, not the team, the one who assumes command as certain humans do in a power vacuum, when the established order breaks down.

I could see it all now: how a month ago in Alexei's absence his carefully constructed team had fallen apart. And the small brown dog up front had been having an especially bad time of it. As Alexei's appointed leader, he'd lost his role. Moved from his patch in Lorino to the unfamiliar scenes and smells of Anadyr, he'd been sitting it out, while brutal pack order replaced the man-made team. Where once there had been the alpha male Alexei, in his place arose Flashy White, and around him subordinate males like Mad Jack snapped

Pack Behaviour

The popular belief is that wolves arrange themselves in a hierarchy – that there are alpha males and alpha females and various subordinates. However, wolves, having learnt to avoid man in order to survive, are extremely difficult to observe in their 'natural' habitat: unlike most bears, for example, they do not as a rule scavenge from human settlements. Therefore, much of the notion of packs operating along hierarchical (as well as co-operative) lines comes from studies of captive wolves, where space and food resources are limited. The pioneering work of the leading lupine researcher David Mech among Arctic wolves (which, because of lack of ground cover, are more easily observed) now indicates that a wolf pack is generally just a family unit, and obviously the parents of any given family will dominate their children. Hierarchical behaviour becomes more pronounced in larger packs and between packs – especially during times when food is at a premium – but typically each pack might consist of a family unit of only seven or eight individuals, a couple of them being perhaps 'aunts' of the offspring who assist in nursing and hunting activities. When the young reach around two years of age, they begin to become more independent; these wandering, lone wolves eventually pair up with others to start their own pack.

There is virtually no reliable record of man having been set upon by a wolf pack, although individual wolves will bite when cornered. Some of the myth of the dangerous wolf might have originated from attacks on travellers' horses and dogs: zoologist Roman Gula, studying wolves in Poland, has found that dogs form a small but significant part of the diet of local wolves (2–3 per cent) – and more than sheep. There is some evidence that dog bitches are attractive to wolves and that they are more likely to pass through wolf country without being hunted down.

and cursed as they fought to hold on to their position.

Just recently, though, to the dogs it had begun to look like Alexei might not be coming back, and out on the ice there was reassurance to be had in obeying me. Thus, today Flashy White had yielded, and the quiet small brown dog could again take up the role for which he'd been trained. And suddenly it was I who was the alpha male.

XX

Yasha showed me the proposed route on my map, one of his short wide fingers steering out across the bay, forging its way effortlessly over the treacherous cliffs and ice cracks that lay in wait, along the Gulf of Anadyr to the only substantial settlement, Provideniya; all too easily his indomitable finger was soon coming to rest safely at Lorino in the Bering Strait.

We shopped for supplies, including a knife for – though, it went unspoken – cutting the dogs loose from my sledge if the ice gave way. We'd fixed our departure for the day before International Women's Day – 8 March – which meant only one day more in which to practise.

Now the two Chukchi women were marching out into the cold, Yasha behind. I walked in their footsteps, the women padding as light as foxes, their furs brushing over the snows and lifting fine silver dust. I paused to watch them go, troubled suddenly that I hadn't given these remarkable women enough attention. I'd come to the Arctic to listen to the men, because traditionally it was men who brought in the calories, hunting them with their dog sledges and kayaks; women it was, though, who kept these calories in the body, stitching and curing skins for parkas, gloves and trousers.

Luda, the younger Chukchi, held my front dogs. She must be warm, I thought; she wasn't stamping in the cold and dancing the way others were today in the wind. How old was she? Eighteen? Twenty-five? Thirty? Through all the fur, I could see only a strip of her face, eyes and skin bright, as if viewed through clear water. She pulled her scarf free so Yasha could hear her calling to him. Her lips were thick and very dark, I noticed, richly red against her white skin as it merged with the Arctic.

Yasha was creating a map in the snow. 'Off you go alone, Benya,' he said.

'Alone? Not a good idea.'

'It's your last chance. You have to. Not far – and I'll be watching.'

Was this his idea of 'not far'? I wondered where Ivan was, so that he might translate. I looked again at his little map in the snow and tried to match it to the features around me. Yasha was expecting me to go on a twenty-kilometre round trip.

Next thing, a drunk Chukchi lady arrived from nowhere – perhaps from wherever it was that Ivan was prematurely celebrating International Women's Day – and insisted on me taking her two little girls along for the ride.

'There!' said Yasha. 'Now you won't be alone.' I didn't want the responsibility of three passengers, one tipsy, the others helpless children. What was my lead dog likely to do – actually obey me for a second day? I hoisted one child off my sledge and pointed her towards Yasha. That left me with the woman and the smaller child.

'Right, let's go.' I waved at Luda. She waved back, released the front dogs and off we sped.

My team leader was again obeying me – at least, when he saw fit. We veered left and right haphazardly across the bay to the first marker, stopping and starting as I intervened with my brake pole. The longest leg now, right to the far black cliff. Once there, with my dogs now turned and ready for home, I stopped. The dogs stood stationary on the smooth, plate-glass ice; the pain of my frostbite was gone and I had forgotten my passengers. We had come all this distance between here and Anadyr, which was barely visible through the crystal vapour. I looked out across the array of ice plates that were spread ahead, tilted and level, orderly and confused, dusted by the snow, metallic in the low sun.

As we slipped homeward, the air around me seemed full of grace and silence, the sledge attached not to a string of coupled dogs but to a flock of migrating birds that was steadily making its ordained passage across the skies. I had at last touched on the freedom to be found in the Arctic.

Yasha's team was coming out of the haze. He was looking for me, standing on his sledge, his hand shading his eyes.

'Where have you been? To America?'

I had misunderstood the scale of his snow map.

'You all right?' he asked my passengers, who had, come to think of it, been rather silent lately.

'The mad Englishman!' the woman said. 'We should have been issued with passports.'

'Are you still drunk?' I wondered, perhaps a touch unkindly.

'I'm c-c-c-cold,' the child said. She began crying. Yasha made her march up and down a slope to warm up, but she bawled her eyes out for quite a while more.

I'm ashamed to say that nothing could lower my spirits. I had mastered my dogs – not for all occasions, but at least for this outing. The tundra was a forgiving place today; I dared hope I might one day cope even when it was not.

We didn't leave the next morning: Women's Day wasn't a festival celebrated, it seemed, for one day, nor by only the women. Ivan was drunk for three days. And during this time I could see the longing in Yasha's eyes: he wanted to be away from here; these towns wearied him. 'If alcohol ever becomes a serious problem on this expedition,' I thought, 'Yasha, you will be the last to succumb.'

But we'd surely be away in the tundra soon, and when our last evening did come I went out to be with the dogs in the dark.

They stirred, hearing me approach. 'They know my footsteps now,' I said to myself, and was comforted. I crouched beside the leader, in my notebook referred to simply as 'Top Dog', who was the only one not sitting up. 'Not wasting his energy on me,' I thought; 'still not prepared to do that for me yet.' Lying resolutely curled up, Flashy White looming over him by way of protection, he put me in mind of another reticent top dog of the tundra, Governor Abramovich. And he, in turn, put me in mind of another tycoon I'd met called Richard Branson. They didn't like meeting your eyes, these two top dogs. That didn't matter – I was shy myself. But it was interesting that it didn't count: they understood power, and that's what made them different from the rest of us. They knew how to work it instinctively.

'Will you let me down?' I asked the dog. 'Or will I let you down?'

I went indoors for a good night's sleep but found myself just lying there, occasionally flicking cockroaches off my face and wondering if things would turn out all right.

In my notebook I filled in the names of the remaining dogs. Dennis and Muttley would have to do for the rear dogs, quiet, sturdy individuals who must have been selected for their lack of initiative. And

Jeremy for Bernard's friend, the dog that resembled a border collie and like any sheepdog was always busying himself.

Flashy White *alpha male, protector of leader*	Top Dog *team leader, reticent*
Mad Jack *likes a good scrap*	Frank *'labrador', a chewer*
Basil *playful, an apprentice*	Blot
Bernard *no tail, doesn't pull*	Jeremy *his companion, 'border collie', intelligent*
Dennis *strong, black and white, loyal*	Muttley *strong, brown, loyal*

My thoughts drifted tortuously to the pieces of luggage, the items that may or may not prove useful on the journey ahead, the survival kit that I'd wear each day, in it the crumpled bit of paper.

We were setting out into the tundra, the dogs were not yet to be fully trusted, and nor was I. And what of those in support around me? The foundations of modern-day Siberia were shattered to the very heart. I could easily anticipate the day coming when the dogs and I might be up against it: ill-prepared, ill-resourced and alone in the Arctic.

Yet still we were setting out tomorrow.

XXI

The thirteenth of March is a clear day, minus fifteen or twenty, and the ice bright and dry, spread like crumbled marble below the immense blue sky. Outside, in my full reindeer furs, I look north out across the bay and find that I am smiling.

Beside me is my sledge, stacked with gear: tent, food, petrol. There's hardly room for me to sit down. Yasha lifts one end up, weighing it. 'That'll be 300 kilos with you on,' he says. 'About right.'

Even with our sledges so heavy, it's hard to hold back the dogs. They've been waiting for five weeks for this moment. And so have I. Last night's doubts are forgotten as I adjust my face guard, covering up cracks of exposed skin; the dogs pace, they howl, they paw at the snow. We are raring to go.

It was a great moment, the dogs so keen but the two majestic Chukchi ladies standing with my lead dogs, not putting up with any nonsense. Again I wished I'd come to know them, these women, stark against the clean ice, strong-boned, strong-hearted. They'd never been surprised at being asked to do anything, and the dogs seem to recognize this certainty in them.

However, one of my dogs, Bernard's pal Jeremy, now escaped. I'd already noticed he was an alert dog, but it appeared that all this time he knew how to slip his collar.

'Doesn't want to go,' said Tolia.

'He can see the amount of luggage,' Yasha said. 'He's worried.'

He was right to be. The first settlement, Uelkal, was 200 km away. A lot can go wrong in tundra over that distance. For this reason Yasha was insisting that Uri and another reindeer herder accompanied us on snowmobiles for the first leg.

We can't wait around any longer. 'Just leave him,' Yasha said to Uri, who was trying to lasso the dog like a reindeer. 'He'll follow.'

Jeremy isn't the only one with doubts. At the last minute, Yasha and Tolia remember they've forgotten to leave an offering to the spirits.

I find it heart-warming. Despite all the world has done to eradicate their beliefs, Yasha and Tolia still look to their spiritual heritage in troubled moments. They may not believe that a pair of ravens brought the world into being, but they still understand what their grandparents meant when they talked of there being no hard boundaries between man and animal, between animate and inanimate.

However, I'm not expecting them to have read up on how to do a ritual in the last couple of days, and indeed they haven't. They ask me for a tin of tuna from my lunch supply and tell Ivan and me to copy them. We observe while they vaguely wave around bits of the cheap Russian canned fish. Then, the second phase: they break up a high-tar cigarette, crumbling it into the snow. It's not exactly a full shamanic ritual, at least not according to the book I wrote on the subject. 'Better the spirits didn't know it happened at all, maybe,' I record in my notes. And judging by the lack of prayers, they don't.

The Chukchi women are still holding the dogs. I go back to my sledge and take a long last look into the tundra ahead. It lies like a

Chukchi Spirituality

The Chukchi Peninsula is unique in the Arctic in that until very recently there has been no missionary proselytizing. Both male and female shamans existed, and they alone had access to the spirit world, using their journeys to cure the sick, predict weather in the highly changeable tundra and sea, and protect boats, men and dogs. The petroglyphs of the river Pegtymel, dating from 1,200 years ago and of uncertain origin, give an idea of the animistic world of the region. Typically the images are apparently of hunting: deer, whales and sea otters followed by men in kayaks with lassos or dogs. However, there also appear to be dancing figures surrounded by mushrooms, which are of monstrous size and probably of the hallucinogenic fly agaric variety. Many are fused to the figures, sprouting from their heads as if to suggest the permeable division between man and spirit.

Bowhead whales were the most significant of the hunted animals in the lives of the coastal Chukchis, and accordingly, while shamans helped ensure that the whale spirits were resurrected and guided back to their homelands, seals and walruses played little part in rituals. Every whale harvested was greeted with words or song, and meals concluded by throwing a piece of meat into the sea to thank the killer whale, ruler of the sea, for allowing the meal to be possible.

Many of their beliefs were shared with the Yupiks, with whom they shared the seas. The killer whale, raven and wolf were sacred and rarely killed. The swallow was thought to protect hunters at sea from the summer fogs and storms, and ceremonies were held to placate the sea mammals before setting out. The killer whale was also a protector, becoming a wolf in winter and devouring the reindeer, unless some of the reindeer submitted themselves to hunters.

'All that exists lives,' Waldemar Bogoras quotes a nineteenth-century Chukchi shaman as saying. 'The lamp walks around. The walls of the house have voices of their own. The skins sleeping in the bags talk at night.' The entire world is animated; it may act, it may speak. Animals as well as humans have souls, and all things have 'masters', spiritual entities controlling them – which humans must engage and come to an arrangement with.

spangled ribbon, the two snowmobiles shrinking into it, Ivan stuck like a freshly caught seal on top of a heap of luggage, fading away as the Arctic bleaches him out. The engines cackle away into the distance for a while, and then that sound too is gone. The tundra looks spotless again.

Yasha was having a last look over his team, nodding with approval and ending with a brisk stroke of Sarah, as if rewarding a corporal for turning out the platoon so well on this big day. 'When dogs greet each other, they sniff. And we Chukchis are the same. When we part, we don't kiss, we hug and smell each other.'

On saying this, he hugged and smelt the two women in turn, pressing his nose into their hair. '*Mei!*' he called out with satisfaction. 'When you have spent time on an expedition, you too will smell of the dogs, the walruses – it's the smell of the tundra, and it's the best smell there is.'

Then Yasha was seated on his sledge, Tolia to the right, ready to block me from the thin ice. He looked back, checking if I was ready. I was indeed, until Luda unexpectedly put her face on to mine, deftly navigating a way between my neck guard and mask to plant a long and large kiss on and around my lips. What was going on here? I'd hardly ever said more than 'hello' to her.

'Oh my god,' I thought as I sat on my sledge, awash with Luda's perfume. I looked up to see those dark, glimmering eyes on me, searching me out from where they lay behind the trim of reindeer fur. I felt her kisses tighten my skin as they froze.

Then I was flying across the bay behind Yasha. I hadn't released the brake: the force of the ten dogs had plucked the anchor free. Luda, along with all manner of questions and answers she presented – on womanly tactics of survival and perhaps much else – was thrown aside. Familiar obstacles came and went: the dreaded highway and its thundering coal lorries, the fishermen and their tempting attendant dogs. All the way, Jeremy was running madly beside my team, unable to tear himself from his place in the scheme of things, which was to be there in his pack alongside Bernard.

By midday we had cleared the bay and were steering through an abandoned military outpost that had suffered severe bombardment – although in the end by way of the advancing tundra and not enemy forces, the advancing armies of the capitalist American empire. Each pane of glass had been blasted out as if by grenade, and the cubicles where once conscripts stopped traffic to examine documents had also succumbed to concerted enemy action. 'СТОП' ('STOP!') a crumpled metal sign said as we swept on through, the barrier bent by winds as if by a tank. And onward through folds of land dotted with surveillance masts and into the empty hills.

For now Top Dog was following the reassuring trail of Yasha's sledge and ignoring my commands. Fair enough, I decided. He's disconcerted by this strange, heavily equipped journey he's meant to help lead through new country for heaven knows what purpose.

The tundra was a glorious place to enter today, the ground smoky with its burden of fine wind-borne snow. Occasionally, life sprung out: rock or willow ptarmigans raced into the air; Arctic hares flipped away. This was encouraging and I kept an eye out for other life – but found none. Not in the skies, not on the land. Then, an hour later, I was rewarded by a single twig. It projected from the snow like a broken car aerial – in fact, at first I thought it *was* a car aerial. I stopped the dogs and examined it, this testament to a dwarf birch more determined than the rest. Newly exposed bark had been peeled by the wind and hung from it like the sharpenings of a pencil. I was reminded of other, hotter, deserts: of crossing the Gobi alone and seeing a coiled snake. It had raised its head, threatened me, but that didn't stop me feeling overjoyed. At last, here was a higher life form! Here was something on my side, the side of the living. I remembered the words scribbled on Janáček's score of *From the House of the Dead*, Dostoyevsky's story of four men in a prison camp in Siberia: 'In every creature a spark of God.' And God in this context seemed to be something we welcomed because we recognized it in ourselves; whatever its intentions, it was more familiar to our core needs than the dust.

The next indication of life eluded me until we crossed a frozen riverlet and my sledge runners passed over ferny leaves trapped as if in aspic. Caught there in space and time were spiralling marsh weeds and strands of what at home I'd have called eel grass, flying like a girl's hair in the wind, although that wind had frozen solid too.

And out here among the rocks and ice, no escape from the cold. I felt depleted as I sat motionless on my sledge, buffeted by the wind, the calories being sucked off me, my heat dissipating downwind – I kept imagining – like the vapour trail off a plane. Surely the tundra would offer us shelter soon.

Yasha stopped the dogs. 'We eat here!' he said.

'Here?' I thought. 'We're going to stop here? Where someone who mislaid his dogs might as well lie down and die?'

Yasha was already settling down as if for a picnic. He and Tolia leant into each other, blocking the wind, creating an igloo arch with their backs as they got on with refuelling their bodies. They were hacking into the walrus, and even though frozen, their picnic reeked.

'Here's yours!' said Yasha, proffering a slice on the tip of his knife. I looked at it: the fat a centimetre thick, the fibrous fishy flesh tinged pondweed green and accompanied by that dustbin odour of old fish. Then I looked longingly at the bread I'd thought to bring from Anadyr. It was now as solid as a brick, and nothing could be found to smash it apart. I opted for a slab of whale meat, chewing the tyre-tread skin and inch of fat through to the finely threaded beefy flesh that you'd hope for in such a grazer.

We wove into the hills – a pounded land, where the snows, even the rocks seemed smacked down. There was nothing soft here but us. And Yasha guided all the way by memory – or some mysterious higher instinct of his. I'd heard it said that the Chukchis even nowadays car-

James Cook and his Ordeal with Walrus

When James Cook inflicted walrus meat on his men, he came perhaps the closest he'd ever been to mutiny. Yet arriving in the forbidding Arctic to find such a source of nutritious fresh meat had seemed too good to be true at first. Cook had ordered his men into boats to shoot the walruses, 'seahorses', which were perched on ice floes around him. Once they'd been cut into steaks, fried and served up, many men simply couldn't help vomiting. A petition went round requesting a return to salt rations. Cook went into a rage and called the objectors 'damn'd mutinous scoundrels who will not face novelty'. Soon men were dropping on deck, fainting as they worked.

ried an internal navigation system; it was in the form of a song. 'A mother sings this to a child in the womb, and later as a lullaby,' a Chukchi mother had explained to me. 'When he or she reaches adulthood, the song acts as a guide. No one may take it away or use it. It's something that will always be there for them, and they add verses as they grow up and life shapes them. These are a kind of song line, drawing Chukchis home.'

It emerged that it wasn't the song lines that carried us safely through the tundra, it was the vague prints of a meandering tractor. That tractor now came into view, coming the other way, trundling back home again.

'Where have you come from?' Yasha called.

'Nowhere,' said the driver, a Russian. He was stiff; his gloved hands looked frozen to the wheel; his breath lay strung like cake icing around his bearded mouth. 'You?'

'Nowhere!'

'Excellent!' said the Russian, exploding into thunderous laughter. 'And you are going where?'

'Nowhere!' The men had a good chuckle together.

What was this confidence that enabled Yasha to follow faint vehicle tracks to nowhere? It was something no professional adventurer would risk, even with the benefit of a satellite phone with facsimile features.

Two hours had passed in the wind, and now I was hungry. 'Should have gobbled up all that stinking walrus while it was offered,' I thought. A further three hours later, and I was looking at the frozen walrus ahead of me, that boulder of granite on Yasha's sledge, and wanting to get my teeth into it. I kept imagining the relief, my energy being replenished as the fat melted inside me.

Four hours on and my cravings had reached Franklin-esque dimensions; I'd have welcomed a portion of *tripe de roche*. Seven hours on, and I could see Michel the cannibal's point of view.

'Shall we camp?' I suggested when we did stop for a snack. It was almost dark.

'Camp?' Tolia said, confused. 'Why does he want to camp?'

'The dogs can get home even in blizzards,' said Yasha. 'They have a sixth sense.'

'Yes, but do my dogs have common sense?' I thought.

'Tolia will stay near at hand,' Yasha said, 'to make sure we don't lose you.'

Darkness gathered and we plunged on into it. My dogs veered from left to right, refusing to follow the scent left by Tolia's team because Mad Jack had been lunging at them all day and the teams had become embroiled in a sad, never-ending tribal war as they sought to defend their brethren. We dropped further and further behind. For a time I could hear Tolia calling to his dogs ahead; then his voice was lost to the wind.

The paws of my dogs were clattering now; we must be on ice. The stars to my left and right were obscured and I guessed we were in a narrow pass, though not one narrow enough to offer up an echo.

I trained my torch beam ahead of Flashy White and Top Dog, but there was no sign of any surface. The dogs skated on over the invisible ice, faithfully following the scent of Yasha's dogs – or a fox, for all I knew.

Sometimes, far away, I glimpsed a light, perhaps from one of the snowmobiles. Then it too was gone. We were floating through blackness, just me and these dogs whom I didn't trust, and who didn't trust me. Finally, as the sledge began slewing from side to side, striking my legs on passing boulders, I decided enough was enough and dug my anchor into the ice. Its teeth didn't bite, but the dogs, like me, were losing confidence and we came to a halt. I heaved the sledge on to its side, in order to jam it there.

I looked at my dogs. They were wanting to give it another go.

'We're not going anywhere,' I said aloud to Top Dog. 'You may be able to smell forty times better than me, but, chum, I can think a lot better than you. And the system is not working.' Then I ducked down behind my sledge – only to find myself with Dennis and Muttley, who'd got there first.

Someone would come back before long. But even if I had to wait out the whole night like this, flashing my torch for would-be rescuers, I'd decided I'd do all right swathed in my reindeer skins. There must be deer out here somewhere in the tundra right this minute, experiencing what passed for reindeer contentment on a night with a windchill of only minus thirty.

That wind seemed thicker now, coming at me in turbulent waves, tumbling along and sometimes rolling the snow over me or thumping it down as if sea surf. Pain spread in spasms from my frost-blistered fingers as I worked harder to keep some feeling in them. My body was faring even worse than expected, exposed as it was to the full onslaught of the tundra. 'I'm the weakest of the expedition,' I thought. 'Yet I've got the biggest plans.'

Eventually, the sound of rescue – the jingle of harnesses in the wind. I waved in the approaching dog team with my torch; two orderly ranks of eyes flashed back, a wolf pack reorganized by man.

Before long we were reunited and pitching the tent for the night. The dogs were digging themselves in, scratching, nudging, squeezing and melting their way into the ice, while we humans, left out here on the surface of Siberia, fought the wind.

I noticed that Uri, normally so overly upbeat, was hugging himself, brooding and silent. 'The wind is wearing away at us,' I thought. 'Hollowing out our will.'

Then Yasha's stove – solid, reliable, Soviet, the type that never fails – failed. My lightweight mountaineering stove was called into service, and although purportedly designed for Everest, this too seemed in a state of shock. I was all for just clambering into the tent, cracking apart a chocolate bar and not bothering to melt ice for tea, but Tolia got down on his knees in the snow, trying to solve the stove's petrol leak. I watched as he jammed a vagrant washer into place, the skin of his hands like industrial gloves, his blunt fingers like pliers.

'These are the people to be among,' I thought as Uri roused himself and ran around in circles, and Yasha lifted morale by blasting off a distress flare. Bang! The night flickered, and we stared, mesmerized by the falling scarlet meteor. 'Happy Chukchi New Year!' Then all was black again.

The Eskimo in Danger

Anthropologist Hugh Brody, with the Inuit for a number of years from the 1970s onwards, found, on an excursion in the tundra, that even in the face of death they were cheery company.

'During one of many tea breaks, Anaviapik turned to me and said, in a matter-of-fact way: "*Mitimatalingmut tikijjajunirpugutqai.*" "Probably we'll never make it back to Pond inlet." I have a vivid memory of the shock of fear that went through me. Although I had known that this was a journey full of difficulty, and while some of the dogs were starving and we were very hungry, I never for a moment supposed that we were at risk . . . neither Anaviapik nor Muckpah had given a hint of worry. Despite exhaustion, hunger and disappointments, they had expressed neither disingenuous optimism nor disgruntled pessimism. The mood never changed. The same balance of quiet conversation, jokes and friendly silence had continued each day.'

'Just look at them, at play here in hell,' I thought. At moments like this, you looked up at the Chukchis and thought you were among the immortals. They seemed a little less likely than the rest of us to die.

Later, in the tent, I twiddled my fingers and toes to keep the blood flowing and with increasing satisfaction lay listening to the wind blowing and sucking on the canvas. 'So,' I thought, 'the tundra at last. And maybe with the help of all of Yasha's strength I will indeed adapt to it.'

My thoughts drifted to Luda. What was she cooking up beneath those thick furs? I tried to picture her face – and couldn't, seeing just the watery depth of her eyes, the rich and fleshy nature of her limbs and such pale, resilient Arctic skin firmly wrapped around them. Once, towards our departure, she'd scribbled childish letters on her hands. Some in red, some in black, adornments that were interspersed with love hearts. A boyfriend, of course. Or someone she was infatuated with. 'B' or 'Ь' or 'в'. Always 'B' . . .

XXII

The wind had dropped. The morning light was rebounding off the snow around us, which lay banked against our tent, against the dogs, the sledges. We stretched, brewed up some tea, and on we went, lurching through loose, loamy snow, ploughing through the virgin fields.

Ahead of me, Top Dog was working himself hard, raising his head, scanning, lowering his head, picking up the pace, slowing it. Though Yasha's team picked the route, he was always adjusting, interpreting. It must be a lonely position to be out there, armed with a dog's senses, waiting for the danger to arrive – bears, the thin ice. And behind you your companions, who were also your competitors: Mad Jack, Frank, Jeremy with his worried eyes flicking over the horizon, Bernard with his heavy, lumbering legs.

I began to miss living things. Dwarf birch, willow, bilberry, crowberry, black bearberry, white Arctic mountain heather, crustose and fruticose lichens, non-sphagnum mosses. They were all bedded down below us, out of reach. Yet there was life nearby: you could detect it in the change that would come over the dogs. They'd enthusiastically lift their muzzles, catching a scent in the wind, or nervously glance around them as they hastened on their way.

'Half an hour ago, maybe less,' said Tolia, stopping to examine polar-bear tracks. 'Lone young male. Moving north – the spring migration. They head for open water about now with a plan in their head: to hunt seals from the ice floes.'

'What sort of place *is* this?' I said to Yasha that night in the tent while drinking tea. My head ached and I wasn't sure how long I could stay awake flexing my fingers and toes for a second night. Had the dogs noticed how badly I was coping?

Dealing with Polar Bears: Notes from Adventurer Pen Hadow

Bears always desire water – looking for seals.

Dogs attract bears.

Dogs will smell the bears and behave oddly.

Don't take your gun into the tent – more and more ice will collect (through condensation) in the barrel.

Don't try pocket-pencil flare – buy a proper one.

N.B. Wrangel Island, just northwest of the Strait, is a bear nursery (only the females hibernate).

Don't shoot polar bears: it's (a) ignorant; (b) unnecessary; (c) against the law.

If you have to kill, report it to police. Keep toenail/teeth for data.

Firearms: anything with gas chamber etc. won't work. Use basic shot-gun. Onus is on you not to kill it. Use whiz-bang cartridge. If that fails, plastic bullet.

Attempt to:

- SCARE IT. Don't try ski sticks over the head. They already know bangs. INSTEAD TRY whistle, zipper. N.B. Pen's secret weapon is rustling a Safeway carrier bag.
- ORGANIZE yourself – or you will get cold (if forced out of camp by the bear, etc.).
- GET FIREARM READY – get your small gloves on, otherwise you'll get frostbite as well.
- IF you resort to shooting, go down on sledge to use as a prop.
- LAST RESORT: heavy shot – obviously centre of body – head/lungs. Or .44 magnum (less than 10–15 m. But would have to be able to shoot it dead! Ideally, .375 rifle, bolt action).

Wolves: not aggressive to sledge dogs accompanied by humans – curious. (N.B. I suspect they may spook dogs, though. The Arctic wolf is one of the biggest. Others have said that even a whole team of unaccompanied dogs, if harnessed, is no match for one big male Arctic wolf.)

'You ask because you think it's miserable. But in a month you'll miss the tundra – even you, who's finding it harder and harder.'

'So, you *have* noticed how slow I'm becoming,' I thought. 'A little bit slower each day.'

'You'll want to be out here, and not in the warmth of the town.'

'He's speaking the truth,' said Tolia.

'Just look at the dogs,' said Yasha. 'Don't you sense their love of the tundra, even though it's such a hard place?'

I did. With all their hearts, they loved it. To run over the glassy ice, to feel the sugary snow fly from their feet, with each step to see and smell anew. Each morning they were coiled like springs, awaiting release. They couldn't wait to savour the blood pumping through them. Only when running, it seemed, were they fulfilled.

'But the dangers . . .'

'They fear nothing except wolves and water. The bear doesn't worry them – until it bashes them. But the water is a killer and they know it. As for wolves, they aren't to be tampered with.'

'There's no wolf blood in your dogs?'

'I hope not! Female dogs do take themselves off into the tundra when sick – for herbs. And sometimes come back pregnant. But the pup with wolf blood in him is untrainable; he'll turn on his owners. We want nothing to do with them. Nor do our dogs! I have friends who'll tell you they woke to find the tracks of two she-wolves running through their camp. Not one dog out of the fifty had barked. They ducked down instead – fifty dogs! No, a clear line separates the wolf and the dog. The wolf, he'll go on killing rages, mauling reindeer and not eating them. Last year, a worked-up wolf latched on to the arm of a herder, but he got that one's head in an armlock and stabbed him, so that was all right.'

The candle blew out and we lay in all our furs, pressed together and clumsy within our sleeping bags like larvae restlessly waiting for the time for hatching.

Once in the night Yasha said, into the darkness, 'But we are sea people, and the animal we truly respect is the killer whale. We never hunt him. We watch and admire him. Our ancestors believed in this creature – his power, his right to rule the seas, to rule the whales. If we sight the killer whale, we let anything we are hunting go, in deference to him. Though the truth is that we love all whales; we sympathize as they dive to avoid being harpooned. It makes you cry to see the family members support the wounded in the water, if, say, a flipper has been bitten by a killer whale. It's a privilege to share the seas with these beings.'

'And a privilege for me to be out here with you,' I thought. 'Keep remembering that.' Whatever their problems, it seemed clear to me now that the Chukchis would survive out here long after the Russians had been forced to pack up and go.

The settlement of Uelkal appeared out of the soft, chalky horizon, beyond ice that was worked by the wind as if by a giant cheese-grater tearing a continuous sequence of knee-deep, sharp-edged divots. The snowmobiles soon had to find an alternative route and we stumbled on alone – until Yasha held up a hand to stop us.

'Cliff,' he said. 'Follow me carefully. To the right.'

'Follow you to the right,' I repeated, and peered forlornly with my dogs towards the drop.

Yasha called to Sarah, and she led, swinging her eleven male underlings behind her in an arc. Away they went, dropping out of sight.

I was hesitant – and not without good reason, I felt. Tolia volunteered to go next. However, he got the angle wrong and my last sight of him was as he sailed through the air a metre above his sledge.

'Benya!' came Yasha's voice from below. 'Your turn!'

'Well, if I really have to . . . *Steeeyyyeeer*!' I yelled to Top Dog, but he stood stock still. Where was his allegiance now? He didn't look back at me. He didn't even hear me. If he'd been quietly gathering confidence over the last day or two, he'd lost it all, standing on the edge of the cliff. His eyes were straining for Yasha, who was somewhere out of sight below. 'I may be a sort of pack leader in the good times,' I thought, 'but Yasha is something like a dog god. The dogs see that he commands me, see that he seems even to command the tundra at times.'

Flashy White was yelping now, looking frantically ahead and then back to the other dogs, wondering what next.

I released my brake, and we were off over the ledge, taking Tolia – found spreadeagled downslope – rocketing along with us. The cliff was by no means sheer. However, at the base of the slope was a fissure, a dark, yawning divide in the ice like the bergschrund you might more reasonably expect at the top of a glacier. I saw that we were meant to be aiming for a little bridge of snow, perhaps two metres wide, which would deliver us over it. Down we careened, so fast that we were over the narrow bridge before I could think about it. We slewed with a sharp smack into Yasha's sledge.

'You must believe more in your dogs,' said Yasha. 'They are not suicidal. They won't take you over a sheer cliff.'

It struck me that dragging me over a sheer cliff was *exactly* what they might do. I remembered the dog driver whose photo I'd seen in Valentia's museum – Nikolai, who'd had his own cliff incident and as a result was sadly no longer with us.

The dogs grew excited at the smells issuing from Uelkal – of the dogs waiting there to be challenged, to be hunted. And so many noises: in the tundra, our every sound had been whipped away by the wind; now, these sounds echoed all around – our commands, even the clicking of the dogs' paws flickered back to us, rebounding off the walls and roads. Yasha guided me in, waving a torch between the treacherous telegraph poles. The dogs, maddened by the possibilities awaiting them here, refused to have any of it, and when we did come to a halt we were wrapped around a lamp post.

'A man died here,' Uri said, as we entered a hut he'd already requisitioned up an alleyway recently topped up with snow. He was flicking a bit of tinned fish and vodka around at the stove. 'This is for his spirit. So he doesn't feel left out of things.'

I waited for him to tell me more.

'That's it. That's all I know that I should do.'

We hung up our gloves, boots, furs; then, steam rising from our underclothes in the warmth, we sat as the kettle boiled. We were stunned, unable to adjust to the sudden quiet of this refuge. All we could do was look around at each other as the heat gathered on our faces. Three days we had been out in the wind; now at last we could savour the peace . . .

For about three minutes, because then a delegation arrived, led by the village administrator.

'Benedict Allen, you are cordially invited along to the Cultural Centre.'

It seemed churlish to refuse – and it was just as well we accepted because a feast had been laid on. In the community hall we found both Russian and Chukchi guests, politely waiting to sit down at a trestle table. They grinned excitedly, their faces lighting up as they examined what had arrived from out of the tundra.

An old lady addressed us loudly in Chukchi as other ladies stood patiently, bearing shots of vodka on a tray. It was a glorious welcome, and though still in shock, I beamed back a smile to express my appreciation. Then one of the ladies with the vodka interrupted the old woman. 'Gentlemen, you must be tired,' she said, yanking the lady to her seat. The aggrieved woman let out an indignant squawk.

We laid into the food while a dance ensemble appeared on the stage. A cassette player was switched on and young men proudly placed their feet squarely on stage, spread and tightened their great ropes of arm muscle and, in the way of some mammal of the sea, swayed side to side with hands flattened like whale fins. The women spread their fingers into flight feathers and rocked their heads, panting and sighing rhythmically like courting birds of the spring shore.

Then the music jerked to a halt and lights began flashing. Two teenagers in tight leotards leapt on to the stage and gyrated to the pulse of Russian rock, offering their fleshy thighs and hips as if on MTV.

'Sexy,' commented Tolia politely.

It was a fine effort, but to be honest, I'd have been happier curled up in my sleeping bag. I'd grown accustomed to the dogs and men of the expedition: the Chukchis in their silence, splicing a rope, stripping down a sledge runner; the dogs always waiting, ready to move on. In the empty tundra, these characters had expanded to fill my world.

After a while we made our excuses and left. Yasha, Tolia and I found ourselves sitting together with our dogs, happy to be out in the cold with them for a moment. I was the last to go indoors. My tears from the wind had begun to freeze, and that set me thinking of the American meteorologist Adolphus Greely, who lay in his tent with a handful of others through the eight lonely screaming months of an Arctic winter, their teeth dropping out, their flesh splitting and hardening like bark in the cold. 'Near each sleeping bag was found a little package of cherished valuables carefully rolled up,' recorded the rescue party, 'and addressed to friends or relatives at home.' Beside Greely had been found Sergeant Elison, both his hands and feet 'frozen off' while foraging for food seven months before. Someone had tied a spoon to the stump of one arm so that he could eat, though what the men were now often eating was their clothing. Yet Elison and Greely had refused to give up the ghost; they remained in their tent, undefeated. But why? Why hadn't they given up the struggle? That's what I had come here with my file of survivors to find out. This type of person refused to renounce their part in the project of living things. 'Like the herbage, I have sprung up many a time on the banks of flowing rivers,' proclaimed Mansur Al-hallaj, the Sufi poet. 'For a hundred thousand years I have lived and worked and tried in every sort of body.' And I was a long way yet from understanding this impulse to persist.

To Be a Survivor: An Eyewitness Account of the Rescue of the Ill-Fated Lady Franklin Bay Expedition, June 1884

In 1881, the American soldier Adolphus Greely (1844–1935) volunteered to command an expedition of twenty-five men to conduct circumpolar weather research over that winter in Lady Franklin Bay, Ellesmere Island, off Greenland. The party pushed further north than any prior expedition to conduct research into weather patterns, but their relief expedition of 1882 failed to reach them, and the 1883 ship also failed to break through the ice. Greely put into action his contingency plan, abandoning his camp, 'Fort Conger', that August and travelling south along the Ellesmere coast in a number of small boats, which were steadily lost to the seas and ice. Finally, at Cape Sabine, after thirty days adrift on an ice floe, they established a camp on 21 October 1883. They persevered through another winter, for the next eight months living off their few remaining supplies, caches left from other expeditions, shrimps, lichens and strips cut from their clothing. Greely had carefully placed his instruments and his two years of collected data in a cairn where it might be found.

The rescue party, arriving in a cutter, spotted the clear outline of a survivor on a ridge. Lieutenant Colwell went to him. 'He was a ghastly sight . . . his utterance was thick and mumbling, and in his agitation his jaws worked in convulsive twitches.' The man identified himself as Long, and once he'd been helped to the cutter, 'in a husky voice, told his story . . . No words can describe the pathos of this man's broken and enfeebled utterance, as he said over and over "a hard winter – a hard winter".'

The other rescuers, meanwhile, hurried to the wrecked tepee near the shore, its pole toppling over and the flaps held down by stones.

'Colwell called for a knife, cut a slit in the tent cover, and looked in. It was a sight of horror. On one side, close to the opening, with his head towards the outside, lay what was apparently a dead man. His jaw had dropped, his eyes were open, but fixed and glassy, his limbs were motionless. On the opposite side was a poor fellow, alive to be sure, but without hands or feet, and with a spoon tied to his right arm . . . Directly opposite, on his hands and knees, was a dark man with a long matted beard, in a dirty and tattered dressing-gown with a little red skull cap on his head, and brilliant staring eyes . . .

'"Who are you?" asked Colwell.

'The man made no answer, staring at him vacantly.

'"Who are you?" again.

'One of the men spoke up: "That's the Major – Major Greely."

'Colwell crawled in and took him by the hand, saying to him, "Greely, is this you?"

'"Yes," said Greely in a faint, broken voice, hesitating and shuffling with his words, "yes – seven of us left – here we are – dying – like men. Did what I came to do – beat the best record."

'Then he fell back exhausted.'

This was all that remained of the twenty-five-strong expedition. The scene 'was one of misery and squalor'. The rocky floor was covered in cast-off clothes, and among them were huddled together the sleeping bags in which they'd spent the last few months. There was no food left in the tent but 'two or three cans of a thin, repulsive looking jelly, made by boiling strips cut from the seal-skin clothing'. It was evident that most of the men didn't have long to live – the heart of Connell 'was barely pulsating'. After a shot of brandy though, 'he could just gather the idea that relief had come, and that he must brace himself to live'.

'Their worst symptom, apart from their weakness, was their swollen condition,' and during the last six months, watching the others pass away, one after another, 'they had learned to recognize this as the surest sign of the approaching end, and although now their faculties were more or less blunted, they had realized that the hand of death was on them, and that a little more would put an end to the horror of existence.

'Colwell gave them . . . a little of the biscuit he had in his pocket, which they munched slowly and deliberately. Then he gave them another bit while Norman opened one of the cans of pemmican. Scraping off a little with a knife Colwell fed them slowly in turns. It was a pitiable sight. They could not stand up and had dropped down to their knees, and held out their hands, begging for more. After they had each been fed twice, they were told that they had had enough, that they could not eat more then without danger; but their hunger had now come back with full force, and they begged piteously to be helped again, protesting that it could do them no harm. Colwell was wisely deaf to their entreaties and threw the can away. When Greely found that he was refused, he took out a can of the boiled sealskin, which had been carefully husbanded, and which he said he had a right to eat, as it was his own. This was taken away from him, but while Colwell was at work trying to raise the tent, someone got the half-emptied can of pemmican, and by the time it was discovered the party had scooped out and eaten its contents.'

Greely dedicated his eventual book *Three Years of Arctic Service* (1894) 'To its dead who suffered much – to its living who suffered more.'

XXIII

We decided to stay for a day and get on with various maintenance tasks.

'I'll fix you a pair of braces,' said Natalia, who'd been commissioned to find a way to keep up my reindeer trousers. 'It's the only solution. Yasha says you are losing weight every day.'

Meanwhile, Yasha was sewing up broken dog harnesses, and Tolia was fixing the sledge bindings, manipulating wire as if it were thread. This was Chukchi culture as Yasha experienced it, not a performance, the half-remembered expression of what used to be. It was about fashioning a sustainable life from the tundra. Once that meant breeding a new strain of dog or adopting the Eskimo's kayak. Now it was about bending an old drainpipe into a sledge runner or borrowing army-issue overalls off a conscript soldier while he was on leave. The sledge too was a tribute to the Chukchi make-do-and-mend culture: the traditional hide stringing (chewed with gusto by the dogs if they could get near it) was replaced by electrical cabling. The dogs ran in two disciplined ranks – a more efficient use of force over long distance – in the manner of the early Russian trappers.

A fight broke out among my dogs. I found Jack standing over Frank, who lay prone on his back. I gave him a cuff. 'He's just a bit uptight at present,' I said to Ivan. 'Feels claustrophobic, perhaps, being in the town.' Personally, I could only sympathize.

'Thump him properly!' said Tolia, giving Jack a blow of his own.

'Tolia must know better than me,' I thought. Dogs don't obey their masters any less if they are beaten. Amundsen, the protégé of Nansen who swept to the South Pole with dogs, would have agreed. 'The right footing must be established from the outset,' he'd said. 'The dog must understand that he has to obey in everything.'

The Traditional Sledge

In his account of his stay with the Chukchis, William Hooper describes sledges constructed for speed 'being exceedingly light, and of an elegant form'. Six or nine arches of wood were set into flat runners, and these supported a seat five feet long. There were whale-bone supports, and at the head were 'runners with thin, springy curves'. The runners were lined with broad strips of whale bone, which 'render friction scarcely observable'. Dogs were attached by a single thong of seal hide, two to ten dogs radiating out from a ring of ivory.

The dogs were given seal-skin socks at times, and the sledge runners were dressed with ice or a frozen paste of moss. The Eskimos might employ only three dogs per sledge, each dog carrying a 40–50 kg load. Critically, the introduction of the gun meant easier hunting, more food for dogs and people, and larger and more spread-out settlements.

In time, both Eskimos and Chukchis incorporated other alien ideas: the traditional fan hitch, the dogs each with their own string, radiating out from the sledge, is still used in eastern Canada and Greenland but elsewhere gave way to the tandem system, which is more efficient in terms of energy expenditure but less safe over thin ice, as the weight of the dog team is not spread. The French command '*marchez*', or 'mush', was adopted by trappers.

'But just keep reminding yourself,' I thought, 'you want your dogs to stick with you when you're all alone.' The great Amundsen didn't need his dogs to do that, nor do the great Chukchis.

Meanwhile, the dogs were watching us as we came and went. They wanted to know what was happening. 'It'll help me,' I thought, 'their insecurity. They'll look to me for leadership.' But not yet, not while Yasha and Tolia are protecting us.

I checked their feet, one by one. They were holding up for now. But the extra measure of safety provided by the two snowmobiles would be gone after the next settlement and I still knew little about my team. What was the point of having Mad Jack along, when he might injure another dog? And Bernard, who was only ever a burden. And the highly strung intellectual Jeremy, who didn't seem to be able to do anything without Bernard. 'They very often form friendships,' wrote Amundsen, 'which are sometimes so strong that one dog simply cannot live without another.'

Presently, Bernard was sitting up to catch the sunshine; he was drooling – the sight of all the walrus meat being chopped by Tolia. His saliva was freezing into spindles of ice. They hung, snapped off, and then others spun down and stiffened to replace them.

Around the supper table there were toasts to Uri, whose birthday it was. And after two vodkas Tolia, usually a man of so few words, felt moved to make a speech.

'Yasha is my companion,' he said, with one hand clenched around the smoothed chunk of meat that was Yasha's shoulder. 'He is my best friend; he has taught me everything. He knows my thoughts, I know his . . .' There was silence as we stood with our glasses, waiting for him to continue. 'Now the task is to get over the bay,' he said simply.

In earlier times, you prayed not to be given a southerly wind, the Wind of the Bad Spirits: the drifting ice would block the bay and stop the boats getting out. As it happened, tomorrow we'd have a northerly wind, the Wind of the Good Spirits.

'Well, that's obviously good,' I said.

'Bad,' said Ivan. 'Apparently, this means the ice gets blown out of the bay. The ice might split while we're out there.'

'Big obstacle ahead,' I wrote in my diary, as the others began drinking in earnest. 'Seems the ice is breaking up. We'll rest the night, then set out. An uncertain crossing.'

I paused, wondering what to do about these drinking bouts. They made life bearable if you lived here, no doubt, but I was afraid for my expedition: alcohol seemed to act like a rotting fungus in these northern hemispheres, seeking where it might advance itself.

'Write something good, because you are responsible for the next generation of British through Chukotka,' interrupted Ivan, lying flat out on the linoleum floor.

'I need him to stand firm,' I wrote. 'Yet his ability to find an affinity with strangers means he's merging with this troubled people. Or, more dangerous, perhaps there's something about this damaging land that he's found a natural affinity with.'

But I reminded myself that things were going the right way. After one night out on the ice we should get to Konergino, the settlement on the far side of the bay. We were still a tight-knit band. So far, the tundra was working to strengthen, not weaken, us.

XXIV

'Once we're out on the ice, don't think about the dogs, think about yourself,' Yasha said as we prepared to leave. 'If you hear cracking, jump clear of that heavy sledge. Just jump.'

I nodded.

'And then run. Just run.'

'Leave the dogs?'

'The dogs will survive better in the water than you, if that's what you are wondering.' Yasha got astride his sledge. 'A friend was out on the ice. Found it sinking below him. He cut the dogs free of the sledge and jumped into his kayak. The dogs swam in perfect discipline to safety, even in their harnesses. He carried on commanding them, left, right, as they swam. They didn't dare disobey him then!'

'And you think even my dogs will do that?' I asked.

'No,' Yasha said. 'No, I don't think that. Not your dogs.'

Leaving town, my dogs were soon getting themselves tangled around each of the telegraph poles that they'd wrapped themselves around on the way in. There were no farewell crowds, just bystanders, including a hunter dressed in white so that seals wouldn't see him sneaking up on them. He stood amazed, marvelling at my incompetence.

However, as we negotiated the usual outlying scrapyard of tangled junk, it was Tolia's team that came off the worst. A dog caught his paw on a rusted nail and was led away limping. That was my last view of Uelkal – not the ailing buildings or lorries buried in alleyways but this dog looking back at us, his head angled sideways as he listened, his eyes tragic and his brow furrowed as he watched his companions leaving him behind.

I was still thinking of how this little injury could have cost me any one of my own dogs when we came to the broken shoreline ice. The bay lay before us, nothing but frozen-up waves to set our eyes on.

Yasha slowed up. 'Tolia's team will go first.'

Tolia seemed to know what was expected of him: his dogs had been specifically trained to go out on to the ice shelves to bring back seals; he even had a dog trained to smell water through the ice. He set off, that water-sniffer dog with its nose to the surface like a bloodhound. The other dogs seemed to be looking at him, wondering if he'd detected any dangerously thin ice yet.

We followed along, lurching over the sastrugi, the dogs skipping over the ice where it reared up like up-ended pavement slabs, me thumping my legs on each jagged blade in its minty blues and greens. I was waiting – waiting for that sharp report which would be the sound of the ice giving way beneath my 300-kg sledge. The scene became one of violence: everywhere the ice around us had been sheared; splinters had been thrown up and tossed aside, scattered in shards along fault lines. And all the time the water, masked by a wafer of ice, waiting beneath us.

Our route took us past a water bird. It lay where it had keeled over, frozen out on the open water during a sudden freeze. 'Not a snipe,' I thought, the long-legged discreet birds Nansen observed; whatever this wader was, from its vulcanized-rubber webbed feet to its pencil beak, it had frozen into a block.

Yes, death could come at any moment. But not for us today. There were no explosions of collapsing ice; just the sound of the dogs pattering over it, the runners grinding beneath me, and all the time, hanging in the air, my ignored commands. Snow fell lightly, and when the wind picked up, the flakes around my eyelashes consolidated, fixing my eyes into a stare.

The two snowmobiles had been taking a more circuitous route, and when I next saw Uri he was singing. He had a bottle in his hand; the vodka had stiffened to treacle in the cold.

'He's not even sharing it!' Ivan said. I noticed that his eyes were fixed and slightly desperate as his snowmobile followed in hot pursuit.

We assembled our tent as the snow whisked about from north and south, circling us in the dark. The next day it had all gone, every flake driven away. Yasha opened the flaps, sniffed at the wind, eyed the sun breaking through the haze, watched his breath rise and dissipate in crystals and said, 'We'll leave right now.'

More snow was on the way. It would obscure the thin ice.

As we went, I was straining for a glimpse of the water, the stuff that was a requirement of life throughout the universe but which might bring us death. With time, I did see the bright glimmer of the water surface – and beached nearby were three ringed seals, slumped there like slugs but in tight suits of black-speckled yellow fur.

'We call them Nerpa,' Yasha called. 'Keep moving.'

Konergino drew near. I knew because the dogs could smell it; they were gathering pace. I'd learnt from Uelkal how the dogs got overexcited on entering other dogs' territory, and began battening down loose baggage as though readying a little boat for a storm. The dogs were yelping with anticipation; Mad Jack was screaming. The town dogs, hearing us, also began working themselves up. Our teams accelerated, and when we finally arrived we were like cowboys riding into a town to shoot it up.

'Keep them from the pet dogs,' Yasha yelled over his shoulder. 'They'll rip 'em apart.'

The large and formidable dogs of Konergino appeared, ready to take a stand, and the bravest charged at us. Sooner or later, however, they were all running for cover. Women rushed out to wave greetings, and then shrieked as our dogs arced round to get at their lapdogs. Two children leapt on their terrier, protecting it from destruction. Not before time, we came to a halt in front of the Administration Block.

'Lydia, Deputy Administrator,' a woman barked out, extending both arms.

Resplendent in furs that encompassed her to her ankles, she also had a fag in one hand which she used like a conductor's baton to point out where the dogs could go.

'Tie them to the lamp posts over there. And unload your luggage here.' She tapped the appropriate spot in the snow with the toe of a freshly polished leather boot and then sped off to our rooms. 'They are simple, clean quarters, you'll find,' she said, as we trotted behind. 'No cold water, but lots of hot.'

She ran a tap. Out came volcanic jets of dark water. Plumes of steam rose from the sink as if from a crater; water swirled with a heavy burden of debris, churning like a cauldron of lava. 'Scalding hot,' she said, chucking her cigarette into it. 'Totally unusable.'

Like Uelkal, the quiet little settlement was a crowded place after the tundra. We felt clumsy and trapped. Soon we were hiding indoors from curious onlookers, clustering together quietly as we adjusted our bodies and minds.

A teacher called Victoria arrived. 'The English class has prepared two cakes. Will you come? You're the first Englishman here that anyone can remember.'

Ivan and I followed her to the school block. As we entered the class, the pupils, mostly girls, stood and clapped. They sat us down to eat their cakes and asked me about Britain: the Queen, Stratford-upon-Avon, Manchester United, the kilts of the Scots. I was invited to stand by the blackboard and talk about places that seemed too far away and too small now to be relevant to anything much.

I suppose I must have given a reasonable enough account of contemporary western Europe, but I was in a daze, dazzled by these Chukchi and Russian faces looking back at me, so fresh, as yet uneroded, alert, open-eyed – vulnerable, like a herd of deer. An hour ago we'd been out on the floating ice and the night before I'd been up secretly staving off yet more frostbite. Now these friendly life forms were all about me. I was mesmerized by their welcoming eyes. Strong survival impulses seemed to be telling me to attach myself to these people, that I should shelter here from the leeching processes of the tundra, because if humans ventured out into it for long they only ever weakened.

I stood by the blackboard, taking in the life force as it flowed towards me from the blue-black inky eyes of a Chukchi called Sveta, who was sitting there dreading that I was going to ask her a question, and a hazel-haired Russian called Tatiana over to the right, her head held erect on a strong, fluted neck. She could hardly speak a word of English, but she stared back defiantly, refusing to baulk as I asked her something she couldn't understand. Here was elegance and life; here was everything the tundra had deprived us of.

Being embraced by this strong community was doing wonders for Ivan as well. From the moment he started mingling with the teenagers he was the easy, lovable person I remembered from before the start of the expedition. Everyone was again warming to him, opening up, letting him in. 'I'd forgotten why I hired you,' I thought, watching as he passed his smile this way and that, from all around him teasing out kindly thoughts. 'How you used to smooth my way.' I'd lost him somewhere en route through the tundra, but now he was back with me again, restored by this dip into a pool of young, intact living things.

I was aware of a silence in the classroom. Victoria and Ivan were looking at me, waiting for me to speak. The whole class was waiting. How long had they waited? 'Bloody hell!' I thought. 'What am I thinking? Is admiring these young ladies the right way to behave?'

I addressed the class. 'So, tell me what ambitions you have. What do you all want to do after school?'

This was a tactless question. What could anyone do here? There was another silence – a really big one this time. Finally, a boy spoke up: he wanted to go to St Petersburg to study computing.

'You enjoy the internet, then.'

'No. Never seen it.'

'I see. Right.'

'I want to be a banker,' said Tatiana.

'Why's that?' I asked. This was more encouraging.

She was confused. 'Why? To see lots of money, of course . . .'

Soon I was wanting to get away from the settlement. The chance came the next morning, when Nikolai the sheriff said he'd take Ivan and me on a jaunt with his snowmobile. 'We'll go to visit the reindeer herders. The third brigade.'

Through the snows we went. No sign of the deer, though – just the herders sitting in a shack having tea. 'We're having trouble with a wolverine,' explained a man with wind-cracked, taut, dry papyrus skin. 'The deer have run off. Every single one.' He thrust a 'carbine' into my hand, then a bullet, and said I must help hunt this nuisance down.

We soon spotted it out there: a bushy-tailed animal with a small dark head and massive feet, a cross between a dog and a bear. It loped along like a shadow against the whiteness, evading our snowmobiles with extraordinary stamina. On and on this animal gambolled over the snows, swerving, ducking, feigning a move to the north, tacking back to the south. Back and forth we swerved across the plain, enacting this terrible dance of life and death, while around us the eternal blue and white mountains looked down. Ivan took a shot and hit the wolverine, but still the beast persevered, blood speckling the snow in its wake. It would not surrender.

Only with a second hit did the end come, the impact of the bullet sending the wolverine cartwheeling. I watched, saddened, as the animal clawed at the new wound; then it gave a deep, despairing sigh and died.

During the pursuit, we had lost the reindeer herders and somehow picked up their dog – a black fluffy creature now with a frosted-up face.

'Let's see. Where's home?' said Nikolai.

'He's teasing,' I thought. Then I saw how lazily he handled the rope as he hitched the wolverine's corpse to the trailer.

'He hasn't a clue,' I said to Ivan.

It was no use looking at our tracks, which wound in hopeless knots around us. We headed towards the sun – southwest, more or less the direction we'd come from. The dog dutifully tagged along behind; unfortunately, it seemed that this hopeless creature was not going to lead us home.

The sun went down, and still we were heading from high ground to high ground, trying to locate a landmark. We came upon fresh tracks, but they were of a polar bear, also wandering around out here. Now even the rolling waves of tundra were hard to discern. There'd been a range of hills to the left and one to the right, we agreed. Which placed Konergino – where? No point in trusting to Nikolai, though he kept up a smiley, unfazed façade. I tried to piece together a map in my own mind, configured around the Pleiades in the sky overhead.

As night came on, Nikolai stopping occasionally to let off inadequate little distress flares, the aurora spread over us in hazy, electric green shafts. Occasionally, these replenished themselves, bursting out afresh, casting vermilion spores across the heavens. These patterned skies delighted me; I loved the way they seemed to be silently giving birth to the dust from which each of us is composed. I looked up to them, even in my growing anxiety. 'No map, no food, no water, no survival kit . . .' I thought. How had I allowed myself to get in this mess?

Nikolai jauntily decided on bearing south, thinking we might intercept a vehicle track. I stopped him. 'Look! That red light!' We wheeled the snowmobile around to shine the headlights at it. The red light blinked at us, like an eye, and disappeared. The tail light of another snowmobile? A trick of the night, perhaps.

After further discussion, we elected to head towards the light, which was inland, west, back in the direction of the bay. At least we'd have the shoreline as reference and might follow it up, or down, to Konergino.

The northern lights were now a menace, obscuring my navigation stars and any light emitted from Konergino. Several times we stopped, seeing the beam of what was apparently another vehicle. The tundra seemed to be haunting us. The wolverine had lured us away into its wasteland lair; now we were paying the price of our arrogance. But wait: I was the only person who hadn't relished the sport of hunting the animal down. Would I be the only one who walked out of here alive? Such were the irrational thoughts assembling in my head.

Earlier we had been able to laugh at our predicament, but not now. All the time I was doing mental calculations, double-checking our progress against my idea of the map. What if we had somehow missed the bay and were heading deeper into the tundra? Was there anything *at all* to the west, between here and Moscow?

The dog was still following us. Sometimes we would stop and see if it was inclined to head off in any particular direction. But he was just a friend content to stick by us, and even that was of some reassurance. Then the chain of the snowmobile broke. It was time to walk.

As we began our march, I wondered how far I'd get with my 15 kg of leather armour and whether anyone was setting out to look for us. Yasha, did he know we were out here? On his final, fateful expedition John Franklin must have taken such comfort in his wife Jane. A determined lady safely back home, she was surely badgering away at the admiralty, demanding relief missions be dispatched as, with the passing seasons, not a word was heard.

We had seen what we thought was a glow on the horizon, so were striking out towards that, not sure yet if it was the northern lights again or some other trickery of the Arctic. One thing to be grateful for: there was no wind. 'We'll last on foot for several hours, at least,' I thought.

Ivan called me over. He'd found what seemed in the dark to be furrows formed by vehicles. We caressed the hard ground with our gloves, smoothing our fingers over the stones as we traced the lines. He was right. It was a piece of good fortune that nobody commented on but which might save our lives.

I forged ahead along the track, marching on in my reindeer skins, still imagining that I was going to need all my powers of stamina. However, turning back to the others, I saw a prick of light emanating from the tundra. There was surely no doubt this time. Another useless flare was set off. I harried Nikolai back downhill to turn on the lights of our skidoo and flash a signal.

The vehicle light was coming nearer – they'd seen us. It must be a rescue party. We relaxed, allowing ourselves the thought of a quick journey back to the warmth. 'I can be honest now and say I was worried,' said Nikolai. He began laughing – a nervous, shrill, unsettling laugh. He didn't seem to be able to stop.

The light that we were all watching went out. We turned off our snowmobile headlamp and peered into the dark. We stared long and hard, willing the life we'd seen to come back out of the night. As we watched, waiting, all was quiet; the tundra had never seemed so deathly black.

The light came again, a glimmer spreading before us across the ground. 'Might be the northern lights reflecting on the snow,' I said. It grew, like a fire coming alight. Then, just what we needed to hear: the sound of an engine. We switched our own light back on. Surely, we would be seen.

Uri drove up on his snowmobile, a bunch of men sitting behind him.

'They are so calm about finding us!' said Ivan, as Uri casually waved hello and turned the engine off. However, all Uri saw was us standing with a broken snowmobile on the outskirts of town, which turned out to be only one or two kilometres away. They hadn't been coming to find us at all.

Uri left us to drop off his friends, and the dog opted to follow him. Ivan and Nikolai had a cigarette, and before they'd finished it Uri was back. We abandoned our skidoo and within an instant were over the brow of the hill and passing the first telegraph pole. Again, I reflected on the thin line between life and death. One moment isolated in the tundra, and precisely sixteen minutes later enjoying the central heating. 'And this thought above all else,' I wrote in my notes that night. 'The wolverine hung on to life beyond anything you might have thought reasonable. Some instinctive urge, a life spirit, a primitive form of belief.'

The experience was to stay with me throughout the journey; it stays with me even now – the death of the wolverine and the manner in which it almost had its revenge on us. And I knew I'd do well to remember how our companion the dog had no compunction in abandoning us. He, like the wolverine, demonstrated life's burning desire to prolong itself, shedding itself of the weak where necessary.

XXV

Our departure was delayed: Uri was having a party to celebrate his farewell the next day. Vodka bottles began gathering on our table, and in large numbers.

Later, a drunk woman with a very strong grip had to be prised off a door frame by Nikolai in his role of sheriff. He put her in an armlock and told us to bolt the door.

'Good night!' he said.

'Night!' added the woman, her eyes red and glassy, determinedly waving her one free arm.

But she might as well have joined us. 'Tolia is plastered, Ivan also out of it,' I recorded in my notes, sitting alone on my bed. 'Still, it's not a good tactic to make a fuss.' But I knew that the drinking wasn't going to diminish with the departure of Uri; the problem would grow. We seemed to have become infected somehow. However, Yasha was still strong, and when he discovered me waiting around with my dogs the next morning he came out to join me.

'Benya!' He smiled kindly. 'When I have a problem with my wife and I'm sad, I also go and sit with my dogs. Some of them ignore me – they couldn't give a shit. Others sit with me sympathetically. Others play around, trying to make me laugh.'

'Do you know how much I'm relying on you, Yasha?' I thought. 'You are the only person I can look to – not one of these dogs, not one of the other team members.'

'You must do something very soon about getting more support for yourself,' Yasha said.

'Do you mean I should fire him?' I said, struggling with my Russian. Maybe that's for the best, I thought: send him safely back to Moscow.

'No. You need him. His mind is more on the job than it sometimes appears.'

'I'm not so sure, Yasha . . .' Then I realized he wasn't talking about Ivan but Top Dog.

'Supposing he gets injured?' Yasha continued.

'I know . . .' I said. 'The thought also occurred to me.' I looked out between the buildings to where the empty tundra awaited.

'With Uri and the snowmobiles leaving, it's up to us now,' Yasha said. 'I'll try to hang back so your dogs have to listen to you.'

He left me with my animals, and I patted Basil and then the other nine dogs in turn. It occurred to me that, what with the cold, I'd yet to stroke these creatures except through my gloves.

The next morning Uri waved us goodbye – and was sent spinning as the dogs launched themselves. Off we went, through the streets of wary well-wishers and fleeing dogs. Past the school, with its flaking green paint, and two mischief-makers given the unending task of digging fresh snow from the windows.

Ten minutes later, we were alone, the Arctic plains lying stretched out before us. Yasha waved to Tolia, and both teams slipped back behind me.

'Aim just to the left of straight ahead,' yelled Yasha. 'Just to the left.' I looked again at the stark land ahead, our planet so bare; here was something powerful and resting, naked and muscular, and stretched upon it, roll upon roll of that thick white skin.

'Dogs, now's your chance!' I said.

Top Dog hesitated. He looked around at the other teams to see if they were coming along. Then he responded to me, leading the expedition across the crusty dry ice and out under the crystalline blue sky. But slowly, too slowly.

'We can't continue at this speed,' Yasha said, drawing up alongside. 'The dogs are scared. Perhaps given a bit more time . . .'

'We don't have time. Not while the weather is so good.'

So we fell behind Yasha's sledge, and Top Dog settled again. Once more I was calling out commands and being ignored: '*Takkkkhté!* For heaven's sake, I said *TAKKKKKHTÉ*!' My lead dog remained steadfastly on the safe tramlines bequeathed us by Yasha, and I was again left to wonder why these animals bothered running without Alexei at all. What was it about them that made them slog on, day after day?

What gene? Where was this passion rooted? In fear, in desire? Life seemed to flow so thickly in their veins.

But I wasn't tearing my hair out worrying about my lack of control over my team. Yes, time was fast ticking away, and I had no great dog leader nor deputy, but what do you expect after a few weeks with a stranger? And there was much in which to take comfort. That same morning, while we stopped to have a bite of walrus, I noticed Top Dog's gaze on me. Even with my back turned it was the same: there was the rest of the team – Jeremy tucked close to Bernard, Frank hiding behind an ice block to escape from Mad Jack – and there was Top Dog, sitting up despite the wind, wasting precious energy just to keep an eye on me. At some instinctive level, the leader understood that I controlled his team's destiny.

The land around us closed in, then opened again, releasing us into a shallow valley and across a river which had swollen as its waters froze; where once it had flowed through the land, now it rested heavily upon it – a giant, obstructive cable of jade. The dogs clattered across it as best they could and on the other side became oddly quiet, self-absorbed, troubled by something.

A fox was lying dead in the snow. It had no legs, no spine, no head. It was, in fact, just a fur ball.

'Wolves,' Tolia said, drawing to a halt alongside me.

'My dogs are worried, I think.'

'Not him,' Yasha said, coming over. He nodded towards Mad Jack. He was straining to pick up the scent, head to the ground. He began whining with anticipation, pleading to be moving forward again.The others were dreading it.

'Put that dog in the front for a bit,' Yasha said. 'He'll give the others courage.'

I moved Mad Jack up, swapping him with Flashy White, and all of a sudden my team was overtaking everyone.

'Christ almighty!' said Ivan from the back of Yasha's sledge as we swept by.

We came to a lone reindeer. He too was freshly dead. His stomach had been bitten out.

'Five adults, all heading east,' said Tolia, inspecting the wolf tracks.

'There'll be a herd of deer out there,' Yasha said, looking about. I noticed it had suddenly become a sunless day; sullen cloud met with sullen ice; in every direction was stretched a huge canvas smeared with oily greys. 'The wolves are heading to their dinner.'

Yasha led off again. We scanned ahead. No sign of life. Not one fresh track. But the wolves were near. We knew that from the twitchy, quick glances of the dogs, their scampering gait and lowered, submissive ears. Every dog the same, except Mad Jack, who was still yanking at the harness. Slowly, as if reluctantly, my own team began to look back to me for reassurance as they ran on into what they seemed to think was danger. Basil was the first to turn to me, then Jeremy and then Top Dog. All the cleverest dogs; leaders, actual or potential. Alexei's ragtag team of dogs suddenly seemed a lot closer to becoming mine.

'Off to the right!' called Yasha. I looked and traced the faint silhouette of a lone animal. We slowed to a halt.

The figure looked like he was in the middle of nowhere, even within the context of the tundra. Set against the vast background he looked small. 'We must look small too,' I thought to myself. It suddenly struck me that these overcast skies were becoming oppressive, wrapped around us like a soiled cotton sheet. 'Wolf?'

'Don't think so,' said Yasha.

I couldn't gauge how far away this figure was, placed against what seemed to be infinity. It might be a fox monitoring us from only a stone's throw away or a distant stag, standing foolishly proud. We strained our eyes, and as we came nearer it showed no interest in going away.

'A fawn,' said Yasha.

'Why isn't it scared?'

'It's scared all right!' Tolia said.

The snow around us had been minced by a thousand hooves, and the story slowly became clear: an hour ago the herd quietly grazing here, sharp hooves scratching through the ice for lichen. Five Arctic wolves slink towards them from downwind, their white coats melting into the snow. The pack splits up, some to lie in wait, some to encircle. A stag looks up, sensing some indefinable change in his world; sniffing, trying to detect this oncoming presence. The lead wolf down on his haunches, pristine fur pressed to the snow, picking out the weak with his gemstone blue eyes. Then a hind spots him, meets that cold, hypnotic gaze, stares right back, transfixed a moment. Is held there, rendered powerless. Then the flight. The herd splitting, rejoining, swerving like a flock of birds, left, right. And now they are gone. And in the confusion, this lone youngster left behind. His mother has lost him. In all this measureless snow, even the wolves have lost him.

'He looks so very lonely . . .' I said, thinking aloud. This is how death was in the Arctic. And if things go wrong for me too, it'll be the same – lonely, very lonely.

'He won't be alone for long,' said Yasha.

'You mean the mother will come back,' I said. 'Maternal instinct.'

'I mean the wolves will come back,' Yasha said. 'Killer instinct.'

The wolf scent was gone – we all knew because Mad Jack fell back. With Flashy White again in the front row, we trotted through the evening and night, rising up through a pass between two severe hills. A silence came over us – the humans, the dogs – as we seemed to glide through the stars.

In the morning we swung out towards the coast. Tolia and his water-sniffing dogs led us out on to an apron of ruffled ice and up the shoreline. Here the ice plates jostled in the currents. Occasionally they gave a sudden snap, but usually they moved around us quietly; they rose and bent and slipped.

Sometimes the ice parted along the beach to reveal water only a few paces to our right. The dogs and I found ourselves eyeing this liquid, peering right down to the bright copper pebbles, which were scattered like loose change beneath. As we watched, the ice would seal them in once again, stretching over the water in a delicate film at first, then tightening, becoming brittle and opaque. Next thing, the sea would be closed off behind giant shields of ice, and Tolia's water-dog would be guiding us carefully over them.

Another night fell, and we sought shelter in a clutch of abandoned huts. Snow extended in thirty-metre-long drifts from each, and all but one was in ruins, broken into by the wind. Excavating the intact house was like unearthing an Egyptian chamber complex from the sands: the door was prised open, torches were shone in. What we found had the eerie sanctity of a lost crypt. Faces looked back at us: a pin-up girl in cheap leathers; beside her, General Secretary Andropov, who hadn't been in office for seventeen years.

From here, the Soviet military had perhaps listened to America, while over in America operators maybe yanked off their headphones, pitched back their chairs and scratched their heads, wondering what to make of this hideout washed by wind and snow. Now the Russians had gone. They had left in a hurry, or else they had just stepped outside for a moment and then thought better of it and never returned. A candle sat mid-table, waiting to be relit. A matchbox lay beside it, half open. A vodka bottle was standing empty where it had been replaced on the shelf. A shovel lay by the stove. And each one of these things was laden with undisturbed soft snow. Beds were laid with snow sheets, a rug of snow was laid across the floor, a quilt of it across a cupboard. There was not one footprint, not a sign that life had been here since humans had closed the door in a former age.

Before settling to sleep I made a last check of the dogs. Seeing me, Basil gave that wagging, winsome greeting I had come to expect from him. He'd become a special friend, though Yasha was always telling me not to let the other dogs know it. But today those other dogs were sitting or standing too. Something was disturbing them, and I flashed the torch around, wondering if I would meet the red eyes of a wolf.

It took a while to discern the problem. I'd tied Top Dog to a post the local wolves were using as a territorial marker. Scattered around was their faeces – the last remains of their meals. Foxes, reindeer, hares, reduced to waste. Inspecting the dunes I saw wolf tracks lacing back and forth; not one or two but many. An hour or so old. A pack scared off by our arrival.

I moved Mad Jack to beside Top Dog. I'd already learnt why Alexei had given him a place in the team: to stiffen the team's resolve in times of danger from predators. The dog's aggressive tendencies might be regrettable, but they made him a good watchman.

The dogs curled into the snow again, dropping their noses out of the wind. Top Dog was the last to settle. His brown eyes remained fastened on me.

I stayed a while, patting this dog, heartened by our strengthening relationship but now feeling the weight of the dependency that came with it. I found myself wondering whether it really was such a good idea for him to show faith in me. I mean, didn't he know any better? He mustn't trust me completely, not yet.

Back indoors I found the others already asleep. The candles had burned a whole inch lower – I must have been outside for half an hour. But when I tried to sleep myself, I couldn't. At what price, I kept asking myself, would this journey be achieved?

Would I go as far as Amundsen, for example, and sacrifice the dogs' lives to gain my objective? He planned for it all along, 'slaughtering the feebler ones' as and when they tired. 'If we ourselves wanted a

Amundsen and the Eating of His 'Brave' Dogs

Amundsen was fastidious in his care of the dogs throughout, beginning on-board the *Fram* as he journeyed south to Antarctica, when he screened them from the sun with awnings and protected them from the damp by placing them on a raised platform. He was proud of 'landing them in a far better condition than when we received them'. He knew that his success in reaching the South Pole was bound up with the health of his dogs. Yet Amundsen also cherished them. 'Coming out of your tent in the morning, one was instantly greeted with joy by one's twelve dogs. They barked and howled in emulation.' Then he'd greet each in turn with a 'Good morning', pat them on the head and say a few words to each. He took time to learn their individual needs and traits. 'It was really touching to see the joy they showed on meeting again,' he wrote of two reunited dog friends.

However, on the way to the South Pole, with the Norwegian team at last up on the plateau, the moment came. 'There was depression and sadness in the air – we had grown so fond of our dogs . . . Twenty-four of our brave companions and faithful helpers were marked out for death. It was hard but it had to be so. We had agreed to shrink from nothing in order to reach our goal.' The place was named the 'Butcher's Shop', a most apt choice. The dogs were chopped up, and 'The delicate little cutlets had an absolutely hypnotizing effect as they were spread out one by one over the snow.' As for the dogs eating their companions: 'all the survivors were not yet in a mood for dog's flesh, and it therefore had to be served in the most enticing form. When flayed and cut up, it went down readily all along the line; even the most fastidious then overcame their scruples.'

Scott's actions, in pursuit of the Edwardian virtues displayed in the 'fine conception' of man-hauling, though well-meaning, resulted in both animals and men suffering. He chose to spread the task of reaching the Pole between ponies, mechanized sledges and men: the latter would drag the loads for the final leg. Although tested by Robert Peary in the Arctic, Scott had decided that dogs would play only a minor supporting role: 'Among those acquainted with the Eskimo dog, I do not suppose I was the only one who was startled on first hearing this,' commented Amundsen. From the start the dogs proved a great success, though the ponies less so. They reached only the foot of the glacier, and there they were either butchered for meat as thought necessary or returned as an act of kindness – although two of these three died anyway. For the rest of the journey to the Pole, 'the men themselves have the doubtful pleasure of acting as ponies,' Amundsen noted wryly. And whereas his men and dogs flourished on the supplies of nutritious meat from the slaughtered dogs – it has been said that they put on weight, such were Amundsen's bountiful supplies – Scott's polar and support teams were starving from day one.

We all know how Scott and the other four scurvied men ended their days as they went about what Captain Oates was now calling their 'wretched man-hauling'. But we forget that even the final support party found themselves in trouble: Lieutenant Evans had scurvy and was saved by his companions Lashly and Crean. The latter heroically dashed alone for help, which came in the form of a dog team.

piece of fresh meat we could cut off a delicate little fillet,' I read, consulting my notes. This way, both men and dogs were provided with nutritious fresh meat.

And who, out of Amundsen and Scott, was the better man anyway? Amundsen, with his clean, cold effectiveness, who respected yet betrayed his dogs? Or his rival Scott, because he trusted to men, not dogs – and they suffered and died instead.

Ivan turned in his sleeping bag, then cried out in his sleep. I listened as his breathing calmed and deepened again.

I suppose that we must each argue with our fellows and with our gods the merits of what we do in order to survive. As for my own dogs, my relationship with them was coming along, and perhaps I should feel satisfied with that. Forget the Bering Strait. Cut my losses; call it a day when I get to Lorino. 'Well, I can make the final decision once safely there,' I told myself. But what if the dogs didn't even make it there? Was that how I was to repay young Basil? Top Dog? As Amundsen put it, 'There can hardly be an animal that is capable of expressing its feelings to the same extent as the dog. Joy, sorrow, gratitude, scruples of conscience, are all reflected as plainly as could be desired in his behaviour, and above all in his eyes.'

'Above all in his eyes . . .' I pictured Top Dog's awaiting, trusting brown eyes.

I put away my notes. I looked again at my companions lying there

Why Scott Died and Amundsen Lived: Notes to Self

Apsley Cherry-Garrard, one of the last to see Scott before he departed for the Pole: 'I have always had a doubt whether the weather conditions were sufficient to cause the tragedy.'

So what did?

AMUNDSEN

(i) Had a single, clear, specific objective: to get to the South Pole.

(ii) His men: chosen especially for skiing experience. One of them, Bjaaland, a champion.

(iii) His dogs: chosen from Greenland, because this breed had been tried and tested by Peary.

(iv) Unlike Scott, was typically pragmatic about the canine habit of eating their own excrement. Dogs were scavengers and could extract fat, protein and certain enzymes.

(v) He appreciated and understood the dogs' characters: 'Hardly two of them were alike, either in disposition or in appearance.'

(vi) Having chosen dogs as his engine, Amundsen understood the importance of prioritizing their health.

(vii) Dogs far better suited than horses:

- They are light: 'If a dog falls into a crevasse there is no great harm done; a tug at his harness and he is out again. But it is another matter with a pony.'
- Individuals within teams interchangeable, if need be.
- Can be fed to other dogs.
- Can be fed to humans.
- Can climb 'up over the huge glaciers that lead to the plateau'.
- Provide companionship for humans. 'If now and then one grew a little tired of one's fellow men . . . there was, as a rule, diversion to be found in the society of the animals.'
- Have thick coats and don't sweat (which would freeze on them).

(viii) For finding food depots, which were placed systematically, he used ingenious traverse markings.

(ix) Amundsen maintained – or even gained – weight ('We did not suffer from a craving either for fat or sugar'). Scott starved. Although the importance of vitamins was not understood, the diet of the Eskimos suggested to Amundsen the value of fresh food, which he believed might protect against scurvy. Sure enough, Amundsen in due course observes how much the dogs 'seemed to benefit by these meals of fresh meat for several days afterwards'.

Rations: simple, easy to calculate (jam, cheese, etc., left at base). (1) Biscuits (which included oatmeal, sugar). (2) Pemmican (which included vegetables). (3) Dried milk. (4) Chocolate. Plus fresh meat from dogs.

(x) Runners on sledges were made extra broad. As much else – the goggles, dog whips, etc. – his equipment was adapted from that of the Arctic natives, 'the Eskimo model'. The Eskimo skins they wore were warm and dry, allowing the sweat to evaporate – unlike Scott's man-made clothing. Although Amundsen greatly admired Franklin for his tenacity and bravery, he also appreciated that Franklin had failed because he didn't adapt to his surroundings.

(xi) Not distracted by 'higher notions' of the means to achieve the goal.

(xii) Pragmatic temperament. On killing his favourite dog, Lasse: 'He had worn himself out completely, and was not worth anything. He was divided into fifteen portions.'

(xiii) At the last minute, the polar party was reduced from eight to five, and this meant even more plentiful rations from the depots.

(xiv) Allowed a very large safety margin. Thanks to the dogs, each sledge was able to carry double the weight of each of Scott's. Plus, the depots were already laid as far as 82 degrees, and on the way to the Pole laid systematically at every degree south (sixty nautical miles).

SCOTT

(i) Mixed science with the polar objective. The collection of geological samples cost him weight and time, when time was against him.

(ii) Members of the final Southern (polar-bid) Party selected for their symbolic value rather than their virtues as athletes. Captain Oates represented a different branch of the armed forces – he was in the army (although now limping from a Boer War wound) – and PO Evans the other ranks (although he already had a bad hand wound). A favourite of Scott's, he was impressively large, but this disguised a possible lack of mental stamina. (N.B. Evans complained that, being so big, he required more rations than the others, which he didn't get.)

(iii) His dogs: chosen from a part of Siberia well south of the Arctic Circle, these were therefore less hardened?

(iv) Scott allowed sentiment (he disapproved of dogs being fed to dogs, and even more so, dogs being fed to man) to get in the way of nutritional needs. Placing advance depots, Scott sent three horses back on compassionate grounds rather than forcing them to their limit and leaving them as meat for the Southern (polar) Party.

(v) Instead of just one choice of draught animal, which would lead to fewer logistical complications, growing expertise, closer man–animal relationships and a clear strategy, he relied on a few dogs (early stages), mechanical sledges, Manchurian ponies and humans.

The mechanical sledges:

- Were an untested innovation.
- Were dangerously heavy – one disappeared through the ice soon after arrival.
- The remaining sledges abandoned after they broke down soon into the march; the most successful lasted 80 km. Lashly and Lieutenant Teddy Evans, in the final support party, would now have to man-haul some 640 km more than their companions, Evans almost dying before reaching safety.

Ponies:

- Were not chosen by the man in charge of them, Oates.
- Sank in snow – as Ernest Shackleton's earlier expedition had shown.
- Danger of being lost to crevasses because of their weight.
- Being herbivores, needed to be brought feed from outside Antarctica; dogs could eat seals/penguins.
- Their feed needed to be carried in addition to any supplies.
- Needed to be led by hand.
- Had to be left at the base of the glacier.
- Were less physically adapted to extreme cold – their coat, etc.
- Sweated – unlike dogs – so suffered as it froze on them.

Dogs:

- Only thirty-three brought, as opposed to the ninety-seven by Amundsen.
- Scott failed to understand dogs' behaviour, e.g. why they ate excrement – called it 'horrid, the worse side of dog driving'.
- Scott had only two men with experience of driving dogs, Meares and Gerof.

The humans:

- Man-hauling embraced heroic Edwardian values, but also a pride not suited to Antarctica.

(vi) Markers en route to Pole: used single, inadequate flags, at irregular distances.

(vii) Equipment failures – paraffin containers leaked on account of leather washers. (Amundsen's were hermetically sealed.) Combined with lack of experience – this was only Scott's second venture in extreme cold.

(viii) Men were not expert skiers, simply using the skis as snowshoes. Bowers' skis left behind on Scott's orders – he wasn't intended as a member of the Southern Party, and in the event had to march 575 km without.

(ix) With a fifth man (Bowers) added to the Southern Party at the last minute, the distribution of rations was complicated and the tent cramped.

(x) The man-hauling placed the bodies of the men under more physical stress.

(xi) Scott's men were starved even as they set out to the Pole – but also malnourished and scurvied.

Rations: more varied, no fresh meat.
Breakfast: cocoa, tea, coffee.
Lunch/supper: pemmican, essence of beef, rice, curry powder.
Snacks: biscuits, chocolate, butter/cheese, sugar.

Although Scott couldn't be expected to know about nutrition, his men were allocated some 5,000 kcal (less correctly but more commonly called simply 'calories') a day, yet required 6,000 kcal – a shortfall of 1,000 kcal per day. (All these figures from Robert Feeney's contribution to *South: The Race to the Pole.*)

(xii) Morale low, having failed to reach the South Pole first. They now had to face 'over 800 miles of solid dragging – goodbye to most of the daydreams'.

(xiii) Scott typically allowed a narrow safety margin (much like Shackleton) – just two depots between the Shambles Depot (below the Beardmore Glacier) and One Ton Depot, a distance of 640 km. He banked on the hope that the weather would not continue to be as bad as it had been at times.

(xiv) Because the horses had failed, the most southerly main depot

(One Ton Depot) was placed 56 km further away than intended. Amundsen's most southerly depot was at 82 degrees, 240 km nearer the Pole. Scott died 18 km (11 miles) from One Ton Depot.

(xv) Scott had no clear plan for rescue. Having helped rescue the final support party, two dog teams set out under Apsley Cherry-Garrard to One Ton Depot to 'hasten the return of the final party'. Cherry-Garrard gave up waiting at a time when Scott was only some 88 km away.

in deep sleep. Now, even a room laden with snow was a cosy shelter for us.

The irony was that should the worst happen out here or, to borrow Scott's phrase, almost the worst, and I was left alive with only one dog, then it would not be Top Dog that I would choose to walk out with me. Nor Flashy White, nor the affectionate Basil. It would be one of the two silent dogs at the back, those I've hardly mentioned and that I hardly ever noticed: Dennis and Muttley. It was they who heaved at the sledge to get it shifting again each time I chose to stop; they who took the strain of the sledge as it threatened to reverse downslope; they who lived in fear of all that deadweight as it tumbled behind them downhill. Dennis and Muttley might not be intelligent, but working alone with one of them, I would take up the role of lead dog myself. I'd put the rope over my shoulder and begin walking with one of these strong, simple, loyal dogs hauling the sledge with me as best he could.

I stopped myself. Then I buckled up in my sleeping bag, laughing at myself for my stupidity. What needless worrying about the dogs. If anyone was going to die out here, it would be me.

XXVI

We crept along the ice shelf, this mash of solid and liquid sea that was a foretaste of the Bering Strait. The dogs didn't like it – the ice dividing, waters revealing themselves, then stiffening and cracking. Plates slammed together and were rent open again by the churning waters and winds.

Once, I saw life out there: a common eider, a drake, black-bellied and very large, circling alone in a pool to keep the hole open. It was a reminder of time passing. Today was 20 March, and I should be readying myself in the Strait itself; I ought to be waiting there, alert, watching the skies, primed for my chance of a crossing.

At sunset there were more birds, king eiders rising from the water to shake their wings, ice blocks shifting around them. Hanging in the wind were red-legged kittiwakes, glaucous gulls, herring gulls. Each bird seemed to be here to tell me that the seas were opening, that I was already too late.

The wind was getting up, and it would be wise to locate the shack near here used by reindeer herders. With the failing light, the wind quickened further and we were still riding the precarious ice of the shore. I saw Yasha exchange a glance with Tolia – nothing much, and nothing was spoken. I prepared my head torch. I began to look around, familiarizing myself with the line of the hills before they were lost to the dark.

The wind strengthened yet more. The clouds above flattened and spread over us. Yasha yelled at me to speed up. We accelerated – the dogs seemed to understand the urgency. Now the visibility was lessening further as stars were blotted out. Snow began to lift from the ground.

Extract from my diary, 21 March 2001:
Yasha was now out of sight ahead. He whistled – both to the dogs and me. Tolia was behind, and Ivan with him. Now the snow in the wind was stinging as it buffeted us. In the torchlight I saw my dogs thrown sideways. Some were turning to me, wondering whether they should be stopping.

Yasha's team was slowing, and from his shouts at them I knew his dogs were reluctant to proceed. I wondered what the wind-chill factor was. My skin was burning, but I thought it was the force of the hard snow rather than just the searing wind. Minus sixty? Minus ninety even? Were the dogs' noses freezing up?

Yasha's team, the most disciplined here, such battle-hardened soldiers, was now hardly making headway, his dogs lying down in protest at times. Mine, confused and frightened, were running amok, unable or unwilling to hear me.

The teams began losing each other; Yasha and Tolia closed in either side of me, closing ranks. It became clear they were sensing danger. We floundered for what I guessed was half an hour, Yasha and Tolia on foot, the beams of their torches whipping through the airborne snow, trying to find a way forward, studying the new ice and assessing how the snows and gravels lay.

Now my dogs were refusing to budge. The wind carried off my head torch – it was that strong.

Ivan came back for me on foot and said, 'Don't f**k about.' There was panic in his voice, the same trilling tone he had when he thought I had frostbite on my cheeks during a storm in Anadyr. 'Ivan is someone untested,' I thought, 'someone not the master of his emotions. Snatching at answers. Does he, this urban kid, think I don't know danger when I smell it?'

It was just as well that progress was slow. Suddenly, Yasha found himself going over a small but sheer cliff. He managed to stop the sledge but the front dogs had dropped from sight. By now I'd retrieved my emergency torch from my survival kit and directed the beam over the ledge. Four dogs were visible in the darkness hanging from their harnesses. Amid the confusion of the humans they looked strangely calm, happy to be out of the wind and patiently waiting to be rescued.

The wind howling into our ears, Yasha made the decision to erect the tent. But how? We battled with the canvas for a moment. Change of plan. 'We head inland!' Yasha screamed above the wind. 'Try to spot light from the herders' shack. Agreed?' We'd give it a go.

But my dogs wouldn't retreat – whatever we tried, they wouldn't shift from where they'd been left behind on the new, i.e. thin, ice. The other teams would have to turn around, descend again on to the new ice and lead my team along it – not a comfortable thought.

A tantalizing twenty minutes passed as we pressed on, flashing lights at each other. Then Yasha flashed a torch inland and there, in the black night, was a light in response that told us we were safe.

Within moments, we were indoors by a stove – again, that rapid transition between peril and safety. We squinted in the bright light; we had found hell out there in the tundra, and suddenly we were back from the underworld.

Around us were short, wind-burned reindeer herders. We were in a cramped wooden place with boots and furs hanging from any available nail. All was silent – or seemed so after the roaring of the wind. Men sat dazed, like the wounded of a bloody war. Mist swirled around the timbers as the snow sticking to these people lifted clear in the heat.

I counted them up: four reindeer herders and maybe ten refugees from the storm. There was hardly anywhere to sit, even on the floor, and if you crossed the room you had to pick your way through the limbs of others and couldn't avoid inflicting injuries.

'Thank God you saw us,' I said.

A blackened man looked up from where he'd been staring at his feet. 'See you? Why would I see you out there? Anyone here see this lot?'

'Someone signalled,' said Ivan.

'He means the tractor,' said a voice.

'Oh yeah, the tractor. It got lost in the blizzard as well. Was meant to come in the daylight to resupply us. You must have seen the lights as it arrived.'

'F**k, you were lucky,' croaked a voice from under a jacket.

I did my best to curl up on a narrow bench that was half my length and wondered if I might negotiate a swap with Ivan's floorspace, but he looked asleep already. I was too tired to think about the way the Arctic did this, threatening to snuff out your life one moment and then giving it back to you the next. It was 1.30 a.m. We'd been fighting the wind for six hours.

XXVII

We woke late and began making ourselves tea with all the other newcomers, people who had been washed up here like the seaweed of a storm tide.

Outside, the wind was still strong but the sun bright. Inside, the reindeer herders were playing cards with old, thick packs. They didn't play for money because they had none – they were paid, they said, in bullets and vodka. Instead, the loser had to do the day's duties – notably, lugging in blocks of ice and melting them for water.

We were all finding it equally hard to adapt. Last night there had been all the space of the tundra and we had had to shout into each other's ear to be heard, but now we were having to learn to see space as a precious currency, something to be spent wisely. Trying to go anywhere, you found yourself having to stand patiently to allow others by.

Yasha had once predicted that I'd miss the tundra, and now I did. It was just as he said: I needed empty space. My mind had reshaped itself to accommodate it, even the horror of it. Yesterday I had been running away from it. Today I wanted to be out there again.

I went for a breath of fresh air but was soon forced to retreat into the hut's outer passageway. This served, I noticed, as a deep freeze. On the top shelf was a whole fox, stripped of its skin; also, a reindeer leg and a polar-bear arm. The second shelf housed the water supply: ice cubes a foot across.

'I'm admiring your bear,' I explained to the herder called Misha, who was wondering what I was up to. I gestured at the colossal naked arm sticking out from the shelf, bent like an unfeasibly well-muscled boxer in mid-bout.

'The bear charged at me,' Misha said. 'Ears down and on all fours.' He winked. 'What could I do?'

Behind him, his colleague giggled. The bearskin was produced – a king-size, shaggy quilt stiffened into an unwieldy board by the cold.

Half a dozen reindeer would be slaughtered today for onward transportation by tractor. The herd was brought nearer. They stood patiently; thickets of antlers clattered as heads turned this way and that. Misha began attempting to lasso some hinds, but after a while he got sick of this, got out a rifle and shot them instead.

The dogs were in an excitable mood, perhaps nervy because of the storm, perhaps aroused by the smell of the deer. We harnessed them up and resumed our journey, finding that the winds had wrenched the old, tumbled ice out to sea and replaced it with a fresh, level sheet.

Inland, we negotiated a lowland spread of rivers and pools. The dogs sniffed suspiciously at the ice, listening to the water currents beneath us and inspecting the strange things held there: galleries of summertime sedge and reed, jellyfish discs of trapped air, bubbles scattered like beads among the herbs and draped in pearl strings through the squat willows.

Further on, squeezed waters broke to the surface, hissing and spitting. It was all too much for Top Dog. He stood, looking back apologetically instead of following Yasha across the river. And for a while he hoped to put off the inevitable, ignoring my commands and leading his team creeping along the bank instead.

Eventually, I led the way on foot, stabbing the brake pole into the ice to test it, while Yasha encouraged my dogs from the far bank.

'And in all seriousness I'm expecting you to attempt the Bering Strait?' I said to Top Dog, his limbs locked in fear and quivering as we stood side by side on the river ice – here so transparent and polished, and over there the stained-glass yellow of resin, grass seeds and twigs caught in it.

We threaded our way between the hills to Enmelen. A vermilion sunset hung around the settlement as we descended through the light-soaked air to the seafront, passing upturned whaling boats and battened-down huts. Children ran out, adults ran out, dogs ran out. We were, a teacher said, the first visitors of any kind for six months.

But we wouldn't stay for long. We repaired our sledges, pacing about with the dogs, wanting to be on our way. The truth was, each of these settlements, although unfailingly welcoming, was bad for us.

The Chukchis were doing their best for me, but with our arrival in each little town there was a waning of intent, a drifting of focus. And this malaise was growing, not diminishing – a certain tiredness in the eyes, a weakening of heart. I'd seen it before among guides in Peru, Sumatra and elsewhere. I remembered the highlands of West Papua: a kindly young porter slumped in the cold, blood dripping from his nose. He was mesmerized – not horrified but fascinated – as he studied his life dripping out of him. And again now. Our life force was draining away.

And soon, in a few days, the coast would begin to turn north into the Bering Strait. The Strait would narrow and then we'd be nearing Lorino. There, I'd face the decision as to whether to launch out alone or not. As things stood, it was ridiculous even to contemplate this. We simply weren't ready.

It wasn't anyone's fault in particular. I was grateful to Yasha, Tolia and Ivan for having remained so resilient until now. But I needed them each to hold out for longer, until my dogs and I achieved what would now have to be a most spectacular breakthrough.

XXVIII

We departed on 29 March, taking with us a backlog of post for Nunligran, a settlement only a day's trek away. It seemed to me extraordinary that not one person had ventured to the neighbouring community to deliver the post – until I saw the terrain.

We ascended to a rocky pass from which the wind had swept all snow. And then came another, and now I was having to lend the dogs a hand, hauling the sledge alongside them over the cracked black rocks.

The wind whistled through gullies, pasting snow against the rock, tumbling it into culs-de-sac, spewing it down from the arêtes in fine mists. The strain of negotiating this alarming terrain of sudden drops and scree slopes got to Frank in the end. Just as he had long ago, when nervous under my command back in Anadyr, he bit through the gang line. My detached leaders sped off down a gully; the rest of us followed, tumbling downslope with Mad Jack and Frank now in the front row.

On this occasion I managed to slow our descent – in the process snapping my brake pole in two – and Tolia flung himself to catch us. But it was another warning: Frank, like the rest of the dogs, only felt secure with me in the good times.

And when, at long last, Nunligran appeared out of the bleakness like a Lowry painting – thin, dark figures against the snow, stark brick buildings that were simple, workmanlike efforts – Jeremy, either because he was an even greater worrier than Frank or because he was the most intelligent dog in the team, slipped his collar. Once more, just as when we were first departing on this journey, he wanted to run away. Disaster, he seemed to feel, though so long evaded, was surely now drawing near.

XXIX

A second dog was left behind, but again not from my team. The dejected character watched as we swept into the distance; his master, Yasha, waved to him tearfully until he was out of sight.

The hill country gave way to a lagoon, and there a small bunch of Chukchis maintained a net that they'd hung below the ice. Alex, the boss, invited us into his shack for some fish. Tolia, sitting on the floor beside a very well-fed cat, cut it up to eat raw, working from tail to head as if slicing a loaf of bread.

'Is this such a good idea out here in the tundra?' I said to Ivan, as the fishermen unscrewed their prized bottle of industrial alcohol.

'Relax, Benedict,' he said. 'We'll dilute it.'

'Doesn't he want to join in?' said Alex, disappointed. I took a token sip.

'Try the eau de cologne,' someone suggested. 'That's the drink for real men!'

'Mr Foreigner,' Alex said, determined to engage my interest, 'there's a Chukchi graveyard nearby. I won't tell you where, because archaeologists from Moscow went there, and after that the walruses wouldn't come any more. The ancestors had been disturbed.'

'A shame,' I said. I noticed that everyone's first shot of industrial alcohol was already gone.

'But we have a solution to the walrus problem. We will open the lagoon with a bulldozer.'

'With a bulldozer?'

'To let the sea and fish in. That'll encourage the walruses.'

'That will be a far greater disturbance to the ecology than a few archaeologists. I mean, what will the spirits think?'

'They will be delighted. They are *our* spirits. Of course they will be happy for us.'

If Russians had said this, it would have been one of their dark jokes. They would have been laughing at themselves and the exquisite tragedy of life. But these Chukchis were laughing at the prospect of turning Russian technology to their own advantage. And they would lose out, yet again. Such is the sly treachery of progress, the sleight of hand of the white man.

We went on our way, and towards dusk stopped by our sledges to eat some more raw fish. A second bottle of alcohol was produced from somewhere. I had reason enough to be concerned, as we climbed aboard our sledges again. The Chukchis were by no means drunk, but you could see that, to dogs so tuned to danger, the slight change in their masters' behaviour – the raised voice, the strange exuberance – was significant. As Ivan began to sing, my dogs began looking back to me for comfort; and though neither Yasha nor Tolia seemed to notice, soon all three dog teams were taking it upon themselves to bunch up closer together, as if for the coming of another storm.

Yet, for all his insecurity, Top Dog would not let me take command. As in any such time of crisis, his nerve failed him; he dumbly followed the other dogs' tracks. I stopped periodically, tried to break Top Dog's concentration and get him to listen to me. It was of little use. The humans were in disorder and he wanted the security of his own kind.

Yasha produced the bottle again – the glass flashed in the last sunlight. Is it about to happen? I wondered. The crumbling away of the expedition that I've been fearing for so long?

Through the dark, now – a waxing moon, a fullish lime crescent. This lit the icescape gently around us and seemed to settle the dogs. A bird of the night flew across our path, its buffered wings silent. 'Snowy owl,' I thought. It swerved and dropped to the ground like a fold of white linen, as we padded through a scene that at times seemed to fly by and at others be so stationary that we didn't appear to be in motion.

However, Yasha and Ivan, on the same sledge, were steadily emptying the bottle; they began yelling wildly into the tundra. 'Faster, dogs, faster!' Yasha's dogs sped faster; Tolia's and mine followed suit. All the dogs were now hurtling through the dark. I could hardly see them but I could hear the sledge runners and pounding dog paws; they were careering along parallel to me on the right, a little downslope now.

The slope steepened – I could feel the sledge tilt. Now the other teams were veering off downhill and we were rising; we were becoming separated. But I was happy to put distance between us for a short while; my dogs – all the dogs – were in a traumatized state, seemingly able to hear nothing but the giggles and shrieks of Ivan and Yasha.

We were high now, riding a hill – and living dangerously; I had to regain control. I looked up ahead to Top Dog running in the starlight, Flashy White alongside.

But now my dogs were slowing; the voice of Ivan was distant, rising from below us somewhere, and Top Dog was listening to me. I was re-establishing order. We were self-contained up here on the rise. Things would work out fine.

Then Ivan's voice came from below. 'Benya! Come on, faster! Where are you? BENYA?'

Top Dog couldn't stand it any more, the isolation from fellow dogs. He had to get back to the other two teams. He turned sharply to the right.

I was aware of Tolia yelling to me. Not drunkenly: this was a warning shout.

And suddenly Flashy White and Top Dog were gone from sight; they just vanished, dropping into the void. Next, the second row . . .

Down the cliff we plunged, the dogs sprawling ahead of me. There was little to do but wait for the impact. We flew – and we fell. 'Maybe it's going to be all right,' I thought as the sledge butted through a shelf of snow. But the sledge was still dropping, and I was thinking how frightened the dogs would be and speculating on whether we would get away with this latest mishap. 'Oh God,' I thought. 'What a stupid end.'

The sledge seemed to spiral with me into the blackness – and in the midst of the fear of what lay ahead, there was the strange peace. Snow was smacking into me, being forced under my balaclava into my eyes, nose and mouth, yet oddly there was calm – until I felt a sharp stab in my right knee and suddenly my leg was yanked back, caught, I knew, in the stray anchor.

Then we were stationary. I sprung up – that surge of adrenaline that hastens you to address a catastrophe. Next the mental check of limbs that accompanies all such mishaps – the same whether scrambling out of rapids, lying winded at the foot of a ladder, limping at the bottom of a precipice.

'It's going to be all right,' I confirmed to myself, rather surprised. 'Nothing broken.'

I lay down among the rubble of the snow and stayed there, motionless for a few seconds. 'The dogs!' I suddenly thought. I felt for my torch, and steering the beam through the darkness ahead, caught sight of Flashy White and Top Dog. They looked back to me: a bit sheepish – quite rightly – but not in distress. Not a single severe injury. And within moments, in the way of disobedient dogs the world over, the whole team was behaving as if nothing had happened. I could see only enthusiastic faces, each looking to me for the next instruction. Somehow, they had pulled through again. Somehow, we *all* had.

'You OK?' Tolia was saying, striding over to me.

'Yeah,' I said, 'fine . . .' I rolled my sledge upright.

The dogs were shaking; the shock beginning to set in. As I untangled their harnesses, Yasha and Ivan remained on their sledge, watching. 'They haven't even got up . . .' I thought.

I was meant to have grown up, to be able now to take responsibility for myself. And although it seemed heartless of Yasha not to come over, I had to face it: I couldn't keep using my guides as props for ever. We – the dogs and I – needed to take charge of ourselves.

After a while we were again passing quietly through the tundra. I was shaken, but we would survive – and that was all that mattered now. I took comfort in the aurora, a bloody haze cavorting through the stars overhead. And I took comfort in the knowledge that my dogs were all right.

Two in the morning, and Yasha spotted a hunting shack. I was now in constant pain, but it had to be done: I began a thorough check of my dogs as the others dug out the shelter and started brewing tea. Fighting to straighten the dogs into a line so I could anchor them for the night, I realized that tears were freezing on my cheeks. I couldn't pretend to myself it was the effect of the wind; it was the agony of my right knee and the way in which I had been left alone to cope with it. A strange anger rose in me, an anger directed at myself. I felt disgusted at this self-pity.

Tolia came out of the hut and lent me a hand. 'He must think I'm a child,' I thought, 'but still he doesn't criticize me.' What to think of these people, drunk on the job one moment and chivalrous knights the next? So much weaker than me, and yet so very much stronger.

Tolia disappeared, and I was left alone again, securing the dogs with a line that kept snapping as it chafed against an old petrol drum. It was aggravating: each time I hauled on the dog ropes, my frostbitten fingers felt like they were being pressed on to a lit stove. However, I knew I was battling not with the Arctic but with a flaw in myself. I must not give in.

Yasha did come out after another ten or fifteen minutes. 'Tea, Benya!'

'I'm coming,' I said, but I mustn't allow myself to go in before the job was done.

I diagnosed the problem: a nervousness had come over the calmest of all the dogs, Dennis and Muttley. Instead of settling down to sleep, they were yanking the sledge forward, trying to get away from it. I went to them and spoke to them a while. They were shaking: going over the cliff had been hardest of all for these two dogs at the back – the fear of being crushed by the sledge as it thundered down after them.

Inside the broken-down shack a passageway had been carved through the snow, and at the end of it Yasha was standing with a tin of meat and a bottle. He was waiting up for me, lit by the candles that had been placed here and there. I noticed that there were hare prints in the snow along the benches. Yasha gave me a swig of the remaining industrial alcohol. '*Mei!*' he said, rubbing his tummy. 'Medicine!' Soon, he was on the ground in his sleeping bag. He blew a cloud of breath, laughed at it, then buried himself and fell silent. Both Ivan and Tolia were already asleep, curled up together on the far bench.

I lay there in my bag. Soon it would be dawn – but not soon enough. I couldn't sleep, the pain was so intense. I had to fight the temptation of opening my bag up to the air in order to numb it.

Yasha's breath was visible rising in the candlelight, gathering in the fur of his hat like hoar frost across a lawn. And as I watched it, the knowledge that I was soon going to be leaving Yasha's protection suddenly bore down on me. I felt acutely vulnerable. The damage to my leg would be as nothing if, once on my own, I didn't get things right. Falling off the cliff had been a shock, but it shouldn't have been. The truth was, I had seen this coming even a month ago.

'I can count myself lucky,' I thought. 'I've been given another warning.' I was fortunate not to be dead already – and I couldn't rely on good fortune again.

I'd come to the Arctic to learn how to pass freely over the ice, but at present I was just sinking through it, like Ivan, like Natasha at the bar in Anadyr, like those famous pioneers of the ice Franklin and Vitus Bering. To watch Yasha and Tolia begin to slip also was especially painful. They were out here to help me, and they deserved better. But my mission was proving too great a strain, and now they were taking me down with them.

Slowly, with a dreadful inevitability, we were moving towards a crisis. The one thing to be said was that if things got worse – as surely they would – I might by then have got the dogs on my side. They were scared – of course they were. After all, they'd just gone off a cliff! But there was no doubting their strength of purpose as they had run towards it.

XXX

I lay there, trying to think. I noticed a mouse trail in the snow around my head. I followed the progress of this little animal's fresh divots from one side of the hut to the other, and then their route in a wide erratic circle back again.

I pictured the team outside in the wind – Top Dog, Basil and Jeremy, the three cleverest dogs. What were their thoughts now? 'That new alpha male of ours, called Benya? Weak. Yeah, useless. The tundra is chewing him up. He's thinner every day – and how's that meant to make us feel? Does he believe in this journey? Is there a sense of destiny about him? Nope. We'll stick with him so long as he feeds us, and then we're off out of here.'

'Useless yourselves, guys,' I thought. 'Who was it who lost concentration and took us all over a cliff? Not me. And, as you rightly point out, who is it that supplies the food around here? Besides, you haven't seen what I can truly give you – which, as it happens, is a lot more than raw walrus meat.'

This was a bit of an idle boast, because I owed everything so far to the Chukchis – and now the indigenous framework around me was rotting.

I reached for my survival kit, which was sitting beside me with all the important gear from the sledge. I opened it and checked it through. The spare stove, the spare bottle of fuel, windproof matches, blanket, kettle, mini-tent, high-energy snacks. And there, curled up in the kettle, the scrap of paper I'd scribbled on at the mission station in New Guinea. I pictured myself there again: still in shock, slumped against the wall, the mud thick on my boots, this very bit of paper in my shaking hands. Very slowly, I'd begun to assemble a few pointers that would help me survive better next time.

To a greater or lesser degree, we all had them, these survival aids: family mottoes, quotes from the scriptures, words handed down. In times of stress, they helped us conduct our lives according to tried and tested procedures; they offered a way forward, comforted us in our hour of need. My own list, written out in the sodden sago forests of New Guinea, would be aimed at the bare heart of it all: what to do when your whole life falls apart – your ship has gone down, your husband walked out, your brother knifed on his way home.

However, I was only aged twenty-four and, until I had more of my own calamities to draw on, I would have to turn to the experience of the great pioneers. Besides, they had more reason than most of us to work out tactics for how to keep on going. Hernán Cortés, H. M. Stanley, Livingstone – they were great teachers because their struggles were so graphic, their skills so honed. They told us by their actions that things could work out all right – if only you took the right steps. The eventual demise of Franklin, for example, offered a most useful cautionary tale.

John Franklin, I'd reminded myself, was aged almost sixty in 1845 and rather fat, not the ideal person to lead the most ambitious Arctic enterprise of the nineteenth century. However, the admiralty was persuaded: his first overland venture – when the expedition members had to resort to eating lichen – had just been unlucky. And the deprivations of a second escapade overland had, after all, given him valuable Arctic experience. He returned a hero and was knighted for his valuable service to geography and his fortitude in bringing nearly everyone back alive.

This new expedition would be altogether different. The best-equipped voyage to the far north that the world had seen, the mission was to find the holy grail of the seas: a passage in a northwesterly direction from Europe through the Arctic to Asia. Two ships, the *Erebus* and the *Terror*, were reinforced with iron cladding and equipped with special steam engines to help them manoeuvre through the ice. They carried three years' worth of provisions, including salt beef, pork, raisins, split peas, oatmeal, chocolate, not to mention 10,000 gallons of spirit, ale and porter. Meat, vegetables and soup were sealed in cans – another exciting innovation of the time.

The steam engines were given a test on the Thames. It was thought that, while not excessively powerful, they'd 'astound the Esquimaux not a little'. The two ships launched gloriously on 19 May 1845 and were last seen by whalers that July, already among the icebergs. Then nothing. Even now, we don't really know what happened. We can imagine them entering the maze of packed ice. There was little chance of rescue, and ahead was a vast uncharted morass sometimes depicted on maps as a terrifying black hole. Into this strange, haunted other world they went, lit by the flickering Northern Lights – and all the while the groaning, creaking, drifting walls of oncoming blue ice.

A note found later reported that the ships had overwintered comfortably at Beechey Island in the winter of 1845–6 – 'all well'. There they sat, a piece of Victorian England secure in the deepest Arctic. And all would continue to be fine – assuming, of course, that the ships were released from the ice's grip in the spring. If not, they'd find themselves prisoners.

Unfortunately, the ships were locked in the ice for a second winter. We know that much for certain – the crew later scribbled an addendum to the original note – and we can guess much of the rest: for instance, that if any one of those crew members had walked up to the captain and asked, 'What now, Sir?' Franklin would have had no answer.

Franklin must have been an isolated figure, even among such isolated men. There was no Plan B. And there was worse to come. Gradually, either aboard the ships as they began to crack up or perhaps standing on the ice floe wondering what to do now, the crew must have come to the sickening realization that more important than a Plan B, an alternative way forward, was a Plan C, a way out. Franklin had not provided them with one of those either. He had given the expedition no escape route, no Emergency Exit. The survivors faced an unenviable dilemma: stay with the dwindling supplies until they starved or otherwise walk south until they froze.

Later, Eskimos reported seeing the men making progress on foot – or, to be more accurate, beginning to drop dead in the snow. Some sailors had been 'driven to the last resource – cannibalism'. As the days, weeks and months passed, even the younger and fitter died – perhaps speared by Eskimos, perhaps clubbed by each other or else just stiffening as they marched through further depths of whiteness. The natives might have recalled another extraordinary sight: a clutch of Europeans weakly pulling a hefty rowing boat – loaded, as it turned out, with books, utensils and crested plates – overland into oblivion.

Just how far the various sailors got could tell you a lot about them, before you even prised their carcasses from the ice for further inspection: how fit they were, how old they were and how much they were able to believe there was hope when there was none. Many other bodies are still out there, yet to be found. There were, after all, a lot of them.

Franklin, then, had shown us the importance of a Plan C. This and other rules of thumb I plotted out on my bit of paper. And perhaps each one of us should bear in mind these nine principles, if we know what's good for us.

Guidelines for Survival – In Full

Remember:

(1) Maintain a Plan C – a way out, an exit strategy – even though all is currently well. This, your fall-back position, should cover the unexpected as well as the expected.

Once disaster strikes:

(2) Face up to your predicament: carefully look at the wider picture and identify what you know and what you don't; what is in your control and what is outside of it. Through this assessment ('reality check') you will locate where you are 'on the map', know what limits you and be in a position to assemble the building blocks to begin to regain control.

(3) Have a clear goal: set your priorities. To get where? To save yourself? Your family?Your companions? Having set that target, do not be distracted by any jealousies, friendships or minor objectives that stand between you and it.

(4) Morale: banish all dark thoughts – e.g. of what you have lost – and think on what you have now and might have in the future.

(5) Break down seemingly 'impossible' tasks into goals that you can deal with in the short term: focus on getting through the next minute, the next hour, the next day.

(6) Adapt quickly to changing circumstances; keep monitoring the scenarios as they unfold.

(7) Play to your strengths, the resources within and around you – your own skill set, the environment, team, tribe, friends – that you have the power to act on.

(8) If possible, work with, rather than fight, forces that are stronger than you and that you therefore don't have the power to act upon. These might be the resources to be had from the terrain or the strength to be had from fellow survivors. If fellow survivors, be wary: man is weak

alone and stronger if he sticks with others, *but* when resources are limited he is a ruthlessly hierarchical creature, so know where the actual or potential power lies – your leader, your enemy – and stay close to that potential power. N.B. You are only as strong as the weakest member of your tribe; however, that seemingly weak individual may one day help you if circumstances change. Indeed, appearing to be weak or irrelevant may be a useful defence strategy – and may be the only option left you.

(9) Don't be afraid to be ruthless and unpopular in achieving anything arising from the above.

These rules were brutal, but they got air-crash victims off mountains and helped lost backpackers escape collapsing sands. They told us that the wisest sort of adventurers planned for a crisis and knew how to prioritize when it occurred: finding shelter and water was probably the first step, making fire the next. And if no help arrived, your feet became your most important asset – not, as the duller sort of survivor might assume, your hands.

Survival, the piece of paper told me, was about regaining control; issues of morality were not addressed. But in the list could be found beauty as well as ugliness. According to these precepts, a leader might have to ensure his own survival first, in order to be able to lead others to safety. Or he might choose to sacrifice himself to enable the survival of the frail.

Here, then, were to be found the workings of the mind of Nansen – at least if my observations were correct – for he understood the truth from the Eskimos: that the far north was too big to fight. He created a vessel with a rounded hull. 'The *Fram* behaved beautifully, as I had expected she would. On pushed the ice with steady pressure, but down under us it had to go, and we were slowly lifted up.' He steered the *Fram* deliberately into the ice pack and used the currents to transport him to within reach of his target, the North Pole. The *Fram* was not crushed by pack ice, and the Norseman did not die like Franklin.

Here also the conquistador Gonzalo Pizarro, who thought to escape the lowland jungles by forging nails from his horse's shoes to build a boat. He knew the value of looking to the resources around him, just as Francisco de Orellana, the man who took off with the boat, knew where the potential power lay: not with Pizarro but with that vessel.

Gonzalo Pizarro

Gonzalo Pizarro, a half-brother of the conquistador of the Incas Francisco Pizarro, offers us perhaps the greatest of all survival stories. In 1541, he set forth from Quito in search of La Canela, the 'Land of Cinnamon', with a 'very magnificent body of men and one well prepared for any adventure': almost three hundred conquistadors, 4,000 Indian porters and a herd of 2,000 pigs. But they were no match for the steaming foothills to the east of the Andes. They weakened in the incessant rain; their shirts rotted on their backs; the porters died of abuse and various diseases. The cinnamon proved elusive, and no amount of torturing the Indians – they were burned at the stake or given to the dogs – seemed to help. With most of their Indians vanished or dead, they had too few men to carry their supplies. Their only luck had been encountering a local chief, whom they had put in chains and forced to lead them onward. Bearing in mind the conquistador's methods, he'd promised them not just a treasure trove of cinnamon but El Dorado itself. However, when he slipped his chains and ran off, they were stuck. But Pizarro wasn't a man to die easily, and he decided to construct a boat and make headway down the Coca river. He sawed up trees into planks, fashioned nails from horseshoes and plugged leaks by sealing cracks with tree resin. By now, they had finished their pigs and were eating their dogs. The one-eyed Francisco de Orellana suggested he take off in the boat to find food. It might have seemed a good idea at the time, but Orellana never came back. Claiming later that he'd been swept onward by the current, he found himself descending (and naming) the hitherto unknown Amazon.

Pizarro turned for home, tying his sick men on to the few remaining horses. As they waded back to the Andes through waist-deep swamps, hacking through the jungle with their swords and fighting off Indian attacks, they nourished themselves by tapping the blood of their remaining horses, even carving off pieces of their trusted steeds and plugging the holes with clay as they stumbled on together. Finally, they slaughtered their long-suffering horses; adding wild berries and anything scuttling across the forest floor, they made soup in their helmets.

When they emerged from the forests, climbing the slopes back to Quito, they'd eaten their 'saddles and stirrup leather, sliced, boiled and toasted'. Only eighty or so of the original 4,280 had survived. They were hallucinating and were clothed in the skins of wild animals.

Here too the stoic Adolphus Greely, who didn't die in his tent; and the reasoning of Ernest Shackleton, who, after the crushing of the *Endurance* in the Weddell Sea, with five men sailed for help aboard the eight-metre whaler *The James Caird*, 'jumping like a flea' over the 1,300 km to South Georgia through the giant southern seas.

I'd always loved the brevity of my survival list, this little nine-point recipe for getting through calamities. I enjoyed the thought that I might turn to it whenever the occasion demanded, receiving these guidelines from the experts as one might when examining the instructions on a tin. For over twenty years it had been a friend, always quietly there for me.

But was this formula all that you needed? Were these the only factors that preserved the life of Livingstone as he stumbled on through Africa with his loyal servant Susi? Or H. M. Stanley, as he descended the Congo pursued by war canoes and warriors calling out 'Meat!' Or Cortés and Pizarro, Richard Burton and John Speke? Was it ignorance of these principles that caused Robert Burke and William John Wills to die their slow deaths in the red dust and spinifex of Australia, wandering forlornly around Cooper's Creek?

Humans were, when it came down to it, exasperatingly unpredictable. While the marooned and desperate always stood the best chance if they did adhere to these nine principles, at times they survived despite woeful disregard for them. Again, take the great pioneers. They had haunted souls; they felt an unusually fierce desire to cast themselves against the raw elements. They craved the world's great stages, and full of this crazed zeal, sought out the Tibetan Plateau and Patagonian ice deserts. Then, often apparently sustained by no more than air and with callous disregard to the laws of survival, they came safely home again. By not dying when they reasonably should, these people spoilt everything. These people had it in overabundance, this commitment to life. They wouldn't be separated from it. But what stoked this furnace that roared so loudly in some?

Animals too appeared sometimes to develop this inner resolve. We've all come across these refuseniks, man's tenacious servants – the faithful old spaniel that hangs on stubbornly, waiting by his owner's grave. And I recall meeting a Mongolian whose camel had sat on his neighbour because he mistook him for a burglar: he refused to move for three days, and only then was the body found, flattened and as cold as the steppe itself.

The Anatomy of Disaster

The expedition was set up by the government of Victoria as part of a competition between Australian states to find the best north–south route across the continent for an overland telegraph. Fourteen men, led by Robert O'Hara Burke (1821–61), a police inspector of Irish origin, marched north from Melbourne in August 1860 with some thirty horses, twenty-four camels, wagons, firearms, eighty pairs of shoes, twenty camp beds, thirty cabbage-tree hats, fifty-seven buckets, fruit and vegetables, and trinkets for the Aborigines. The explorer Augustus Gregory had advised the inexperienced Burke not to start out until the middle of summer to avoid much of the heat. Before long, as they headed north, Burke found himself arguing with his second-in-command, George Landells, and appointed William John Wills, an English surveyor, to replace him.

Progress was slow – too slow for Burke, who feared that a rival expedition (sponsored by South Australia and led by John McDouall Stuart) might reach the north first. He began discarding equipment. On reaching Menindee on the Darling River, he forged ahead with eight men to set up a depot at the halfway point, Cooper's Creek.

For a while they waited in vain for the others, led by William Wright, to arrive. After six weeks, Burke decided to wait no longer; he'd make a dash for the north coast with three men. William Brahe was left behind to await the relief supplies, having been told he should not leave unless it was absolutely necessary. They would be back within three months.

But the small party – Burke, Wills, John King and Charles Gray – took two months to reach the northern coast at the Gulf of Carpentaria, and even then they were prevented from getting to the shore because of swamps. Their outward journey had been acutely hot and dry. Now, on the return leg, they were plagued by incessant rain. Their rations diminishing, their last camels weakening, on 17 April 1861 Gray died, perhaps from starvation, although days earlier he seems to have been beaten up by Burke for cheating on rations. They spent a day burying Gray, and four days later, their legs half paralysed, they reached Cooper's Creek. Brahe had left. A message carved into a tree read: 'DIG – 3 FEET N.W.' They dug, and found a few supplies and a letter telling them that Brahe, having waited a whole month more than was deemed necessary, had finally departed with the other men only eight hours before. The day that Burke had spent burying Gray had proved fatal.

Sitting exhausted in the camp, the ashes of Brahe's fire still warm, Burke overruled the opinions of Wills and King, who wanted to pursue Brahe. He was, after all, starting out fresh. They would instead try for Adelaide via Mount Hopeless and a cattle station 240 km away. Burke left behind a note, ending with the words 'Greatly disappointed at finding the party here gone.' He signed the message and added: 'P.S. The camels cannot travel, and we cannot walk, or we should follow the other party. We shall move very slowly down the creek.'

Burke, Wills and King headed off with the two remaining camels but were soon on their last legs. Brahe, meanwhile, encountered the rearguard party, led by Wright, bringing the long-overdue relief supplies. They decided to return to Cooper's Creek to see if Burke had turned up yet. They arrived on 8 May but saw no sign of Burke, Wills and King, who had erased all traces of their presence to stop Aborigines removing the note for any rescue party. No one thought to check beneath the 'DIG' tree. Instead, seeing no obvious sign, Brahe headed back to Melbourne to organize a search party. Burke and his companions were presumed dead.

As it happened, though, they were still only a few kilometres away. Having realized they were too weak to make their intended journey, the three men had decided to return to Cooper's Creek. From the Aborigines they encountered over the next few weeks they received fish and the wild grass seed nardoo. This proved insufficiently nutritious, at least for Wills and Burke. Both starved to death, Wills first. His last diary entry was on 29 June: 'I can only look out, like Mr Macawber, "for something to turn up,"' he wrote. 'Starvation on nardoo is by no means very unpleasant.' Burke died two days after leaving Wills. King, the sole survivor, lived off crows that he shot. He was found by Aborigines – 'they appeared to feel great compassion for me when they saw I was alone on the creek'. On being shown the remains of Burke 'the whole party wept bitterly'. For the three and a half months it took for a rescue party to arrive, the Aborigines looked after King.

CONCLUSIONS THAT WE MAY DRAW:

Burke managed to turn a well-resourced expedition into a disaster. How?

We can confidently agree that:

(i) The expedition suffered a structural failure, mostly, but not wholly, centred around the leader's failure to devise a Plan C, his fall-back position.

Arrangements for the depot awaiting Burke – and follow-up supplies – were inadequate and vague. There's no sense here of a leader planning for the unexpected, of a man playing to his strengths – one strength being Wills, an English surveyor, who had common sense and some bush skills, another being those extensive supplies, which might have provided advance depots. Burke does not seem to have been someone who might measure the resources around him, keeping the expedition in control of its destiny. Instead, here was someone who allowed himself to be distracted by the 'race' with Stuart to reach the north.

(ii) Burke, a stickler for discipline and subject to mood swings, was unable to maintain morale – as suggested by his early dismissal of his second-in-command and later by his beating up of Gray.

(iii) Even his own lack of bush skills might not have mattered if he'd acknowledged that the land – home to the Aborigines who roamed freely in this country – was a resource. Burke fought the terrain all the way, and it was too strong for him.

Only when the expedition was brought to its knees did anyone truly adapt to the arid terrain of central Australia, grinding grass for carbohydrates as the Aborigines did. By then it was too late.

As for the rest of us, we crave life in varying degrees. And this made a mockery of my little bit of paper. What was this Moral Fibre that made some of Franklin's crewmen give up after a few weeks and others take step after step to nowhere? The thought of an impending miracle, perhaps. But where would the miracle come from in the Arctic?

Some of us, but not others, battled on. You might practise the arts of survival until you were blue in the face, but they were insufficient in themselves. Something lay beyond. And so, over the years, I'd been filing away press cuttings and photos and jottings on survival and survivors. Now, twenty years after scrawling my guidelines in New Guinea, I had come here to Siberia to ask of the tundra what that something was.

I closed the survival pack, dug into my sleeping bag and again tried to sleep.

XXXI

We were up again early, before last night's tea could freeze in the thermos. We carved butter and meat from their tins, and ate the chunks from the end of our hunting knives. Outside blew a relentless, buffeting wind.

Dennis, the black-and-white back dog, was still traumatized from the cliff fall, and when I began loading the sledge he slipped his harness. He ran almost out of view, and as I prepared the remaining dogs for departure, he stood watching from afar. Soon, he was wanting to be recaptured.

'He has no option,' I said to Ivan. 'Like us, he can go nowhere alone.'

'Actually, we aren't leaving now,' Ivan said. 'Yasha says there'll be a snowstorm.'

'I can't tell you how relieved I am,' I said. 'My leg needs a day's rest.' Sitting was one thing, but how would I push the sledge if it snagged on a rock? How would I dive for it if it sped off without me? Ivan and I sat and chatted for a while. It was a moment I valued. Just lately, I hadn't been able to get this close to him. Ivan – brilliant, genial, mercurial, flawed – how I missed him when he wasn't there, lightening the spirits of all those around him.

I went to Yasha to advise him of the injury, make a clean breast of things.

'April Fool!' he said, before I could get a word out. 'We're going!'

'So it's April the first,' I thought. Already a week later than my target for crossing the Strait.

Once we were on the move, I was thankful to be out in the cold. The wind acted on my swollen knee like an ice pack. But not for long. The dogs were still shaken by last night's tumble and took short cuts across the rocks to be near the other dogs. All morning I was hobbling along, freeing the runners whenever the dogs jammed them in crevices. Despite my best efforts, a grisly temper again overtook me. 'I look after you, I feed you,' I muttered, 'and what reward do I get?'

It wasn't long before I was wanting to hug them again. Descending, we came to a large, lazy river, its frozen tributaries in gleaming ribbons, its frozen springs in silver cords. The river itself was so silky smooth that Tolia's team, ahead, was carried sliding sideways across it by the wind. My dogs looked horrified: they trembled in a huddle, sniffing the air and listening to the pressured water rising through the cracks, emitting a last weak gurgle as it met the air and then lay deathly still, frozen in thick new rolls. Yet Top Dog decided to give it a go. The team followed, scrambling over the polished surface, falling like novice skaters, picking themselves up and falling again.

Nearing the far river bank, Yasha got off his sledge to come and congratulate me. '*Mei!*' But the dogs must have been fuelled by the terror of what lay behind them – that cliff – not the pleasures ahead, because they raced right on by him. And on, tumbling down a steep incline, and finally chucking us all into a chasm. Again we got away with it, but again my dogs were making me want to cry.

Sireniki was meant to be a respite for us all. It was not.

Tucked away in the cliffs by the sea, the settlement was like a James Bond film set, a Soviet hideaway where 007 might have pulled off a mission amid ammunition-dump explosions. There were two massive radar shields perched over the craggy cliffs, hidden petrol depots, army barracks with wooden watchtowers. Once, the US military might have done whatever it took to get spy photos of this frontier base, which – hazarding a guess – had missile silos; now, there was only one soldier on duty that we could see, a youth who never quite got around to finishing getting dressed.

We were installed in a wooden house, and tied the dogs up outside as best we could. That evening, examining their paws, I found that the pads of Dennis's hind right paw were worn on the outside due to the extra leverage he'd had to apply, splaying his legs as he heaved the sledge over the hills. Just as serious, Flashy White, the dog lending such vital physical support to Top Dog, had cut a front paw. 'I only have you ten,' I thought. 'Hang on in there for me.' However, the truth of the matter was that all the dogs were wearing down.

Everything was. Tolia dragged the sledges indoors and began stripping them, rebuilding the components with bits of scrap wood and screws extracted from the hut walls. He, Ivan and Yasha all looked like they needed fixing as well.

The weather worsened. My teammates quickly sought out alcohol from the hospital.

'This is what we do in bad weather,' Ivan said.

I noticed his use of the word 'we'. He was now one of them.

I joined in a half glass to show camaraderie. 'Yes, we're actually drinking 95 per cent strength surgical spirit,' I thought, as more alcohol of dubious provenance was poured into a teapot to be mixed with water.

Soon, Ivan was in what I'd learnt to recognize as his ugly phase. 'I told you to bring carabiners and harnesses for the dogs, but you wouldn't listen.'

'Because I'm here to learn the local way of doing it,' I said.

'And the local way is to use whatever is lying around,' Yasha explained kindly to Ivan.

But Ivan was beyond listening. 'Benya, you are so arrogant.'

Yasha initiated an amiable contest of arm-wrestling with a friend and, between bouts, ate snacks of walrus borrowed from the dogs' supplies. On his way to bed, he stopped, noticing Tolia lying in the corridor. Swaying, but undaunted by the task, he gently collected him up as you might collect a lost puppy, placing him on his shoulder and delivering him to his bed.

In the morning, the winds were screaming around us. Outside, I found it impossible to stand; I had to crawl on all fours to reach the dogs to treat their paws.

The day went by. The wind howled, the three men drank and slept. The dogs huddled together as the remains of their snow bed flew away. Out at sea, the gale was wrenching open the pack ice and agitating the water. I watched the snow jetting past our window, finishing its long journey from the interior of Siberia, spinning off the cliffs in white ostrich plumes, then dropping, at last, to rest below.

My diary of the following day:

Yasha asked me to feed all the dogs – all thirty-two of them. '*Все в порядке*?' ('That all right?') he asked anxiously. It's virtually his

> last gasp as he sways, helplessly. '*Заебись!*' ('F**k me!')
>
> I dressed in my skins and went to the dogs; I was happy to be outside with them in the wind. And I was happy to do a favour for Tolia and Yasha. Hadn't they done more than enough for me? But as I lobbed the walrus chunks at the dogs – first my team, then Yasha's, then Tolia's – I was wondering where this was going to end. Just how strong was I going to have to be? 'This might be the low point of the expedition,' I thought. 'Or maybe it'll get worse! Maybe I'll look back and wish it was as good as today!'
>
> From time to time, a drunk would totter by. Sometimes they would insist on trying to help me feed the dogs, sometimes they would wave merrily, sometimes they would just collapse in the snow with a quiet thud. With each passing drunk, the dogs became more unsettled. Tolia's dogs waited for Tolia, while Yasha's dogs waited for Yasha. Even my dogs seemed to understand that the human matrix that supported them had collapsed. Instead of ducking down, each and every dog was sitting up, watching the hut, listening above the wind to the sound of the carousing.
>
> Each time I visited my dogs, the youngest, Basil, would dig his muzzle into my leg, seeking attention. Flashy White, when I treated his cut paw, tried to play. He rolled, he supplicated himself. This was the beast that had once threatened me; now he too was like a puppy, whacking me with his great forepaws, left and right. It was touching and it was pitiful – these dogs who could sleep unprotected at minus fifty degrees and who were now needing comfort.

The future did not, on the face of it, look promising. From where we were now, it was only another day's ride to Provideniya – 'One day,' Yasha always said, whatever the distance, and it always was, whether it meant arriving at dusk or midnight. With the help of the dogs' night vision, a day was a very flexible unit of time.

With luck, we would set off on 5 April and arrive the same day. Reaching there would be a milestone. It was a huge settlement, kept open by ice-breakers – or at least it had been in Soviet days. It also marked the beginning of the narrowing of the Bering Strait.

Of course, the temptations afforded by Provideniya hardly bore thinking about. Yet I couldn't help wondering – and not without considerable feelings of guilt – if the deterioration in my colleagues was just what my dogs needed. Steadily now, I might be able to take the initiative. Indeed, what other option was there? This was that moment that we all recognize, when it's suddenly up to you and no one else. Silently, you turn away from your companions and loved ones; there's nothing they can say or do to help you any more. You must somehow find the necessary resources within yourself.

XXXII

I must now begin to gather my thoughts, mustering whatever useful notions I carried within me. This was my side of the bargain, my side of the contract with the dogs. Survival, I reminded myself as I lay in my sleeping bag that night, is what we all do daily. It's normal – we mustn't panic about it.

If we have doubts as to whether we can find enough inside us to struggle on, this one thought can surely lend us encouragement: that in our everyday lives, without knowing it, we continually find ways to persevere. This impulse comes to all life quite naturally. I remembered the island of Surtsey, which was created by a volcanic eruption beneath the seas of Iceland in 1963. For three and a half days, the North Atlantic rumbled and spewed forth crimson lava. But then a fly was observed to land there. Two years on, a sea rocket was in flower, and soon seals were observed lolling on the black beaches. We should take heart at the obstinacy of these living things, the blossoming of that Icelandic volcano. It was true whether at sea, in the jungle or here in the Arctic wastes: even unthinking bacteria struggle onward, joining with a thousand other species to transform sterile rock into thick, mossy, verdant forest.

Thus we practise our alchemy. We find ways to get through dark winters just like trees that drop their leaves, salvaging what they can of the chlorophyll before they decommission them. Even if our lives veer off course and we appear to be heading with unseemly haste towards death's door, we must remember that we are not alone. None of us is.

This comforting thought carried me through the rest of the night as my only steadfast teammates, the dogs, waited outside for me to come up with something.

What Is Life?

Recently, Lynn Margulis and Dorion Sagan have tried to pin down what we define as life: 'A tornado risen on the plains doesn't go "whoops" as it wanders into a mountainous landscape that spells its doom; but even the simplest life form effectively does, actively responding to its surroundings to preserve and protect itself.' But just like Erwin Schrödinger before them, they came up with no definite answer. No one ever does.

However, we may prefer to think in terms of the Second Law of Thermodynamics, whereby all isolated things in time dissipate their energy, heading irresolutely to absolute zero. Living organisms are exactly *not* like that; they resist this decay into disorder. We, mere soft vessels of organized material, fight against the state of what Schrödinger refers to as 'thermodynamic equilibrium'. Instead of dissipating, we living things suck up what energy we can, bringing about a negative flow of entropy.

We can say that all animal and plant life is in the same business: each living thing reveals some inner urge to perpetuate itself. 'For all of us organic beings are striving,' wrote Darwin. 'If any one species does not become modified and improved in a corresponding degree with its competitors, it will soon be exterminated.'

Hence, the California pine cone retains many fertile seeds even in good years, releasing them only when fire sweeps through, resulting in what an ecologist might call a 'substantial recruitment of new cohorts'. Or the cicada: different species emerge at different times – some at seven years, others at thirteen, others at seventeen. And if these numbers seem familiar, it is because they are all prime numbers, divisible only by themselves and one; if a cicada emerges in these years, it's hard for predators to achieve a cycle that is in sync with them.

It has been this way since the beginning of life itself, which began somewhere on earth among a soup of amino acids over 3.5 billion years ago: lifeless molecules were transformed by the finger of God, or a single freak chemical trigger, and from that moment exhibited the behaviour of the living. They acted as if to better themselves. They developed a metabolism, they reproduced. From that point, the living would always be divorced from the chemicals around them, which showed no inclination again to create a living organism. We've known the truth since 1859, when the young French chemist Louis Pasteur, boiling up meat broth in a flask, sealing it and showing that no micro-organisms grew from it, disproved the theory of spontaneous generation. No, it was clear that life began way back in time, and once life had begun, there was no stopping it – life begot life, which begot life. 'It only had to arise once,' wrote Steve Jones. And it got everywhere, to the highest mountain, to the deepest ocean trenches, to scorching geysers and acidic caves. Some 4,000 million years on, here we are.

9(a) Towards the end: the formidable Flashy White now supplicating himself before the new alpha male.

9(b) Top Dog, with battle scars.

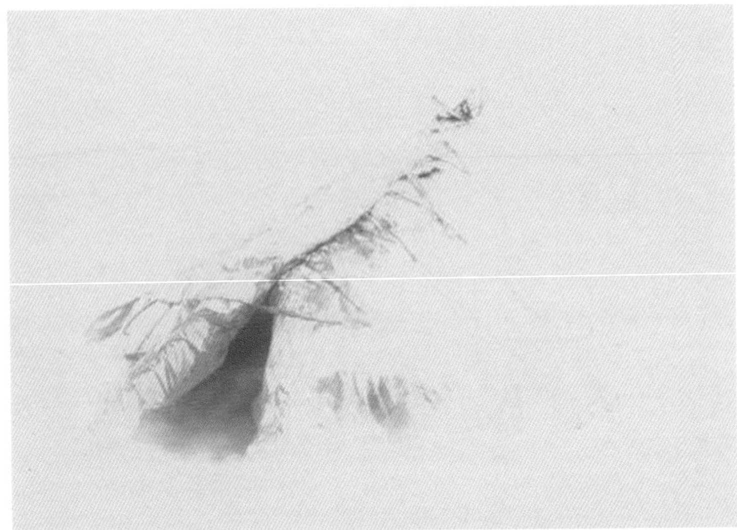

10(a) The traditional yaranga tent of Chukchi reindeer herders, as the wind gathers.

10(b) Wolf country: Top Dog looks back for reassurance. Young Basil, third row, has his tail characteristically high; Bernard, second row from back, is, as usual, not bothering to pull.

11(a) Discussing the oncoming weather at dusk.

11(b) About to leave for the Bering Strait: saying goodbye to Bernard, while his companion Jeremy looks on anxiously.

12(a) Heading off alone into the Strait. Bernard (nearside, second row from rear) joins the team unharnessed, content just to be back alongside Jeremy.

12(b) Devoid of all 'back-up' in the Bering Strait; Top Dog as usual with his eyes on me.

13(a) Melting snow to drink, the tent up as a windbreak. The ice of the Strait is comparatively smooth as yet.

13(b) View from the end of Asia: about to head east from the Russian cliffs towards Alaska. The previous night the dogs, nervous of wolves, had bitten through the gangline and slept heaped against the far side of the tent.

14(a) About to cross a pressure ridge: the lead dogs lie down, saving energy. Jeremy (second row from back, Bernard far side) is about to take over, leading the strong rear dogs Dennis and Muttley.

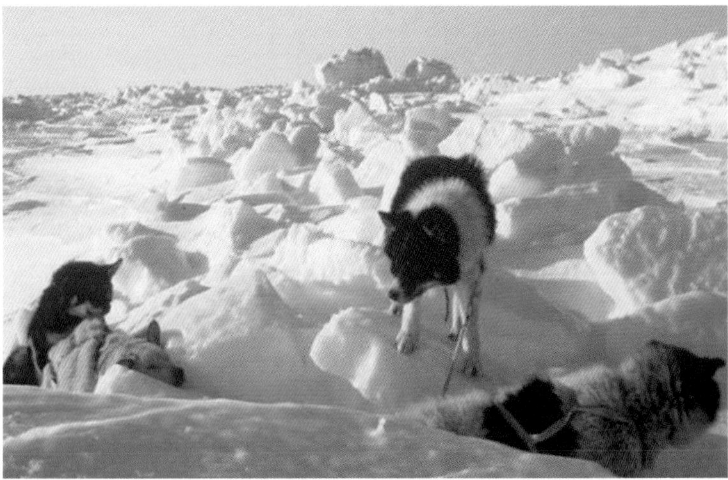

14(b) Jeremy (centre) takes charge: Muttley and Dennis wait for my order to take the strain, Jeremy prepares to lead – and Bernard still daydreams.

15(a) A quiet word with the leader: Top Dog with me, while Flashy White looks on.

15(b) The dog team safely back in Lorino. The lead dogs are mentally exhausted, Flashy White protectively in front. Mad Jack is carefully pinned by my left arm, while Frank hides from him on the other side.

16 A Chukchi herder lassoing deer.

XXXIII

The passage out of Sireniki was fast and unlike any other. I was happy to be moving again – as were my dogs. They wouldn't wait for the other teams to ready themselves and I was swept away through the settlement, clinging on as best I could. We hit not a single telegraph pole – my dogs wanted to be rid of here, as if they had learnt something that man had not: that settlements in the Arctic brought about sickness, that out here in the tundra all higher creatures – whether hunter or hunted – must keep on the move.

I was reunited with the other two teams on the edge of town. Below us lay a river outlet, frozen into an ice rink and being used as such by children skating in their everyday boots.

'Benya, your dogs . . .' called Yasha from alongside me. 'They are obeying you!'

They weren't. At least, not all the time, not yet. They just wanted to be gone. And soon they took a short cut off a high ledge, just to keep up with him. As I got to my feet, they accelerated away again, sending me sprawling in the traces.

We slowed for a sentryman in white camouflage and then we were on our own in the white silence. The scree on the hills vanished as gentle snow fell, and a stillness descended around us as we accommodated the tundra in our minds.

My dogs were calmer now, again listening for my orders. I watched Flashy White, that damaged paw of his protected by a sock. Would he make the distance? He seemed to be holding back.

Time went by. The dogs were still obeying me; I wondered again about this change in them.

'A hitch-hiker!' laughed Yasha, pointing to a rock the shape of a curled corpse ahead. Everyone was in a convivial mood. 'They'll be looking forward to meeting old friends in town,' I thought. 'Perhaps they're also starting to think of home.'

Yasha guided us through the valleys and out into an immense bay sheltered by high walls of blue and black rock. We paused to look at the mirrored surface, the dogs reflected to the heavens as they stood panting upon it. 'Not far now,' said Ivan. I sensed he was beginning to celebrate.

'No need to stay long in Provideniya,' I said. 'Got to keep moving.'

A machine was coming this way. It looked like a tank; the caterpillar tracks were chewing the bay ice, spitting it out in little cubes as this chunk of Cold War technology rolled towards us. The driver undid the hatch and stepped out. He was the ex-administrator of Provideniya, one of the old guard booted out by Abramovich.

'Where's your other lovely snow machine?' Yasha asked.

'Down there,' he said. 'A hundred and fifty metres deep, they reckon.'

We looked at the ice at our feet. Perhaps Abramovich had been right to replace him.

We got on our way, over the smooth, frozen waters, the hills rising steeply to their shattered pinnacles. Ringed seals rested by their holes, happy, it seemed, to able to bask through the longer daylight hours.

'Somewhere very near here,' I thought, 'came the *Plover*' – the ship that brought Lieutenant Hooper on his fruitless search for Franklin. The Chukchis had piloted them towards a natural harbour, and among the next Chukchis to come along to visit them were a clutch of women. Hooper tells us: 'one of them was presented, as a jest, with a small tallow candle . . . It was, notwithstanding, a very pleasant joke to the damsel; who deliberately munched it up with evident relish, and finally drew the wick between her set teeth to clear off any remaining morsels of fat. This was rather too much for some of us . . .'

Provideniya rose from the shimmering ice. The ships at this distance were like toy boats locked into a frozen pond, the dockside cranes rising behind like reeds. Soon, I could pick out the reassuringly solid and obstinately socialist apartment blocks.

Nearer, these looked a lot less solid. Our dogs didn't care. They seemed to have forgotten all the traumas of the last settlement and ran excitedly towards whatever this one offered. We parked them beside a workshop maintained by someone called Vanya, a Chukchi friend.

'Good,' I thought. 'Safely in Provideniya.' The bulk of our trek was behind us and everything was reasonably fine for now. The dogs had been fed, were now settled in good thick snow, and Vanya was making me feel welcome.

'We use this shack to prepare skins, mainly,' he said, slicing a seal open. Swiftly, like an anatomist wielding his scalpel, he dissected the corpse into little heaps of organs, skin and bones. 'Anyway, you're welcome.'

'We won't be staying long, but that's great, thanks.'

'Well, enjoy your stay, however long it is . . . By the way, no electricity till 11 p.m. – the whole town is rationed.' He offered me the seal's eye. 'Best bit.'

I looked at it. It looked back at me. It had a sizeable amount of clear jelly and the pupil was staring out blankly from dead centre. 'Like Tolia's glass eye,' I thought.

I said I'd give it a try. But too late – Yasha made a grab and was scoffing it down. 'Sorry! Couldn't help myself.'

That night, Ivan and I stayed in one of the Soviet blocks, and Yasha and Tolia slept in the shack – or tried to. They were kept awake by a metal coat hanger that Vanya had covered with old dress material, declaring it to be the 'house spirit' that would protect his valuables.

'It kept looking at us,' said Yasha.

'It didn't have any eyes,' I said.

'Yet all night, just staring!' said Tolia.

On the second day, when I suggested that we should be thinking about leaving, Yasha and Tolia entertained half a dozen of Yasha's Chukchi female 'cousins' in the shack. Soon the whole day was gone and we found ourselves in a bar.

Tolia and I got talking about the location of the whale bones erected in prehistoric times north of here. By all accounts, they stood as proudly as the columns of a cathedral, the bones rooted firmly in the permafrost and resisting all winds as they solemnly arched to the sky. No one knew quite why they were there.

'I'd love to see them,' I said. 'Any chance?'

'Wiped out this very winter,' Tolia said. 'Swept away by the snows.' He smoothed his right hand in a circular motion over the table, as a barmaid might clean it with a cloth.

'You hear that, Ivan?' I said. 'They've survived hundreds and hundreds of years, but this winter has been too much for them. That's so sad.'

The lights went out – another bout of electricity rationing – and the manager scurried for candles. Ivan must then have gone on to drink a lot under cover of darkness because when he next spoke his voice had been transformed.

'It's not true,' Ivan said to me. 'I've heard they are fine.'

'What are?'

'The whale bones. They are still there.' I recognized the tone, that belligerence that overcame Ivan at a point somewhere between four and five vodkas.

'No,' Yasha said. 'Tolia is right. Whale Alley has been pushed flat by ice.'

Ivan stared at Yasha. A coldness settled over his eyes.

'These men are honest, Ivan,' I said. 'You know that. They believe what they are saying. Let's leave it for the moment. I'll check at the museum.'

'I don't know what they are playing at,' said Ivan.

The Chukchi cousins then turned up and settled at the next-door table. I danced with Lena, an angular-faced, pale and sad-eyed girl with the fine, light bones of a creature designed for flight. A tragic figure, she fluttered about me like some sort of doomed Siberian snow bird. When next I noticed Ivan, he was sitting looking into his glass and snarling.

'Yasha lied to us,' he said.

'Why would he?'

'In order to get on home.'

'Leave it for the morning. That's time enough.'

'I need to confront him.'

'Don't, please, Ivan.'

'Better confront him.'

'This could jeopardize everything,' I thought. I tried again. 'Please, Ivan. Drop it.'

'He's lying to me.'

'Please.'

Ivan said nothing, but kept his surly gaze fixed on the vodka.

The evening began to slow. Lena danced on, alone; her skin seemed to thin, as if the alcohol was finally dissolving her away. Later she sat with her friends, leaning on them, crying and chewing her lip bitterly, seeming to become more and more like a plaintive bird mourning the extinction of her kind.

Tolia came over. He shook his head, saying to me sorrowfully, 'Yasha . . . Ivan, problem.'

'They've been arguing?' I went over to Yasha. 'You all right? What's been happening?'

'OK!' he said. I looked into those rich, warm, tender eyes of his. He was trying hard to put on a brave front. 'Benya, ya OK!' But there was no disguising it: he was very hurt.

'F**king liar,' said Ivan.

'Ivan, what have you done?' I thought. I gave an apologetic smile to Yasha, and he smiled back as best he could. The situation looked salvageable.

'Let's leave,' I said to Yasha. He shrugged his big shoulders, then stood up.

'We go!' commanded Yasha, gathering up Tolia and the girls.

Ivan swayed where we had left him – cross-eyed and resentful, a defeated dog – as the rest of us put on our coats.

I asked Yasha to wait while I found Ivan his coat. Somehow I needed to sober him up – I didn't have the address of our flat.

'We go!' Yasha repeated.

'Just coming!' I said, reaching for Ivan, whom I'd now propped for convenience between the coat hooks.

'No. *We* go. Ivan stays.'

'I can't just leave Ivan,' I said. Yasha stomped outside and waited there, sitting down in the snow at minus twenty. He wasn't drunk. He was making a point.

We joined Yasha and together made it through the town to the cousins' apartment.

Extract from my diary, 5 April 2001:

In the flat, all got ugly. Yasha began cursing at Ivan. From where he sat on the kitchen floor, he started waving his huge fists and punching the air. The girls intervened to calm him. Ivan sat back in the kitchen chair, pouring scorn on Yasha while the women plied Ivan with vodka to disable him.

They handled Yasha and Ivan easily. 'Women business,' one of them said, keeping me sat down as Ivan tried to snog first one girl, who appeared to leave in tears, then the no-nonsense flat owner. She dealt with him briskly. Then Ivan began hitting her with my BBC camera, breaking it irreparably.

Sasha, partner to the no-nonsense woman, came stumbling out into the kitchen. He announced that he wanted to arm-wrestle with me. I noticed he had vast muscles on his right arm, less on the left. His drunken gaze then slowly turned to the corridor, where Ivan was hitting his girlfriend and she hitting him. We all spotted Sasha's head turning – him registering that his girlfriend was being attacked – and realized there was going to be trouble. We kept him down for a while, but then he made his way slowly over to Ivan, hampered by me and the girls as we hung on to him. He laid a couple of punches on Ivan, who collapsed in the corner, bewildered and small. I blocked more of Sasha's blows, adrenaline rushing, thinking this was going to get far worse – probably for me rather than Ivan. But Sasha ambled to his room and instantly fell asleep.

The girls decided to eject Ivan, which they did – into the sub-zero snows. He was wearing my large indoor shoes on his little feet.

I had to go and rescue him. 'No, no, NO!' said Lena, deploying one of her two English words. But Ivan wouldn't get to our flat in his state, and I couldn't just leave him out there. He pounded on the door to be let back in again, banging on and on for the entire time it took to explain this to the girls in Russian.

Eventually, I carried Ivan in, took my shoes off him and put on his boots. This meant having to manhandle him on to the bed (with Sasha, that force of danger, asleep on it) to do his laces. I told the girls I'd come back the next night at eight (in the end, I couldn't face it) and away we went. I tottered with him back through the snows for a good hour. He would throw my arm off, turn away, stagger a few metres and collapse. Three or four times I felt like abandoning him to die. He'd kick and shove me. 'Please, Ivan, I'm your friend.' Already, in the cousins' flat, I'd caught his wrist when he tried to swing at me. He'd looked startled.

Got to the apartment block finally. As I was in the middle of trying to haul Ivan through the snowed-up outer entrance, while cross-examining him about the number of our flat, two youths wanted to sell us key rings. Trying to gain my bearings, I abandoned Ivan in the stairwell. He began calling to me more often for help. I tried the key in lots of doors. Then Ivan miraculously – with surprise, as if waking up – said, 'That's a coincidence! We are near our flat.'

'Of course we are!' I thought. 'Where the hell do you think I've been trying to get you for the last hour?'

'Number 14,' he finally uttered. So I tried that door and it worked.

I kept him locked indoors all the next day, despite his pleas, and at the museum met Igor, a fluent English speaker who laughed when I asked if I could take his number – there'd been no funds for his phone to be reconnected for quite a while.

With nothing else to do but talk to my dogs, who waited around like beleaguered airline passengers in an airport lounge – starved of information, bored, worried and restless – I set about filming Vanya in his shack. He appreciated the situation and, smiling sympathetically, led me past the comatose Yasha and Tolia to reveal, behind a curtain, the pelt of a polar bear. The third I'd seen hunted illegally on this trip, it hung dripping from a line, like a mighty rug hung up after cleaning. Around us were the dead leaves of the cucumber plants he had planted in May, almost a year ago. 'Not long now!' he said. And he was right. Spring was fast coming along.

'Yesterday it was only minus fifteen at midday,' I thought. 'Today it was briefly plus five.' More cold would come, but this was the beginning of the end. The Bering Strait ice would soon be breaking apart.

I brewed a cup of coffee, tiptoeing over the bodies of my companions. I dug through my bags, rummaging through my notes. Finally, I found what I wanted: the indestructible plastic file labelled 'Survivors'. It was in pieces. The plastic had shattered like glass in the cold. Shards of it lay everywhere among my expedition papers. I picked through them: 'EXPLORATION OF THE STRAIT', 'WHY SCOTT DIED AND AMUNDSEN LIVED', 'NOVICES AND THEIR DOGS' . . .

I moved Yasha's thick, heavy leg aside and spread the contents of the 'Survivors' file on the table. I began digging through the sheaves, picking out examples I'd collected over the years of how and why living things sought to endure. Nature's inexorable imperative, said H. G. Wells, is adapt or perish. I sieved through various organisms: tree frogs that carried their offspring on their back, fish that spat at their prey. And the human that used its head.

I reduced the pile: all examples not directly involving man I put aside. I wasn't interested in the silent, blind mechanism of evolution but in the here and now, in what any of us might do to help ourselves live another day. What did sustain the survivors of the Greely expedition in their tent, through 'the horrors of existence', month after month, gums swelling, teeth dropping, eyes sinking? Why should a limbless, starved man bother to 'brace himself to live', as he was encouraged to do by his rescuers?

I sifted through these comforting instances of human doggedness, occasionally picking out another plastic splinter. I assembled passages from specialists and non-specialists alike, assessing the evidence, wanting to know how adventurers had spun out of whirlpools, limped through glacial moraines, bounced off hideous black cliffs to safety – not forgetting the grimness that we each have to face from time to time without venturing anywhere much.

'I gave a motivation speech for clients of Lloyds TSB in Chatham,' read one of my notes. 'Neil, one of the organizers, says that clients try all sorts of techniques to get a loan from him. For the men it's mainly dressing up their projects and themselves. But the women, of course, flirt. Sometimes they go further. "It's called a groin loan," he said.'

We all have our own favoured strategies: we bite, we cross our fingers, we tussle, we manoeuvre, we joke, we follow our nose. Thus, we stand up, draw breath and shout out to the disinterested winds: 'I am alive.'

Soon I found myself hurrying, as if there was not a moment to lose – and as far as my own expedition was concerned, maybe there wasn't.

'Come on, Prévot! Our throats are still open: we must keep walking.' Antoine de Saint-Exupéry to his companion, their aircraft having crashed in the Sahara.

'No one had lost courage; with such comrades one should be able to manage under, I may say, any circumstances . . .' Among the last intelligible pages from the diary of Salomon August Andrée, Swedish balloonist on his attempt on the North Pole, 1897.

'On seeing that the game was up, I decided to forfeit everything except my life.' Sven Hedin, discarding his baggage in the Taklamakan Desert.

She was known as the Yargee girl. She sold yargee, the home-grown tobacco, in the market – and she was fading away in my arms. Or rather, not fading. She was fighting to live, kicking and writhing, as I tried to spoon a sugar solution into her mouth.

'That's it, fight!' I thought. The village waited, seeming to expect me to begin the Christian magic that would give her back her life. But my hands were not the healing hands of Jesus.

There was little doubt in my mind that she had cerebral malaria – and was past recovery. But even later, in her unconscious state, she fought. And afterwards everyone agreed that, despite the tragedy of it all, we had all been moved by this spirit in her. My diaries, Kandengei village, Papua New Guinea.

'We all hope to meet the end with a similar spirit.' Scott, after failing to persuade Oates not to walk out to his death.

'I'm in trouble,' I say aloud. My head is so heavy; I can't walk back yet. I'll wait for the heat to go. With the cool I'll be stronger.

All day I fight against sleep, squeezing a sharp pebble in my hand. The sun starts to turn down. I get up, fall.

Time to make the emergency signal: I must light a fire. Micky said it works every time.

I throw a match. The first three do not catch. Then I wait as the grey, oily spinifex smoke rises. The wind gusts, the flames rip. Soon, I have to crawl away so as not to burn. I'm left with a low shrub to lean against and it has no more shade than chicken wire. While the fire gushes, the sun moves, and I shift to keep in the shade of the bush, such as it is.

But no one has come yet. Fear takes hold – I'm to die out here.

I look at the damage my fire has inflicted and am pleased. The lust, joy of destruction in those flames – their dazzling appetite. I've put up quite a fight.

The sun is weak. No help has come from the sandalwood camp. It's up to me.

Around me, destruction. The flames have died. My fire has eaten trees whole or sometimes just their roots, felling them. Red dragon tongues stretch over the blackened sand – paths of underground fires. There are spouts of escaping air from cooking roots. The soil has risen like pastry into orange, Vesuvian cakes. Sticks smoke like fag ends, ash tailing them. All this I've destroyed in order to live.

Dusk arrives. They aren't coming now. A small scorpion emerges from the sand near my face. Then another. Even with all this destruction, creatures are going about their business. Everywhere there were survivors. And finding myself among them seemed to be good for me, a reminder of the resilience of living things. I raised myself to my feet. My diaries, while separated from Aborigines in the Gibson Desert.

'Each time the moran, the fighting class of the Maasai, moved in, he would take out his false teeth and show them off. It always did the trick.' Joseph Thomson, negotiating the 'dread' Maasailands, despite the warnings proffered by H. M. Stanley.

Mungo Park, meandering along by mule as he sought to find the direction of the Niger: sometimes to get out of trouble – and he was in trouble a lot – he plucked off one of his silver buttons and presented it to the local Moorish ruler.

In the bar, talk of another three people dead on the road.

'Usual story.'

'Usual? Three people dead is usual?'

'Usual pattern, mate. They always leave the car – first mistake. They start walking, and then they take their shirts off to keep cool – second mistake.

'Yeah, always the same. We find the body of the man nearest the car. He's sacrificed himself – given his water to his wife and child. Then we find the mother, further along the road. Under her, sometimes alive, there's the child. The child lasts longest – the mother too has sacrificed herself. She has given her water to her child so that it might live.' My diaries, Wiluna, Gibson Desert.

Joe Simpson, the climber remembered for crawling, hopping and rolling down a Peruvian mountainside after his rope had been cut, taking one rock at a time. He talked of one part of him saying, 'Keep moving!' The other part was just 'looking around'. He had to try to listen to the part that wanted to live.

We are taught how brave, bloody Hernán Cortés brought down the Aztec empire with a handful of men. To concentrate their minds, he scuttled his eleven ships on arrival. The little cluster of 508 soldiers, 100 sailors and sixteen horses were left on the alien shore, their only hope of retreat gone. It was a great motivator. Now there was no plan of retreat.

But what we are not told is that Cortés arrived here in Mexico needing to protect his rear. He'd learnt of a plot among his men to seize a ship and retreat, betraying him to Diego Velázquez, who was his superior, his enemy and the Governor of Cuba. Viewed this way, we see that his tactic is less rash: less to do with ambition and more to do with survival. (He seems to have hanged two of the ringleaders, another traitor was released – he was a clergyman – and another had either one or both feet sliced off.) My diaries, Sierra Madre Occidental, Mexico.

Conversation with the Afrikaner selling me three camels:

'Agh, *man, you want three like* this?' *He nodded towards the strong one and turned back to me with a look of disdain.*

'Well, yes, I do actually . . .'

'And every step you take into the sand, these three strong camels will know that you are the weakest of their herd. They will then calculate how to get rid of you. No. Don't take strong camels; rather take weak ones and then hope to be their leader. Look: a man has nothing to offer a camel in the desert. Nothing to offer but his determination to carry out his strange plans.' My diaries, Kalahari, South Africa.

No Need to Die – *title of the survival manual by Eddie McGee.*

The camel called Jigjig now made his big move. He rebelled at the perfect time: I was days from any help. Ahead stretched a belt of hilly dust. 'It's true what I've been warned about,' I thought. 'When it comes to survival, the camel is a master tactician. His whole life is about bettering the odds. I, being weak, am lessening the odds, and so he has to do away with me.'

I still had two camels that were sticking by me – for the moment. Bert had one hump instead of two, and one eye instead of two. But at least he carried luggage, unlike Bastian.

Now there was nothing to do but demonstrate to them that I was the leader with greater purpose. I tried to lead the other camels away, while Jigjig called indignantly at them to follow him. But they did follow me, first Bert and then Bastian. And so my life was saved not because I was strong but because I had a sense of intent coupled with a human's even better tactical brain: and I'd chosen to employ the weakest camel I'd ever seen. My diaries, Gobi Altai, Mongolia.

In Glasgow I bumped into a mountaineer who had just come back from a hike with Ranulph Fiennes. 'I called him "the terrier". Always at me heels. Always a pace behind, however steep we climbed. Pursuing me with bared teeth – jeez, I couldn't get rid of the sod.'

Yesterday, Pete Goss talked about why, even though caught in a terrible storm himself, he turned back to save a fellow round-the-world sailor: 'It was really quite simple. It wasn't a decision made by me but by centuries of ocean-farers . . . Once you've been deep in the valley of life you know its value.'

'Below stretched a vast basin of sand with a group of trees in the middle, bounded on the far side by range after range of dunes. We were standing two hundred feet above it, on the brink of a drop that was very steep indeed. The obvious and prudent course was to unload the beasts, lead them down one by one, then return to man-handle the baggage after them. Neither Ibrahim nor I had the strength left for that. We looked at each other, not needing to speak our minds.

'"We try?" he added. I nodded.' Geoffrey Moorhouse, Sahara.

XXXIV

Extract from my diary, 6 April 2001:
Yasha was sheepish when I saw him. I gave him a warm smile and hopefully all will now be brushed over. He said to me, rather sadly, '*Передай привет Ивану*' ('Say hello to Ivan').

It'll be put down to drink, let's hope. But I need to think of distancing myself from the others now. It'll be dangerous without Yasha, but his presence, unless we can rid ourselves of the devil which is in Ivan, might begin to be too much of a threat to all I've come for.

I always hoped Ivan would bring me closer to the Chukchis, but he's taking them away from me. I suspect he thinks I want to be a hero, and we do not like heroes unless they are far removed from our everyday lives: Odysseus, Jesus of Nazareth, war veterans, fabled pioneers and God do very nicely. A hero is an inspiration but also a threat to you at close quarters. The glory-seeking colonel might not mind dying, but most people just want to get home from a war alive. They don't want to be led to their death.

I walked around, feeling alone out here. Igor, at the museum, was the only level-headed voice to listen to. 'Educated,' I thought. 'So does that mean that "education" is the only answer?' I hope not, but Igor does provide a release for me, an escape from the bottled-up angst that is released by the others through drinking. Besides, it's a question of either talking to him or talking to the dogs.

The next day, we didn't leave. Tolia had not come back that night; we wouldn't be going tomorrow either, at a guess.

I talked to Yasha over the map, overseen by that dreaded 'house spirit' and also by Ivan, who I called in to clarify things. It was time to break the news that I still wanted to go it alone in the Strait.

I began by floating the idea that only Yasha should guide my team onward from Lorino.

'*Можно* . . .' ('Possible . . .') he said. 'My dogs will try anything.'

'And I would then go on alone into the Bering Strait . . .'

Yasha was silent. Waiting for more. But there was no more.

'*Что?*' ('What?')

Ivan had to repeat it. There was genuine shock. 'But he doesn't have control of his dogs, he doesn't know their characters. They might do anything out there.'

'I know, I know . . .' I said, 'of course it doesn't sound sensible. There's also the danger of cliffs.'

Yasha gaped at the map. Then he gaped at me. Then he gaped at Ivan.

After a while I filled the silence by suggesting that I did a trial run anyway.

'You could try along the coast a bit,' Yasha said reluctantly.

'Absolutely!'

'And what would happen to me, having left you? Who would see me safely home?'

'He's even scared of being alone out there himself . . .' I thought. I reassured him that we would talk more in Lorino. This made him feel better. Perhaps he thinks I'll forget the idea, as Ivan thought I must have done a long time ago. But I won't; it's what I'm here to do . . .

Before our departure, Yasha – rather silent now, full of misgivings about my intentions – asked me to give blessings to the spirits. For good measure, I sacrificed a piece of each luxury food item: chocolate, jam, bread, Choco-pie . . .

'In three directions,' Yasha said. 'Especially to the north.'

'Why three?'

'I don't know. Our grandparents said so. Anyway, it seems to work. The weather was good to us because we did an offering before we started.'

And it was true, the weather had been good to us – although it might not have felt like it. And while in Sireniki we had avoided a severe storm. Apparently many Chukchis had been caught out, and their dogs had suffered frostbitten muzzles.

My team looked well rested. I would keep a sock on Dennis's paw, I decided, and keep treating Flashy White's pads. But all in all, the dogs looked in good physical shape for what lay ahead.

We wove onward to the nearby settlement of Novoye Chaplino, Vanya taking our sleeping gear ahead with his snowmobile. And although I didn't feel comfortable travelling even a few hours through the tundra without such vital equipment, we were reunited with it sooner than expected. There it was, ahead of us in the middle of the arid whiteness, chucked out into the snows.

'What's he playing at?' I asked Ivan.

But we all knew. Soon we came upon Vanya himself. He was driving round and round in circles, singing. I waved back at him. I was no longer surprised or disappointed. Not even later that day when I heard that this charismatic man, who was so wonderful to me in Provideniya, had shot at his friends during one such drinking spree.

Novoye Chaplino, like Sireniki, was largely an Eskimo settlement – that is, the Soviets had chosen this particular spot on which to deposit whole communities of them. The houses were swamped with snow. Roofs poked from drifts that were five or even, if you were really unlucky, ten metres deep. For the first time we were in a settlement that used sledge dogs, and we veered left and right through the roof tops, attempting to keep our own dogs from where they pranced and howled at us, attached to the guttering and eaves.

We were offered food, we were offered drink. As I left to go for a walk, I saw Yasha restraining himself, fighting not to join the others on the road to oblivion. It pained me to close the door.

I had wanted to investigate a colossal brick structure that I'd noticed on arrival. Was it a storage depot or did it have some darker purpose? A man found me wandering about and invited me to his house. 'My wife's just making some bread!'

I followed eagerly behind, trotting along like a befriended stray.

'Which way is your house?' I asked.

'Down!' he said. Access was via an igloo tunnel to an upper window, and descending into the house was like easing your way into a cave. The lower floors would not see daylight for another two months.

The man's wife served up a round loaf of fresh bread the size – and almost the weight, it seemed – of a scooter wheel. A little girl watched me, this abandoned creature her father had rescued, as I gratefully ate up the whole lot.

Back at our house, everyone was flat on their backs. I noticed that the walrus meat had gone – the dogs must have already been fed. 'I judged my companions too harshly,' I thought. 'And not for the first time.'

I woke later to the sound of Tolia crashing about. 'Hey, Benya . . .' came a slurred voice through the dark. 'You fed the dogs?'

'You mean that you haven't?'

'We were drinking . . . and . . .' Tolia began, embarrassed.

Ivan's voice said, 'Benedict, you prick! How could you let down your own dogs?'

I wanted to protest, but he was right. No excuses were good enough. I should have checked properly. How could I have let the dogs down – and now, of all times, when they were standing by me? I tossed and turned bitterly through the night, and in the early hours got up, turned on my torch and flicked through the plastic file, again with an urgent need to know the minds of these survivors – and more precisely, the source of that desire in us to keep on living.

'My position is this: I have an apparently terminal disease which doesn't allow me to make any realistic plans for more than a couple of months ahead, a voice which stopped when my cancerous tongue was removed, a diet completely dependent on the food blender, and a fair to middling amount of pain on most days. To add insult to cancerous injury, I neither feel the need of nor can I discover any comfort in religious faith . . .

'With so little time left for living, what is there to live for?

'The easy answer is Philip Larkin's about none of us ever being able to get out of bed in the morning if we had any real sense of our own mortality, and it seems to be borne out by the mortality statistics. Depressed and fraught as we're all meant to be with our fast and unliveable modern lives, last year only 5,000 or so of us were so desperately unable to cope with it all that we killed ourselves . . . Even if we don't know what to live for, we all want to carry on living. Well of course we do – it's what we're programmed for. A species which could take life or leave it alone wouldn't get anywhere like this far . . . Why am I happy? Because I'm alive. And the simple answer to the question "What the hell is the point

of it all" is this *is the point of it all . . .'* John Diamond, *Observer*, 31 December 2000.

Whatever it is, this survival urge, this primeval instinct, it's so central to our existence that it rewards us with joy when we acknowledge it. Andrew Eavis, the caver who's discovered more underground terrain than anyone else, wrote to me with an account of his time caught in a flash flood in Pierre Saint Martin in the Pyrenees:

'As we sat in the gloom hour after hour, there was no sign that the angry flow of water was going to abate. We told each other our life stories several times over . . . Families were discussed, friends analysed, but the difficult conversation, however, never moved towards the current situation; it was almost as though we were not psychologically prepared to weigh up the chances – I guess we thought they were low!'

He was fifty-five hours underground, and in a neighbouring cave two Frenchmen were drowned. Yet, after climbing out:

'As my senses returned, it dawned on me how utterly unbelievable those hours had been. Life at two hundred metres from the bottom of one of the world's deepest caves had never looked so good.'

The first bullet, from a rifle, seemed to part my hair, in much the way these things do in adventure comics. It was clear that this was not a warning shot. As I paddled my canoe, my back an easy target, I waited for the second shot. I paddled as fast as I could – of course. And my mind was racing, yet waiting, waiting for my execution, the thump of the bullet in my spine. And still the second shot didn't come. At last, as I rounded a bend and was about to disappear out of sight, I turned and saw why I hadn't been finished off. Each time the trajeta *raised his rifle, the canoe prow swung to the left or right. He had to put the gun down and pick up the paddle. Then pick up the rifle again. It was funny – almost. He was a really poor assassin. He couldn't 'multitask' – paddle and kill someone at the same time. Or could it be that I survived because I cared more about life than he cared about ending life?* My diaries, regarding being shot at on the Putumayo by *trajetas*, the hitmen of Pablo Escobar's Medellin cartel.

'When she created us, nature endowed us with noble aspirations,

and just as she gave certain animals ferocity, others timidity, others cunning, so to us she gave a spirit of exalted ambition, a spirit that takes us in search of a life of, not the greatest safety, but the greatest honour – a spirit very like the universe . . . It is master of all things; it is above all things; it should accordingly give in to nothing . . .' Seneca, the stoic (c. 4 BC–65 AD), letter CIV.

'Hey, you!'

'Me?' *It was the Colonel in the corner – he had already finished his bottle.*

'Yes, you. I want talk to you! About the war.'

'The Cold War?' I said, a little apprehensive.

'No, no. Other war. The war we had in Crimea.'

'That was a long time ago.'

'It was first modern conflict,' said the officer. 'Big guns, and the French had first accurate bullets. But also you Brits on your horses. Running into Russian guns, with the sword held in hand! What stupidity!' He stopped. 'But we also find something to like in these crazy heroes, is not true?'

'It's true,' I thought.

'"C'est magnifique, mais ce n'est pas la guerre." *So, buy a bottle for me and let's drink to glory we see even in most foolish bravery.'* My diaries, Moscow airport.

The Darkness Beckons – *title of the caving book by Martyn Farr. But what exactly is beckoning? What do people find attractive in a place where one 'becomes, effectively, blind'? Farr writes of the joy of the challenge, of 'pitting one's wits and resources against the cave', of the 'boundless elation' of triumph, the camaraderie. But it's all very unsatisfactory – he concludes only that 'To most, this eternal darkness holds little attraction, but to a select few . . . it is their life blood.'*

'I cannot say that I felt anything except a pleasant exhilaration.' Freya Stark, attacked by brigands in Persia.

At the Royal Geographical Society, standing among a bunch of mountaineers: 'I love the simplicity,' one of them said. 'On mountains everything is made so simple. You descend the mountain or you die.' I looked at them. I pictured Doug Scott descending from The Ogre in Pakistan for six days through a blizzard with two bro-

ken legs, Bonington with a broken rib. Herzog getting off Annapurna even after losing his glove – and therefore his fingers. Was that the answer? They did it because they preferred the everyday struggle that we are all *doomed to face in our lives reduced to something much simpler to understand?*

'Then a small boy was running towards me, trying not to spill what was in the bowl . . . This was the most beautiful thing in the world, more beautiful by far than the stained glass of Chartres, than a fugue by Bach, than the moment after ecstasy with the woman you loved, or the moment when your son scrambled to squeeze the breath out of you and say, "I think you're smashing, Dad." There was nothing in the world as beautiful as this bowlful of water.' Geoffrey Moorhouse, on reaching a Saharan oasis.

Extract from my diary, 9 April 2001:
Leaving Novoye Chaplino, our hostess came out and tried to get me to drink with the others. I was simply cross; normally I am at least polite. There we were, about to head into the tundra – and wasn't it warning enough to Yasha that the dogs had not been fed last night? Everyone had copious last swigs as they stood outside, me sitting with my dog team, waiting to go.

Later, once we at last got on our way through the wilds, I stopped my dogs. Beside me had appeared Yasha's sledge – with him not on it. His dogs, confused, had been trying to catch me up to alert me. I called to Ivan, but he was semi-drunk. Tolia heard me calling, though, and turned back to look for Yasha. He found him asleep out there in the snow. Yasha reappeared, very embarrassed – shocked at himself, I think. But not long to go now, and I think I'll weather this storm.

I was fully aware of what I must now do: bide my time, gradually building my independence from my companions, just as they were from me. Any chance of pulling off my plan was up to my dogs. 'Think only now of readying yourself,' I thought. 'Of establishing control where you can.'

What we are perpetually seeking is a level of control over our surroundings, I'd thought, shuffling through the file at night. *We better ourselves in our careers, in our gardens, in our kitchens.* This is, surely, nothing more than an extension of the life urge – *the universal effort of living things to impose their pattern on randomness.* Thus:

Admiral Peary's desire to be immortalized as first man to the North Pole:

In childhood: 'Remember, Mother, I must have fame and cannot reconcile myself to years of commonplace drudgery.'

In adulthood: 'There is something beyond me, something outside of me, which impels me irrestistibly to the work.'

Supposedly at the Pole, possibly having faked it: 'The prize of three centuries . . . mine at last!'

On his return (Ellesmere Island): 'What I saw before me in all its splendid, sunlit savageness was mine, mine by the right of discovery, to be credited to me, and associated with my name, generations after I ceased to be.'

On his final resting place: 'Faced with marble or granite,' he ponders, musing on a fitting style of mausoleum. 'Statue with flag on top, lighted room at base for two sarcophagi?'

Joe Simpson seems to have decided *to live. 'I'm insanely stubborn. I do like to have things my way.'*

In order to maintain our dreams we must know ourselves:

'By climbing mountains we are not learning how big we are. We are finding out how breakable, how weak and how full of fear we are. You can only get this if you expose yourself to high danger.' Reinhold Messner, the mountaineer.

'Because this *is who I am beneath. Lose a sense of who you are and you lose a sense of absolutely everything.'* Wilfred Thesiger, outside his hut at Maralal, explaining to me why he was wearing a fine English tweed jacket in the middle of the African savannah.

Knowing ourselves, we can decide what strategy is acceptable to us. The checklist of a prince, after consultation with Machiavelli, might include:

Take loads of advice, but adopt it only when you *choose. Learn from the fox and the lion: the fox in order to recognize traps, the lion to frighten off wolves. Men are wretched creatures who don't keep their word, so you don't need to – and don't honour your word if it disadvantages you. Try to win a reputation as someone of outstanding ability. Better to be feared than loved, but always avoid being hated. Be generous, but if possible, only with things that aren't your own.*

A saying that's used a lot here in Siberia: 'НА БОГА НАДЕЙСЯ, А САМ НЕ ПЛОШАЙ' – *'You can rely on God, but don't let yourself down.'*

As we travelled, I worked harder on my team. I made the dogs stop, turn left and right, right and left. The procedure was simple: make them do everything that they didn't want to do. Again and again and again. 'The sooner you obey, the sooner we get to the next settlement,' I explained to them. Mad Jack, Frank and Basil began copying Top Dog's lead, swinging their weight behind him, leaning into each curve. And after five hours even Flashy White, not the sharpest of the bunch, was getting the idea. With every passing moment, the dogs were consolidating as a team, shaping themselves into something more reassuring than the disorder surrounding us.

The people of Yanrakkynot welcomed us into their community as other communities had done before. Top Dog chose to spend the next two days sheltering like a refugee under Flashy White, who had adopted the habit of standing patiently to offer him shelter from the passing revellers.

Vanya turned up, and by way of apology for his own drunken escapade, took us on his snowmobile to the whale bones of Yttygran Island, the alleyway that Yasha thought had been washed away. But there they were, standing resolutely in the snows, jaw bones of the bowhead whale, twice the height of a Chukchi and tinged green with lichens. They had withstood even this severe winter, dividing the winds that otherwise passed unhindered through the Arctic. A few stood like sentries in isolated pairs, but even more impressive were those which formed the aisle. They rose like giant arched sabres, a corridor leading to nowhere and from nowhere. In this unkind tundra it was a statement of defiance. Only man could have erected them, and only man could pull them down.

How could each such glorious arch, curving like a rainbow, speaking of such intent, be a mystery even to the people who worked the tundra today? 'What do you think?' I asked Vanya. 'Were they a tribute to the whales? Perhaps the people who built them hoped to win favour with the spirits of the sea.'

'Whatever they were built for, they were made by heroes of the tundra,' Vanya said. 'People who were here before the Europeans, before the arrival of metal. That's the most important thing to know.'

Yasha and Tolia need hang on only a little while longer. We were two days from Lorino. 'Think only of that,' I thought. 'Before you know it, you two men will be on your home turf, and you dogs will be on yours.'

And I too would be where I wanted. Lorino would be my launch pad, my chance. At last the time was coming.

As we again tumbled along through the tundra, the future seemed to beckon brightly through the snows. My leg injury was manageable, the dogs' paws healing up. I looked at the team – the dogs were running eagerly, heads up, smelling the wind as it glided over each passing scene. They could detect the sweet scent of home, and we were still fifty kilometres away. Should I accept Yasha's judgement? He said I didn't know the characters of the dogs, and although I felt I had a fair idea, I must assume he was right. I should count my blessings – we've had some great times. But how would I ever know what we *might* have done? 'I can't end things here,' I thought.

> *If maintaining a 'positive outlook' helps us persevere as individuals, then dissatisfaction is the key to survival of man – why he looks around the world for new challenges and solutions.*

Back in Yanrakkynot, I'd talked it over with an old Chukchi called Leonid. Regarded as a font of knowledge, he had hard, deeply set, dry inkwell eyes and a face like a slab of rock worked on by the Bering Strait – fluted as if by ice, gulleyed as if by rain, burnished as if by relentless wind. In addition, he had short, blunt teeth. Short, blunt fingers. He was a short, blunt man.

'Did they tell you I'm the only survivor of a boat carrying ten people?' he asked, bothering me with those sunken, blackened eyes. I said they had. A storm from out of nowhere had capsized the boat and he had clung on to the keel for seventeen hours, finally being rescued by a fishing vessel.

'Almost drove me mad, the swirling waves,' he said. He looked down to his hands now lying in his lap, the horny fingers that had been white and wrinkled and washed by sea foam as they gripped that keel. 'But to answer your question about whether you would survive alone with your dogs, these things aren't altogether in our hands.

We Chukchis believe that certain people are born dead. They will have accidents sooner or later and will die.'

'Nothing you can do about it?'

'Nothing.'

'And how do I know beforehand if I'm one of those people?'

'You don't,' he said. 'Though in the case of you and your dogs, I think you might be able to hazard a guess . . .'

Now, spinning through the Arctic, the day passed quickly – I wanted to make the most of every minute with my workmates the dogs. I looked for cliffs, treacherous ice, anything that would challenge them and reveal the limits of our relationship. But I had to be content today with testing them on dry, flattened tundra plains. Again and again we'd peel off like scouts on a lone mission and swerve over the snows before returning to the main expedition. On each of these ventures, the dogs obeyed without question.

The night came, and still we were hurtling along. And out of that great darkness came a light, about a mile away. Or just a few hundred paces away – we couldn't tell. It flickered like a candle as the snow passed across it and threatened, it seemed, to snuff it out.

'What's ahead?' I called to Ivan.

'Not sure.'

'Nomads,' shouted out Yasha. 'Reindeer herders. Keep the dogs under control.'

We had stumbled on one of the last bands of nomadic Chukchis. And not until I drew up my dog team beside their *yaranga* did I know just how much I'd needed this – not an ex-Soviet apartment but a tent much like a squashed tepee, sunk progressively into the ice by the warmth it harboured. This dwelling hadn't much changed since Hooper came across the coastal *yarangas* supported by whale ribs and overlain with walrus skins – 'tightly stretched and neatly sewn' – that were so well cured they were semi-translucent and acted as windows. In the antechamber, sledges were unloaded and dogs slept, 'the faithful creatures ever seeking to lie close to their masters at the edge of the inner rooms, and even thrusting their noses into the heated atmosphere'.

Having seen to my dogs, I joined Yasha, Tolia, Ivan and a clutch of herders around a central fire. A woman stirred a pot that hung from a rope; the wick of a seal-oil lamp fed a flickering amber flame. We sat in almost total silence, stilled by the soft, smoky light, our tea mugs sinking into the ice. The structure around us was encased in the tundra – and a continuation of it. Boulders hung by ropes from the main cross poles; a sleeping chamber had a thick underlay of insulating grass. Even here indoors, ice was never far away; it spread around and beneath us – and yet the air was warm, as if an agreement had been struck with the elements presiding outside. One such agreement had certainly been struck with the reindeer: everything here owed itself directly or indirectly to that animal. The tent fabric of cured skin, the rugs, the fur trousers, the shoes, the jackets. Even the wood poles and cooking pans had, like the lamp, been traded for skins from coastal people in a tradition dating back to before the time of James Cook.

I retreated to the sleeping chamber, a little skin compartment like a central, vital organ. Inside, lit by a tray burning seal oil, I pulled myself free of my outer clothing and spread out among the fur blankets. I was warm and secure, held protectively inside this inner body. This was the most peaceful night I'd ever experienced in the Arctic, and I knew there would never be another like it. Here was my last sanctuary. From now on, everything would be different.

XXXV

At daybreak the men fanned out towards their reindeer herd. They moved the deer over the snows, stirring them, watching them. The herders were no longer protecting their animals from the wolves; now they were predatory wolves themselves, selecting their prey, identifying the slow, the lame. Dividing and re-dividing the herd, they looked about with the same hungry eyes, seeking whom they'd devour.

They made their move, diving in, casting lassos. Ropes were fastening on antlers; a hind was fleeing, a man being dragged. Then, the rest of the pack moved in and the victim was being pressed to the snow. And sudden calm. All was as before: two hundred deer stood in all their elegance, as peaceful as gazelles in the Serengeti when the lions have done their killing.

We were under way again. The breeze was picking up. I looked back at the *yaranga*, knowing it might one day be important for me to remember that people could live comfortably out here in the tundra.

The wind blew. Soon we couldn't tell if it was snowing afresh or whether the snow striking our eyes was merely being shunted from here to there across the plains. For ten or fifteen minutes at a time, we lost sight of each other and had to stop to regroup. Each time, I thought Yasha was stopping to announce that we should head back to the herders.

'Shit!' Ivan said. 'My hands hurt with the cold. That's the first time on the trek!'

'But I've been in pain every single hour of this trek!' I thought. 'Even in the towns sometimes!' And all this time I'd been assuming Ivan, Yasha and Tolia were just being braver than me.

The snow piled upon us, weighing us down. We were floating as if through thick cloud and I couldn't even see Dennis or Muttley, running right in front of me. Not even this wind, though, would stop my dogs now. They had no interest in following Yasha but pelted along beside him. 'Your dogs aren't concentrating!' he called out. 'They are thinking only of getting home.'

'It's not just my dogs, actually,' I thought. Soon Yasha's dogs were so unruly he was forced to stop. He grabbed a spare harness and whacked the members of his sledge team, one at a time, starting with the ones at the back. Further up the row, the dogs waited mournfully. They knew the routine.

Tolia went on ahead, alternately battling with and encouraging his dogs. I followed, slowing my team to establish order and then making them jive to the left and to the right. I began enjoying the sight of what we had accomplished together. 'If nothing else is achieved,' I thought, 'then at least I'll have had this moment.' Today my dogs were better disciplined than either Yasha's or Tolia's. 'Why not end it here?' I thought. 'Why not just stop in Lorino? Why risk spoiling a happy ending?'

I watched Yasha's dogs disobeying his commands. If at times they did this even to him, what chance for me? His lead dog Sarah was beginning to take risks; she galloped blindly on home, cutting over thin ice, flying off slopes.

At sunset, we headed along a shoreline where whale bones had again been erected by unknown prehistoric peoples. I stopped my dogs for a moment to look one last time at these monuments standing up to the wind. The snow streamed by us, reddened by the low sun and split by the line of bones like hair divided by the teeth of a comb.

Lorino came out of the darkness. I saw the lights and knew that very little now could stop us getting the remaining dogs safely home. Ahead, a settlement with seventy dog teams; a community that not only understood the dog but was reliant on it. Like little vessels we cut across the frozen harbour, making our way to human shelter.

Yasha was having problems even getting his dogs to go left and right. He kept stopping to thrash Sarah. 'Pull yourself together!'

I went on ahead, trusting Top Dog to take us through the blackness and wondering where in the town we would end up. Was he following the scent laid down by Tolia's team – if indeed Tolia was ahead? Or some old doggy friends of theirs? Or would we turn up at Alexei's doorstep?

'Where to?' I said. 'Where's home?'

I let the dogs make the decision.

We were heading up a slope, buildings rising to block the stars on the horizon. And then my dogs stopped. They seemed to think we were there. I discerned the eyes of another dog team, and a voice came from the night. 'Benya!'

Tolia. My dogs had elected to stick with the dogs they'd grown familiar with in hardship. Yasha came up alongside and stopped his dogs beside me. 'Benya!' he exclaimed. 'For the first time just now I saw that you were a team.'

Tolia's relatives had been busy unharnessing his dogs, and now partially seen hands were doing the same for me. All around, the wagging of tails and sneezing of dogs; they milled about, as if congratulating themselves. I had never seen such celebratory behaviour in them: instead of trying to bag the best piece of snow in which to lie, they were sniffing, stretching and licking my face as I sat on the sledge. They were back on home territory and they were content.

We were put up for the night by a quiet, pensive young Russian named Andre. Hardly sensing who or what this thoughtful, generous figure was, we hung our frozen clothing around his flat, and as it thawed and dripped, fell asleep on his floor.

Extract from my diary, 13 April 2001:

Only the next afternoon was there any human celebrating. After a lunch laid on with great aplomb by Tolia's family, we went to the evening disco. We all know how the evening will end . . .

Yasha, though, did not drink himself senseless. He sat alone in misery. Ivan, rallying himself, said, 'Poooor Yasha, no one met him on his arrival. He might as well have kept going. No one noticed him.'

Yasha began crying. Then he pulled himself together – you could see him tussling with, and finally suppressing, the feelings that threatened to surge out of control. This man who had been cheery in the storms, smiling at a wind chill of minus seventy or eighty degrees. He raised himself up to go, as Ivan pushed the vodka at him again.

Yasha left, indicating to me with his fingers that he was just going to walk about in the night snows. I tried to tell him that he had to remember he had children who adored him. During the day he had brought around two little skipping girls for me to meet, Tanya and, a little older, Valya, who's brown from the sun at the Black Sea – one of the extraordinary trips to paradise paid for by Roman Abramovich for the impoverished. But Ivan was well beyond translating and soon was knocking shelves down – the flat had been adorned with images of communist heroines and photos of Fidel Castro.

'As for me, I still have the dogs and the Bering Strait,' I thought. 'And I'm not about to rest.'

XXXVI

In the morning I found the dogs wondering what was about to happen, just like me. Further downslope, children were snowboarding on bits of guttering.

Basil rose to his feet. The other dogs did the same, stretching, yawning – as if limbering up. Seeing this spirit in the dogs, my own spirits rose; so much outpouring of life. I played with the dogs a while, wishing I could express my thanks to them for getting this far.

I remembered Edward de la Billière, who'd run a team in the Iditarod, talking in a London pub of his devotion to his dogs rather as a young lieutenant would of his platoon that had got him out of scrapes. 'You'll miss them afterwards.' And the words of Brian Gillett, another who'd heard about my trip and generously came to offer advice: 'They'll get you into trouble, but by the end you won't want to say goodbye.'

I looked out at the pack ice. It looked very empty, very unaccommodating to the needs of man: a terrible, yawning, lonely place. I retreated to my diaries and opened the shattered plastic folder, easing the papers out.

> *Loneliness,* I thought. *Strong in the consciousness of survivors is the fear of the unnatural lonely state – of being separated from our own kind:*
>
> *He lay on his back in the shanty town, a cluster of children around him. The man seemed to have been killed with a six-inch nail, which had somehow been forced up through the roof of his mouth. Someone had planted a candle beside him.*
>
> *'To accompany him,' a little old lady explained.*

'He was a good man, I'm sure,' I said, by way of offering my condolences.

There was an awkward silence. 'No,' the woman said. 'No, he was not a good man.'

'Oh,' I said.

'He was a bad man,' chipped in another bystander.

'Very bad . . .' nodded a third.

'I see,' I said, backing away. What had this man done that so many people were willing to speak ill of the dead, and right in front of him?

The little old lady said, 'But we give him a candle anyway. We will all be journeying alone one day.' My diaries, Brazilian Amazon.

Joe Simpson: 'I didn't crawl because I wanted to survive; I wanted to be with someone when I died.'

Why a headhunter need never be afraid:

'We are never alone,' the Iban elder said. 'Even when we stray off the jungle path and are threatened by Pontianak.' (He was referring to the worst fate of any man, an encounter with the female demon who collects testicles.)

'But even if you die, the dead are never beyond reach.' My diaries, with the Iban, Sarawak.

'One shining, incalculable asset remained – the tight, warm friendship of men together in misfortune. While we remained together hope could not be quenched.' The Polish cavalry officer Slavomir Rawicz, sentenced to twenty-five years' hard labour in the Gulags.

'Being pack animals like my yaks, we take comfort in others.' Herder, Uvs, Mongolia.

Lieutenant Belgrave Ninnis fell to his death down an Antarctic crevasse in 1911. He took with him most of the food of his two companions and the only functional tent. 'It was to be a fight with Death, and the Great Providence would decide the issue,' commented Douglas Mawson, one of the two remaining men.

He and Swiss mountaineer Xavier Mertz still had six dogs, and they survived the next days by eating them. Finally, they killed their last dog, the ever loyal Ginger. 'Had a great breakfast off Ginger's skull – thyroid and brain.'

When Mertz died too – of excess vitamin A, from too many dog livers – Mawson stumbled on, attaching planks of wood to his feet in lieu of crampons.

He began to lose hope – especially when he fell into a crevasse himself: 'It would be but the work of a moment to slip from the harness, then all the pain and the toil would be over. It was a rare situation, a rare temptation – a chance to quit small things for great – to pass from petty small exploration of a planet to the contemplation of vaster worlds beyond.'

Why then was he still walking seven weeks later? It was 'in the hope of reaching a point where my remains would be likely to be found by a relief expedition'.

Shackleton's ability to inspire loyalty was based on two premises, both of which appeal to our inherently tribal nature:

(1) Never ask anyone to do anything you aren't prepared to do yourself.

(2) Make every crew member feel that their contribution, however small, is important.

Bernard disappeared. He had slipped his harness – something he could have done at any time, I now realized. And perhaps every one of the dogs could have done the same if they'd chosen to – there'd just been little incentive to run off and hide in the tundra. I found Bernard: he'd apparently been patrolling the streets in search of Sarah. She was in season and Bernard was staring deep into her eyes in a way I thought only people did to each other.

He escaped again soon after, and again I tracked him down.

'In love,' I thought. 'That's what you'd say of a human.'

But it turned out, in a way that seemed entirely characteristic of Bernard, that he was the only dog in my team who had somehow avoided being castrated.

'The rest of the dog team are anxious,' I said to myself later, as I fed them. 'They know that something is imminent. They, like me, are preparing themselves.'

The difference, I thought, rummaging through the 'Survivors' file, is that a dog's needs are simple:

Our chances of survival over a period rest on our ability to glean something of sustenance from the future. We must acknowledge that we seem to be different in this respect from other animals: our powerful minds make but also break us. We need inspiration.

'He who has a why *to live for can bear with almost any* how.' Nietzsche.

More die descending mountains than ascending. Because they are a spent force? Or because the goal they have striven for has already been achieved?

'The Admiral, according to his custom, told the men they had gone thirteen leagues, for he was still afraid that they would consider the voyage too long. Thus, throughout the voyage he kept two reckonings, one false and the other true.' Columbus, fabricating the ship's log in order to sustain belief.

'There is something about this show which is missing. It is what I would call the Shackleton touch, which made the ward room a brighter spot as soon as one went into it.' Captain John King Davis.

If you live in the wilderness, you might want to look around for a non-human role model. You might envy certain powerful animals their niche. A jaguar, say, top predator of the Amazon – strong, agile and intelligent:

Pablito of the Matses, River Javari

Or a crocodile, a reptile with a 120-million-year pedigree – highly territorial, powerful, yet with strong nurturing instincts:

Joel of the Niowra, Papua New Guinea

In individualistic, urban civilizations more useful is a belief in an Almighty not so dissimilar to us: he can empathize with us personally but also serve as pack leader, an alpha-plus male.

One of the wives of the victims of the Kursk: *'We carried on praying – now asking God that just* one *of our husbands had been spared.' They had been asking the Almighty for everything, but now they were willing to negotiate.* Moscow.

Handing over responsibility to higher powers is the age-old solution to life's oppressive burdens:

A healer came today to read the entrails of a goat. The future of everyone is good, he says, and we feel better for it – the tendency of ours to look for a pattern in things. It satisfies our desire to make sense of the world. Our ancestors' lives relied on their ability to distinguish between threats and opportunities in the dappled shade of forest. My diaries, with the Himba, Namibia.

Extract from my diary, 15–16 April 2001:
When I came across Ivan the next day, I was diplomatic. 'Hello,

Ivan! How are you today?' He looks at me, and I'm conscious of having spoken like a doctor to a patient.

'Was I mad again last night?'

And I love him again; he's suddenly back at my side.

However, he was soon off once more. That night he didn't come home. Yasha hasn't been drinking since coming back here, which means virtual isolation from much of the community. He's out by the dogs, hacking at the walrus meat or swinging it with a hook into a cold store like the holes traditionally used by Chukchis for stowage of meat from the summer – but this store is actually a snow-buried hut.

In the queue at the bakery, I met a man I'd been thinking a great deal about. I recognized him immediately: Alexei, the owner of 'my' dogs.

'You brought them safely here!' he said. I remembered how much I'd liked him the last time we'd met, with Gena, when he'd looked a wreck, having been up whaling all night.

He happily agreed to come along and tell me the names of the dogs. Wearing a splendid black fur hat and gigantic, astoundingly flashy sunglasses, he accompanied me through the town, chatting away in response to my questions.

'The only man in the world who knows these dogs better than me,' I thought. It gave us an uncanny bond. I felt close to this person, as if we were long lost brothers.

'These four know left and right,' he said, indicating Top Dog, Flashy White, Mad Jack and Frank.

'Some of them more than others,' I thought.

'He's not a strong leader,' he said, patting Flashy White, 'but he knows how to get out of a tangle with his harness! Notice that?'

'Er, well actually . . .'

'Great, eh?'

Muttley, the brown dog at the back, turns out to be the senior member of the team – twelve years old. It explains his exhaustion, the way he sits heavily on the ground, slumping whenever he can. Bernard, however, is only seven!

'So, this dog,' I said, pointing at Bernard, 'why is he in the team?'

Alexei laughs. He knows what I mean. But I can't understand his explanation in Russian, however many times he repeats it.

'Wait for Ivan to wake,' he says in the end.

'Might be next week,' I say.

Alexei then invited me to go seal hunting. It would give me a chance to drive alongside his other dog team. 'I always knew there must be another one,' I thought. 'The A Team.'

Yasha was coming too, it seemed, because he woke me at 4.30 a.m., by which time there's already a lot of light. I could see immediately, even at that hour of the day, that he was still troubled. He filled my thermos, then met me outside with my dogs, having already begun harnessing them. He was still trying his best for me.

Alexei's other dog team arrived. They were very young. 'Yes, we're definitely the D Team,' I thought.

Alexei would lead out on to the shore ice, which meant that his dogs were trained for thin ice. Off we rode, Alexei's commands abrupt, barked, I noticed, the actual orders no different from those taught me by Yasha.

I became nervous: I hoped my dogs wouldn't embarrass me in front of Alexei – and in front of the other dogs! This new, super-fit young team seemed very swift. 'Rather too pleased with themselves though,' I couldn't help saying aloud to myself.

Out to the ice edge – and this was ice as I'd never seen it. This was what Gena had meant, long ago, when he talked of 'new ice'. Spongy, mushy, flexible, the sort that might (or might not) form overnight to bridge the Strait.

Strapped across the back of Alexei's sledge was a seal-skin canoe – to act as a float if the ice collapsed. Ahead, clear, restless water. On the lip of the ice a small ringed seal lay on its side, as if gazing at the sky. To me it was rather a gentle thing, a labrador with no legs; to Yasha and Alexei it was a pair of gloves, boots, a meal for ten.

The seal flipped back down into its water hole. We moved along; all the while, as the new ice flexed, my dogs remained calm, trustworthy even, as the sea water sloshed up through the seal holes. 'Self-assured,' I thought. And I can see that Alexei expects no less of them. They didn't panic even when a hunter behind us went through the ice. He gave a startled yelp and shouted to his dogs, and they went into some sort of emergency procedure, doubling their efforts and finally plucking him and sledge from the water.

'So,' I think, 'my dogs probably won't fail me on sea ice. Should I go? Should I?'

As for Yasha, the man I must leave behind: yesterday we went out on a trek together, and the tundra acted as a remedy for him. I even made him laugh. Presently, though, nothing will lift him from the misery of having been failed by someone dear to him.

Life is especially worth fighting for if we know it might get worse otherwise: 'The terror of what lay behind them, not the pleasures ahead' – the words I wrote earlier on what motivated my dogs to cross a frozen river.

A Dutch explorer survives:

'Where could I fly? Where conceal myself? I saw the terrific monster ready to swallow me; I saw his eyes glaring, and his throat swelling with fury.

'. . . By seizing upon every projection, and holding fast by every cleft, I at last reached the edge of the rock, and drew myself to the top.

'[I had] ascended this, to all appearance, insurmountable barrier, the fear of instant death having lent me courage and address. In no other circumstances would I have attempted it; the mere idea would have made me tremble, and deprived me of the power to execute it.' J. Haafner in Ceylon, 1821.

If we have already come through considerable adversity, our resolve stiffens:

Clemens Forell was possibly the Gulag prisoner whose fate, together with that of his dog, had worried me as a child. His canine friend was Willem, a sledge dog given him in the course of his escape. Over three years the prisoner fled 12,800 km west across the breadth of Siberia from the Chukchi Peninsula. Sure enough, his dog Willem did not die at Forell's hands: he was machine-gunned down by guards some while later. Forell took this cruel blow as he had taken so many others: 'He would miss his dog, as he missed those other friends whom Fate had snatched from him, one by one, year after year, as though it were decreed that this man should fight and suffer alone, to the end of his days.' Why did Forell continue? Because the land beyond was bound to be a brighter place than Siberia.

Extract from my diary, 17 April 2001:

'Five days!' said Andre's wife, in whose flat we've been staying.

She was referring to the time Ivan has been drunk since our arrival in Lorino. 'I so sorry,' she said in English.

Last night, I'm ashamed to say something in me snapped and I seized Ivan by the throat as he tottered in the street.

'Benya, you are hurting,' he said. He promised he wouldn't drink, as long as I didn't lock him up. I released my grip – it was hopeless. Off he went to get drunk.

Later:

The decision: I must just go off to the Bering Strait . . . Thank God for Yasha, who remains solid. He also remains unpaid. Thousands of dollars dangle around Ivan's neck and can't be taken from him. I continue to give Yasha money to keep him going in the meantime.

Yet when I got into trouble with an officer from the FSB for filming a government warehouse that happened to be burning down, Ivan did come to my rescue. The no-nonsense officer – he had the cold flounder eyes of fellow KGB man Vladimir Putin – escorted me to my accommodation, and there I found Ivan in bed but actually sober enough to talk. Sometimes, even now, he springs into action like this. He functioned brilliantly on this occasion – though he hasn't functioned at all for almost a week. Something deep inside him, buried in the Soviet past, seemed to tell him never to mess with the KGB.

It was fright; a survival mechanism kicked in. And Ivan may pull himself together now. Either way, I'm going to make my bid to cross the Bering Strait.

XXXVII

I unpacked the satellite phone and walked around in the snow until I could get a signal. Once I'd got hold of John, my film producer friend, I spelt out how things stood. Next, I told him my intentions – that I would head off alone with my team and see how far we'd get. I'd have food for ten days. But this would be a dash, nothing prolonged; there was a plane out of here in six days which Ivan was aiming for, and I'd told him I would too. I had every confidence in my dogs. The authorities would not allow me to take a rifle, but the Chukchis were saying that the bears were heading north up the coast, not into the Strait. Based on long-term experience and everything I'd gleaned here, I felt the dogs and I would come back safely. I would be leaving the satellite phone behind – I'd done my duty to my guides by bringing it along until now. The transmitter I'd take with me, though I couldn't guarantee it would go all the way. 'No need to worry about anything. I expect you'll hear from me within four to five days.'

Alexei helped me load the sledge with walrus meat and human food. We worked fast, and I was worried that we were *too* fast – what might I have forgotten? Yasha stood watching a while. Then he began harnessing up his own dogs. He'd see me to the other side of Lavrentiya, he said.

'No need,' I said. 'But thanks.'

'I do need,' he said. 'I do need.'

As I checked everything over, Bernard managed to slip his collar again. He sidled up to the front of Yasha's team and placed himself squarely in front of Sarah. She lay down – not because she was being submissive but because she was not interested. 'She's very difficult to please,' said Yasha, with considerable feeling. 'Bernard mustn't be put off.'

Bernard wasn't going to be put off. However, it was time for me to go, so I dragged him back to my team. But then I thought better of it. Bernard didn't pull anyway; he used up valuable food. He should stay.

'His heart isn't in it,' I said to myself, watching Bernard plod off again to win the heart of Sarah. I noticed his friend Jeremy was straining at his harness, wanting Bernard to come back. He seemed to be aware we might leave without him.

'Sorry, Jeremy,' I said, smoothing his head. 'Best he remains here.'

There were no farewells – I can't remember Ivan even being there. There was just Alexei watching his dogs disappear down the slope as we wheeled to the left behind Yasha's team, on out of Lorino. I looked back, wanting to see what expression was on Alexei's face – this man who might be seeing his dogs for the last time. He wore his outlandish, dazzling sunglasses and I couldn't see his eyes, but he was smiling a very large smile. I thought to myself, 'He's not worried about his dogs, he's proud of them.'

Lorino was soon gone, and the dogs calmly taking us up the coast. Only Jeremy was looking back now. Why this insecurity in him that he needed to be with Bernard? And why had Alexei tolerated that overweight underachiever in the team anyway? I'd never quite got around to finding out.

'I hope Bernard isn't important,' I said aloud. It was a joke. He obviously wasn't, except to Jeremy.

Jeremy needn't have concerned himself, anyway. When next I looked at my team, Bernard was running alongside with us. In the end the tribal bonds had been too strong. I didn't bother stopping to harness him up – such was his contribution to pulling the sledge – and we carried on north without a break. The dogs knew the way to Lavrentiya; they were still on home territory. 'Nothing unusual about this journey as yet,' I thought. 'No reason for them to be concerned.'

And what about me? Plenty of reasons for being concerned. And if I was to make serious headway, I must allow myself only a few hours' sleep a night. That was all right; for a year or more I had been gathering myself – and this was my moment. I reminded myself: walk to the North Pole in this new millennium, and you were likely to find someone walking ahead of you; scramble up Everest, and you might be overtaken on the way. However, cross the Bering Strait and you would find no footsteps ahead. Here before me lay a range of unquantified challenges. It would be just me and the Arctic; I wouldn't be dissuaded.

Our desire to make our mark on the world, I thought, *is to do with establishing territory but also perhaps to do with an unconscious desire to distinguish ourselves from the inert, the un-alive.*

Joe Simpson spoke of his fear of losing the spark that defines the living, of 'becoming part of the rocks, where I was never going to move from'. Particularly hard for him was that bad moment when no one answered his cries for help: 'I lost something. I lost me.'

And when he did arrive at base camp, the man left behind there spoke of his fear of The Thing he saw coming his way: 'I was holding back, feeling that it can't be human.' Simpson's fight for life was a fight not to merge with the cold mountain.

It was a bright day, the air still, as if at long last taking a rest. 'Minus fifteen, perhaps,' I thought. Yasha, ahead of me, was looking around. 'He's thinking of bears,' I thought. 'Wondering if we'll meet any.' Twice, a hare soared out from the rocks, flying lightly over the snows and causing both our dog teams to surge off the track. All in all, though, everything was as it should be. The sun shone; the Strait sat to the right, patiently. Occasionally, Yasha flicked a stone at Fatty to stop him getting up to mischief.

We entered Lavrentiya. Pet dogs, as usual, charged, skidded to a halt and fled. Drunks, as usual, stood in the road, tottering and swivelling.

'Tea!' said Yasha. 'Let's stop a moment to have some tea.'

'I want to press on.'

But there was no changing Yasha's mind. We tied the dogs between lamp posts and walked up some icy stairs and into a flat. I was pleased to find our host was Vladimir, the bespectacled Chukchi from the Ministry of Agriculture. 'We must celebrate!' he said.

'Oh . . . must we?'

'In the summer you said you would come, and you have.'

'And soon I must go . . .' I began. But two bottles appeared, which multiplied like flies. Yasha rubbed his hands. '*Mei!*' he said, trying to jolly me along. 'Yasha feels responsible for me,' I thought. 'He's trying to slow me down, waste precious time.' It was dark before I managed to winkle Yasha away.

'Careful,' Vladimir called down the stairwell, 'There's a pack of seven wolves on the beach.'

My dogs chased after Yasha's team as best they could in the darkness; we were, as far as I could tell, tackling the broken-up ice of an inlet. It was hard going: lumps of whiteness loomed from nowhere, thumped the sledge and snagged on my legs. 'He's going round in circles,' I said to the dogs after a while. 'I'm almost sure he is.' We stared into the night to see. Finally, my sledge collided headlong with an obstacle. It was Yasha. He was snoring.

'Sorry! I fell asleep! Would you believe it?'

How could I be angry? Yasha cared for me – me, the white man who knew nothing but his little dreams. Indeed, Yasha cared for the whole world even though it abused him. What's more, driving along drunk into the bay at night was no more foolish than setting off across Arctic waters alone, without a gun and without any means of communication. Nor was I taking a seal-skin boat; after much agonizing I'd judged it would be too unwieldy as I heaved the sledge over pack ice.

In due course, Yasha soon found what he was looking for, a deserted shack immersed in snow. While I fed the dogs, Yasha got out my shovel, put on my head torch and dug like a miner two metres down to the foot of the door.

This would be my last full night of sleep. 'Enjoy it,' I told myself. I thought of what lay ahead, a scene less charted than the moon, less charted than any land on earth. It was within reach now, creaking, churning, restlessly turning; lingering out there, this untamed monster, expanding and contracting as if breathing; mysterious and dangerous. But fragile, soon to be gone, swept away like an insect with the changing of the season.

XXXVIII

Dawn. Yasha shaped a large snow figure outside our hut. 'A bear,' he said. He grinned at his handiwork. 'See, it even has eyes!'

He handed me the flare gun. I took aim, the cartridge exploded and the flare smashed into the snow, fizzing and sparking where it lay embedded in the belly of Yasha's bear.

'Blimey!' said Yasha.

'Good, eh?'

'But you were meant to aim at the bear's feet,' said Yasha.

Not that a flare would stop a very hungry polar bear. That would be the job of the two little sacks of walrus I'd prepared, which would be at hand at the front of the sledge to be flung to the stalking bears. It had seemed a great idea back in Lorino. Now, I looked at the dogs, harnessed to the gang line like Roman slaves to their galley, and wished I had a trusty .44 magnum – its long barrel, its reassuringly weighty bullets, the first chamber containing a 'soft round' for maximum spread of impact. But I did not.

I checked the dogs over and strapped my survival kit around my waist. Everything looked set; everything felt right. 'It's my last chance to pull out,' I thought. However, this was not the time to falter.

Yasha led me from the beach down on to the ice. It was smooth – maybe a week old. 'I'm in luck,' I thought. 'I'll make fast progress. Maybe have a fast retreat.'

To our left, coastal cliffs, broken, ripped. Ahead, the band of glassy ice. To our right, out at sea, a jumble of ice blocks. I could expect them to become more discordant as we came upon the currents of the central Strait.

I stopped Yasha. 'So, Yasha, it's time . . .'

Before he could reply, I thumped my gloved hand into his.

'A little journey, all right?' he said. 'Not a big journey . . .'

'He still thinks I'm just journeying up the coast a bit,' I thought. 'He doesn't believe I'll head right across the Strait.'

I promised to make it a short journey. Could twenty-five kilometres up the coast and one hundred and five kilometres to Alaska be counted as short? My dog team had managed a hundred in a day before now – though, of course, if you slipped into the Bering Sea after only one metre you might well die.

I sat back down on my sledge and took a look at the waiting dogs and – beyond their expectant faces – this flexing icescape. Dead, yet alive with movement. I took a deep breath to calm myself. I stretched my back and adjusted my posture as if about to walk out on to a theatre set.

Departing words of Pen Hadow: 'As you well know, a ship in harbour is safe. But that's not what ships are built for . . . Bon voyage.'

Top Dog was waiting. I gave the signal: 'Hup!' My sledge moved off, as if slipping its moorings, leaving the safe waters that Yasha had always done his best to provide for me.

We were away, the sledge runners squeaking beneath me, the dogs' claws clicking and clacking on the marbled blue ice. Far away was the line of bright silver that expressed all the beauty and terror that is freedom. Here was a panorama that man had never touched. The untrodden view offered an absence of security, but with that lack of security came release, the freedom of Adam and Eve setting forth from Eden, armed with the fruit of the tree of knowledge. It was what we were designed for.

I looked back. Yasha was following at a distance. He stopped from time to time, got up, peered at the snow – looking for wolf tracks, wondering where the local pack was. Later I saw him again, now a small, ant-like figure on the cliff top, his arms like antennae as he shielded his eyes, turning this way and that, inspecting the Strait. We watched him together, me and the dogs; winced in the glare of the ice to catch a last sight of him. Then he was gone. For a second, we all paused on the ice, uncertain.

Chris Bonington, over dinner: 'I'd never climb a mountain with someone who isn't afraid.'

Why We Co-operate: Some Thoughts

Humans, like dogs, understand the need to work together, the benefits of co-operative behaviour. However, in humans this sense is greater than in any other species. Chuck a load of chimps together in a crisis and they will not pull together. Why do we seem to help even complete strangers? Because we evolved in small groups where there *weren't* many strangers. If you acted like a Good Samaritan, it was noticed. You were advertising your usefulness.

Although both dogs and humans start out in life as entirely selfish, dependent entirely on our mothers, we become less so as we grow older. It's important to continue being selfish in part; we each need to develop personal skills. But gradually we begin to recognize the importance of fostering selflessness in ourselves so as to be able to have access to the benefits of society: the group hunt, the collective pool of knowledge and resources.

Some of us, though, are better than others at learning to be selfless. We need to enforce this ethic, to make sure all members of society contribute. We need a judge, a policeman. Having a god who will oversee a moral code, we all benefit.

In summary, we co-operate because:

(1) Co-operation in itself brings obvious rewards, whether it be in an office team or among a pack of dingos.

(2) In social activities, if we do not share, we tend to feel a lack of fulfilment. We are not exhibiting the social behaviour that we are programmed to exhibit for sound reasons of survival.

(3) Even seemingly weak members of society can bring an unexpected contribution. The alpha male might drag us to the kerb after a motorway pile-up, but he may not have the calming ability of the little old lady who lived through the Blitz, nor the skills of the child who has done First Aid at school. Therefore, we must look to the weak even when we are strong: they might help you if (a) the power structure collapses in the future, and you are now the weak one; (b) they have assets which presently aren't, or don't appear, relevant.

(4) Deep down, we are aware that the 'weak' person might one day be us.

On we went. It was up to me to watch for animal tracks now. I wondered what I was sharing this ice shelf with. Hare droppings rolled in the wind; I passed the old prints of a solitary bear heading north.

With Yasha gone, I again felt a surge of enthusiasm for this venture: now it was up to me and the dogs to work this out together.

We followed the line of the shore. I checked and rechecked our position, the best lines forward, the best lines of retreat; the dogs interpreting, reinterpreting. We trundled along, thinking, pulling, each in our own way working for the pack's survival. You could almost hear the collective effort, the faint hum of the motor of life.

But what if the wolf should come – what then? I was thinking of Prokofiev's *Peter and the Wolf*. Me as Peter, tripping lightly and innocently into danger. And sure enough, before long we come across a wolf. Or rather, the fresh trail of one. He was alone, heading east, trotting purposefully seaward. Why? Just scouting about perhaps.

'Be ready to grab the lead dogs,' I thought. 'Get Mad Jack to the front.'

Yasha had thought the local wolf pack wouldn't attack the team, even after such a hard winter, though they 'might make a grab for the walrus meat'. The greatest danger was that, sniffing around, they would spook my dogs. At night, that might cause them to flee, leaving me behind.

The dogs were slowing. Top Dog had, it seems, still been hoping that Yasha was coming along on this trip. Jeremy and Basil were flicking their eyes up to the cliff top for signs of him. Soon, the only dog that wasn't looking around for him was Mad Jack.

The scent of that wolf. I busied the dogs with commands. An hour passed, and we negotiated a first patch of ice rubble. I watched Mad Jack: he was alert, but less excited now.

By mid-morning I'd reached Nunyamo, the last mark on the map, the last human impression on the tundra. I stopped and looked up at the snow-daubed cliff, the overhanging shaggy turf of ice, beyond which lay the broken walls and wind-gutted huts of an abandoned settlement.

In summers not long ago, Eskimos came in kayaks across the Strait to these coastal settlements. In winter, it was said, they crossed with dogs, on calm days when the ice lay like clean bed sheets. Mothers, gathering herbs among the cotton grass and mats of yellow marsh saxifrage, wore mittens of seal skin; their children ran behind, each wearing bells to stop them getting lost. Up the pebbled beaches came the seal hunters. Wives would run out with a ladle of water to give the spirit of the seal they'd harpooned a drink. Later, the skull would be taken to a space in the tundra reserved for all hunted things and added to those of foxes and wolves, facing east.

No sign of this life now, nor of the Eskimos swarming upon a freshly landed whale to remove everything but the skull. Nor the sunken larders set in the cliffs, the shallower ones designed to thaw in the spring, the deepest serving as a freezer through the warm months. No more the seal-skin tents, carved wooden birds perched on top. And no more the brave men who were known at times to hunt whales not with harpoons attached to seal-skin floats but by jumping on to the whale's back and plunging in a knife. When the whale dived, the men were said to breathe the air trapped in their tunics.

One day, further up the coast at Naukam, someone had invented a new dance. It celebrated not the animals of the tundra but the arrival of electricity in Anadyr – the burly Russian workers digging in poles, ascending them to fix the wires and swearing as they flailed in the wind. But one warm afternoon in July 1958, the order came. Some villagers half expected it, and everyone agreed they should obey. Whatever these Soviets were up to now, they did know a thing or two. It must be for the best. The settlement was to be emptied in the next three days. It was part of a countrywide campaign of the 'termination of villages which have no future'.

'Loaded into boats, we were,' a walnut-skinned old Eskimo called Nina had told me quietly. 'The last thing we did, assembling on the shore, was to do a celebratory dance, just as we did when whale meat was safely gathered in for winter.' The women stripped to their waists, peeling back their furs. They danced on that summer day for the last time. Beads swung from their necks; the seabird feathers in their headbands rattled in the breeze.

For a while, many of the Eskimos found themselves deposited here at Nunyamo – 'with a whole lot of reindeer herders', Nina said – before this settlement too was proclaimed to have no future. There were fights with the Chukchis, there was drinking. 'We began to forget we had been happy before.'

The dogs and I stood and stared: gone, all gone. Even having worked our way nearer, up a gentle incline, we found only communist wreckage: picked-apart woodwork and strewn Soviet bricks. Where walls still stood, even the paint had been scratched off. Had there been wallpaper here? That had been carried away by the Arctic too.

My dogs wanted to move on – the clacking of shattered, swinging doors, maybe. Or that unhappy, moaning wind, the tundra's unwavering reminder of its power to destroy.

Now, imperceptibly, the obstacles facing us grew in number. Once, we had skated easily over plates of ice with an even sheen; now, we were having to avoid ice blocks that were bigger than the sledge, higher at times than me.

The dogs behaved impeccably; I began trusting Top Dog to use his initiative to duck and weave between the pressure ridges. Our progress began to seem natural and right; we still had our understanding. We travelled along in silence, the dogs still with this common desire to obey me, who passed for their pack leader. 'If we continue like this, we'll be fine,' I thought.

The old saying: 'The world steps aside for one who knows where he's going.'

The ice we faced that afternoon was an altogether more serious matter. It rose up as if in great armies to stop us – long ranks of debris that surely no amount of dog and human initiative could circumvent. All of a sudden, things were not looking so positive. 'We'll try our best,' I said to the dogs. But I couldn't help but be disheartened. We were now having to stop, start, go back. We were having to tack our way between long piles of ice rubble that seemed to have been bulldozed there like heaps of breeze blocks and pre-stressed concrete, the last remains of a magnificent, once orderly structure judged past its time. And the ice ahead promised only more of the same: bank after bank of building-site rubble.

There was no way around. I got to my feet to give the dogs a hand over the first ridge. I hoicked Top Dog up the jumbled blocks, walked him over the top, then slid back down to haul the sledge with Dennis and Muttley. Surmounting this first crest left me breathless. By the second obstruction, I was breaking into a sweat. The third left me with an ache in my ribs and a feeling of despair: there were hundreds or even thousands of these same ridges ahead of me. I leant against the next barricade, saying: 'Dogs, this system is not going to work. But we can't just give up and go home, can we?'

Both Flashy White and Top Dog looked at me; they were both more than happy to do just that.

I drank from my thermos.

'I'm like that wolverine that ran around and around in the blinding whiteness,' I thought, 'pressing on, regardless of the odds.'

'And this thought above all else,' I'd written in my diary – I remembered the words even now – 'some instinctive urge, a life spirit, a primitive form of belief . . .'

'Belief,' I thought. 'That one immeasurable factor in determining who amongst us will survive.' It always came back to that. The greatest adventurers all shared this one thing: an utter belief in their ability to fulfil their mission. They weren't suicidal; they didn't think for a moment they weren't going to return. They even roped God in, positioning him firmly (and often without asking) on their side.

Take Columbus – although there are any number of God-trusting plunderers. Sailing in search of the Indies he expected God's assistance (as well as demanding one tenth of any precious metals found, hereditary titles and the position of viceroy over any lands he discovered): 'All these good signs' – dolphins, birds and weeds – 'came from the west, whence I trust that the high God, in whose hands are all victories, will very soon give us land.'

Or consider those who did not ask assistance from God: Sven Hedin, for example, crossing the Taklamakan Desert, the sun like a 'red-hot cannon-ball on a dune' in the west: 'I did not want to die: I *would not* die in this miserable, sandy desert! I could run, walk, crawl on my hands and feet. My men might not survive, but I had to find water.' He was half right about his companions: despite drinking the blood of their last sheep, one man 'had already begun his death-struggle'. The other came to life only in the cool of the evening. 'With his hands clenched, he crawled up to me and cried pitifully: "Water! Give us water, sir! Only a drop of water!" Then he crawled away.'

And when these explorers did die, they did so with an unqualified commitment to their mission: 'You need have no fear of any failure,' said Colonel Percy Fawcett, donning his hat and setting off into the Mato Grosso – and that belief carried him for weeks before the jungle did him in.

Belief: that our existence is justified, that things will get better, that God will intervene. With all hope gone, it came down to our sense of self-worth. Alone, facing death on a mountainside, we wonder if our lives are valid. Together, sheltering in a huddle in a lifeboat, we look to a leader who will reassure us. 'Don't we count?' we ask ourselves. Living things are fragile and transient, so we reach up to God or philosophy, or any other stable platform to help us out with this question. What does the world care about us? Are we just the same as sheep, ending up as a morsel on the end of a fork? This is the challenge. Sitting on Annapurna or standing here in the Bering Strait is no time for modesty. We have to believe the world needs us to remain around a while longer. 'Koba, why is my death necessary to you?' an old friend of Stalin wrote to him from his prison cell. And each of us ask that very same question of God – or whatever else might be in charge of our destiny – hoping that He might, just like Stalin, keep our scrawled plea in His desk to consider from time to time.

'We'll keep going,' I told the dogs. I anchored the sledge and walked on by myself, scouting for passageways. But the truth was I'd noticed something unfamiliar in the ice. Since I'd first come to Chukotka I'd been observing its nature: how tracts of it were crafted by the wind, thumbed and moulded; how it bedded itself down in lead-crystal leaves. This ice, though, was different: it wore a sheen, as if freshly varnished. Here and there it was bulbous, as if molten; it looked blistered or waxed. This ice had melted and refrozen – and more than once. The temperature was now regularly above zero, and for periods long enough to thaw the top centimetre. Next time the ice melted, it might be the end of us.

The coast curled northward as we inched our way along. I watched the ice surface and began to be obsessed by this one thought: that I was being held up out of the water by water itself. And now it was midday and I too was melting. My clothes loosened up as the ice crystals unlocked. The warmth became a hindrance. The dogs were beginning to pant. We – the dogs and I – were encased in furs designed for temperatures thirty degrees cooler than this. I began to sweat. It was strange to see that my breath didn't freeze but instead gathered as beads on my balaclava. I noticed that I had to drink more frequently – and that the tea wasn't freezing in the thermos. My hands felt different too. What was it about them? My damaged fingertips: they were no longer aching.

The season was changing about me. And now that the cold was gone, I began to wish it back again. The cold preserved the ice; it kept me alive out here.

I climbed another jagged ice block. More batteries of ice, as far as I could see, and yet to succeed here I had to somehow find a way of going faster.

When I returned to the dogs, I noticed they were all looking at me, waiting to hear my conclusion. 'We continue,' I said. But where was the point in all this? Where the sense, and therefore where the belief? 'Barrier after barrier after barrier, that's what's ahead, if you really want to know,' I told them. Immediately facing us was a chunk of striated ice the size of a two-storey hut; otherwise, the ice was as before – and not worth dying for, was it? There was little that was inspiring any more, just these disheartening, smashed-up remains, something left of a civilization after an unwelcome visit by plundering hordes.

I looked back the way we'd come. My retreat, the Plan C, how was it looking? Up until now, if I had fallen off the back of the sledge, I would probably have been all right. With my survival kit I'd have managed the twenty kilometres to Lavrentiya. From here on, I couldn't be so sure. And if I died, the dogs wouldn't get back either. Whether we liked it or not, our fortunes lay together now.

We were right amongst the ice stacks now, winding along narrow corridors. The dogs were becoming uncomfortable. They were creatures of open spaces, and here they were hemmed in. They kept turning back to me – and to each other as if to share their doubts. Even I was feeling claustrophobic in this maze. Besides, I didn't like not being able to see clearly around me. Where, among this whiteness, were those white bears?

The strain was beginning to tell. Next thing, a fight broke out: I found Mad Jack pinning down Frank. 'This is neither the time nor the place,' I told him. I pulled Mad Jack away – and in the scuffle, he sank a canine into my left hand.

I gritted my teeth, then counted to ten. 'Let's call it a misunderstanding,' I said to Jack, holding his muzzle firmly shut. He looked grateful to be forgiven, and there was little more that could be done. Mad Jack, a highly strung dog with a temperament you wouldn't wish on anyone, was the only animal here not afraid of wolves. When all was said and done, I felt better for having him here with me.

The bite was not going to hold me back today – any infection would take hold tomorrow or the day after that. To clean the wound I let the blood flow and then applied a snow compress to reduce the swelling.

We battled on for another hour. I noticed that the dogs were keener when our route took us away from the north: they were hoping to encourage me to turn for home. 'Not yet,' was all I could say. 'Not yet.' Although I was running out of reasons to continue. Why carry on with this? Even now a bear might have his nose to the air, catching our scent. I stopped the dogs. 'You're right. We should turn back while we still can,' I said. But Top Dog got to his feet and the team started running of its own accord. Well, we might as well press on. 'Who knows,' I thought. 'We might reach America after all.'

In the days of early mankind in the savannah, we needed something to make up for our physical weakness – and those with a tendency to believe in things bigger than themselves survived to pass on their genes. From then on our minds were set: if gods didn't exist, we had to invent them.

Two years: *the extent of the unique meteorological data kept safe by Greely while his men died around him 'in the ground consecrated' by their great achievements.*

Sixteen kilos: *the weight of rock samples carried by Scott and companions to their death. 'Had we lived, I should have had a tale to tell of the hardihood, endurance and courage of my companions which would have stirred the heart . . .'*

Also on Scott's last expedition was Apsley Cherry-Garrard who, in the Antarctic winter of 1911, undertook the 'worst journey in the world': 'These three embyos from Cape Crozier . . . were striven for in order that the world may have a little more knowledge, that it may build on what it knows rather than on what it thinks.'

We are nowadays accustomed to thinking of Scott as the loser, the man who failed to get safely back from the South Pole due to misplaced pride and an unhealthy spirit of amateurism. Amundsen was, we like to think, the professional – the first modern adventurer, perhaps. However, Scott's ambitions were greater than those of the adventurer. As well as his ambition to claim the Pole, he had a wide-ranging scientific programme of exploration.

Scott died, it's said, in a blizzard, just 18 km from One Ton Depot. Actually, the truth is that the blizzard had probably blown out, and Scott's two companions, 'Birdie' Bowers and Edward Wilson, might have reached it. They died perhaps not wanting to leave Scott. Loyalty, sacrifice, duty and honour were more important to them; or at least these values were what they wanted to demon-

strate to the world by going to the South Pole. And now survival of the ideal had become more important than their own survival, and by not letting it die, they achieved a victory over Amundsen.

A cold breeze now began to pass over us. It grew into something more than just tiresome; it developed into a gusty and pernicious force that spat. By dusk it was bringing with it hardened pellets of snow from off the land. The dogs were struggling as the snow flurries ran over the ice, stinging their eyes. They winced; they stumbled.

Drawing up at what seemed a relatively sheltered spot in the lee of a promontory, I anchored the dog team and assembled my tent, heaving the material against the wind as a seaman might yank his canvas in a gale. Once it was up, I weighed it down by shovelling heavier blocks of snow around its skirt and piling my sleeping gear inside.

It wasn't enough. The wind took hold, and the tent spun away like tumbleweed, threatening to leave me behind to freeze solid. I dived, and caught it, paused a second with my eyes closed as I contemplated what might have been, and between the gusts dragged the tent to my sledge and fastened it there.

There was a lot more to do before I could rest: feed the dogs, melt ice for water. The wind spiralled and the snow twisted. When I did crawl into my tent to eat, I felt like I was surrounded not by wind but heaving seas. The winds punched from all around, and I was rolled from left and right.

I checked the map and found myself to be at 65° 40' north, 170° 30' west. Could be worse. In the space of my first day I had reached the northernmost point of my journey. From here I could cut east, out into the Strait.

I ought to go outside and do one last check on the dogs. 'Is it strictly necessary?' I asked myself. 'Will they really run off into this weather?' I unzipped a flap and saw only blackness scoured by slanting snow. I went out and found the dogs with their heads half-buried. Many had their eyes screwed shut, like children who don't want to look. My biggest fear of this venture had always been that the dogs would abandon me – startled, perhaps, by wolves; excited, perhaps, by a scavenging fox; afraid, perhaps, at being alone with an inexperienced human far from home.

When I woke, it was to find the night very dark and calm. I was reminded of Yasha's story of the wolves that passed through a camp at night – the quietness that overcame the dogs. 'I should check on my own team,' I thought. 'Something's maybe not quite right.'

Although leaving my sleeping bag was the last thing I felt like doing, I told myself I must: my life might even depend on it. Reluctantly, I put on my boots, took my flare gun and eased out of the tent in all my reindeer clothes, not feeling very happy about walking outside into what might be the company of wolves.

My torchlight found the dogs: they were sitting up, looking around. These ten, energy-efficient creatures were doing something that was not natural to them: exposing themselves to the cold. I looked about me at the surrounding, shadowy figures of ice.

Then a movement off to my right. I fired off a cartridge. Bang! It thumped into an ice block, bounced and skated. The scene around me was lit with an eerie, otherworldly green light. As the flare fizzed, we were like specimens captured in a goldfish bowl thick with algae.

Of any wolf, there was no further sign.

'Reload,' I thought. I went to the dogs and patted each one in turn, looking around me for whatever might or might not be lurking. Finally, I retreated to my tent. 'Can't hang around all night, you know,' I said to my video camera.

I did try to stay awake, reminding myself that it was important for our survival. But the very next moment, it seemed, I was bolt upright in my sleeping bag, scrambling for my torch and flare gun. Had I dreamt that howling? I leapt for the zip of the tent, bracing myself for what was going to greet me. I might see wolves padding into camp, or worse, nothing at all – my dogs gone.

I opened the flap again and what I saw in the torchlight was a bulky creature with his head pitched back. He was howling, howling for all he was worth into the night.

'Bernard,' I thought, 'always so unprofessional.' Was he lonely, his sledge dog's heart aching for Sarah? Whatever the explanation, Bernard's inner pain was better than seeing my dogs gone. First thing in the morning, I'd feed them again, I decided. It would do no harm at all to remind them that I was the commander of their food supply.

But the night wasn't over yet.

I next woke to a hazy mauve light rising from the east. Only half awake, I lunged to open my tent and reassure myself that my dogs were indeed still with me. But when I parted the tent flaps there was not a sign of them. For a full five seconds, I must have stared at where the dogs had been, knowing what would be the consequence of their departure. I felt the full, dread, cold weight on my heart. The dogs were going to be the death of me.

Then I heard snoring. Bernard. He had moved to sleep right against the tent. And he wasn't the only one. The dogs had chewed through the anchor line and heaped themselves beside my tent to be near me. They thought I'd keep them safe. How dogs work on the human psyche, plucking at our heart strings! I wanted to embrace each one of these animals for the faith they'd shown in me, which I knew I didn't deserve.

Soon the tent was down and the sledge packed. 'Perhaps,' I thought, 'I should secure the dogs and reconnoitre on foot out there in the Strait. It would save time in the end.'

I left the dogs, marched out to the east, and – preoccupied with tracing a route for the sledge – couldn't find my way back to them. The evening came, and then the night. My emergency stove then began to cough and splutter. It was a worrying few hours; looking at the film footage now, I see a face that is controlled but also sad. But I'd secured the dogs well on the ice and they were waiting along this shore somewhere, and indeed, all was well in the end. In the morning, the dogs and I were reunited.

'Treat it as useful practice for a *real* emergency,' I thought. And as it transpired, that is exactly what it was. For now, though, it was just a nuisance. I had lost valuable energy. I made a little depot of provisions. It was here also that I left behind the emergency beacon, camera and all that I'd filmed. I felt better for having done that. By reaching the Bering Strait, filming all the way, I had completed my obligation to the BBC. Now it was up to me, the dogs and my map and compass. I was free at last to do what I had come to do.

I stood above my camp on the rocks at the shoreline and looked out east. As far as the eye could see, and beyond, all was destruction. Like the remains of the settlement of Nunyamo, everything was reduced, leaving nothing but brick after brick of smashed-up ice, everywhere the confused remains of something that had once been whole. But I had done valuable work on foot: we'd get further than I'd dared hope.

However, time was slipping from me. I had pressed on through every hour of daylight, but from now on I'd have to do the same again, and also through the dark. I called to the dogs. 'Ready? Then let's go to America . . .'

I took out my compass and pointed my dogs directly due east, away from the Old World and towards the New.

XXXIX

In and out of the ice we went, me and my little tribe, over and between the chunks of minty substrate, each veined by successive freezings, layered like ancient cross-bedded strata, pressed by the surging winds, massaged by fluctuating currents. And all the while I was adjusting and reforming my plan, the dogs doing their best to interpret it. Around my neck, the ice spikes hung ready. I rehearsed how I'd clamber out of the water. I wouldn't have long. 'Shock and pain slows the heart, creating fatal arrhythmia,' my medical notes had said, 'and a reflex gasp for breath. Cold shock – hyperventilation, lowering CO_2 in the blood, decreasing its acidity, resulting in tetany of the muscles and loss of consciousness.'

Over the ridges we climbed, the dogs skating and scuttling, my sealskin-soled boots slipping. Time and again there was nothing for it but to trust the dogs to wait for me as I reconnoitred. First I'd scan around for any fox or hare that might excite the dogs into a chase, and next I'd point the dogs carefully towards a cul-de-sac. Then I'd quietly leave them.

Three hours later, I had to face the fact that no amount of scouting ahead was going to get me around all this shattered ice, untold miles of which still spanned ahead. We needed a miracle, and it looked unreasonable to expect one.

But one came nonetheless. As I was yanking the lead dogs over the ridges, cursing and groaning my way towards America, I discovered why Bernard was in the team.

Since first I had set eyes on him, I'd held on to a couple of theories, but with diminishing confidence. Perhaps he was a guard dog. He might stand boldly as the others dogs cowered in the presence of encircling wolves, facing them down. However, Mad Jack had from the start seemed an altogether more promising watchman. So maybe this odd character existed to offer short bouts of brute force alongside Alexei and the rear dogs as they heaved the sledge in rough country. I could live with his lack of stamina, if that was the case. But his lacklustre performance in the hills had long since told me that I shouldn't look to Bernard for any physical contribution ever again.

However, there was a third explanation, and it revealed itself today, not in the tundra where over the last weeks I had grown to know these dogs but out on the pack ice for which Alexei had assembled his team. I began to see, as we surmounted each obstacle, that Top Dog was redundant. His eyes remained on me, but now he was the one sledge dog lying down. As I heaved and hauled at the sledge with Dennis and Muttley, praising them for the effort they were putting in beside me, the front dogs had nothing to do. They could only wait with their harnesses slack. What a sledge master needed at these times was not a lead dog at the front but a diligent dog near the back, someone to unsnag the gang line and take up the slack in front of you as you heaved. The dog that took up that role was Jeremy. Resembling a border collie, he also had the temperament of one, the sort of animal that needs to be kept busy with tasks.

Somewhere out on the sea ice Jeremy – the worrier, the intellectual – must have become very valuable to Alexei, valuable enough to be given all he wanted. And what Jeremy wanted above all, or so it seemed, was his companion, the redoubtable Bernard. Why? Perhaps they grew up together. Perhaps like Nansen's Old Suggen he was a treasured friend. Whatever the reason, Bernard was important to Jeremy and he was allowed to stay.

We found a rhythm, out here in the chaos. A way of riding these frozen, broken seas. I called 'Huuk!', and Dennis and Muttley took the strain. Ahead, Jeremy led the gang line clear and ducked to left or right as ordered. Bernard daydreamed; Top Dog lay down and watched; the other dogs stood and waited.

So exquisite is the world, when you are making headway in it. Every breath you take with satisfaction, believing you are fulfilling your destiny. I was in a place that was rent and torn; I was beyond the reach of most living things. And yet we were fine.

We made progress. Stunning progress. I stopped only to light the stove, drink and refill the thermos. Nor did I feel tired. There would be time enough later for rest.

Between the crumpled zones of ice, lying like harrowed fields to the horizon, were smooth, thin, zig-zagging avenues that took us further. Sometimes I would see prints of bears – but old ones. The droppings of hares too, but they had rolled a dozen miles from the shore. For the time being we had been left alone to do our mission, suspended on our platform of ice.

By late afternoon I estimated my position at 65° 55' north and some 170° west. I was losing sight of the Siberian mainland, twenty-five kilometres away in the clear frozen air, and there was still no sign of the Diomede Islands, my navigation point forty kilometres to the east northeast. I felt adrift at sea, as if the ice was shifting. Maybe I was. I must not lose my conviction though; I must claw together all the resources at my disposal. This was the last push.

*Vanya and I had talked about the last putsch (*Путч*), which saw the fall of the Soviets. 'What are these people doing, throwing away their medals?' he said. 'Are they saying those years of their life are wasted? I was a communist because I believed in it. That's all that matters.'*

Belief, conviction – but I had terrible, dark moments of doubt. Soon I'd be sledging out of sight of both America and Eurasia like an astronaut out of all contact on the dark side of the moon. 'Not to panic you, dogs, but no one on this planet knows exactly where we are,' I told them. 'No one will find us if this goes wrong now.' It was a glum thought: the snapping beneath us, the howling as we surrendered ourselves to the Arctic. And I began to worry at this good progress we were making. The further we went, the further we would have to come back. 'This is a risky thing we're doing,' I kept reminding myself. More than once I stopped, feeling sick at the thought of it. Perhaps it was already too late. I might be about to end my days like Franklin, drawn here by an unreasonable sense of hope.

But mankind's genius lies in his ability to imagine new possibilities, I thought to myself. *And was it developing this facility that allowed early man to spread rapidly from Africa 100,000 years ago, after so many failed starts? Around 50,000 years ago he was painting on cave walls. We know that by at least 40,000 years ago*

> *he was burying the dead. Was this the answer? His ability to visualize a different future?*
>
> *With my supplies gone and nothing but sodden rainforest on all sides, I had nothing left of my own but my imagination. Every day, as I walked through the dripping leaves, my clothes and skin beginning to rot, I imagined placing a new brick on an imaginary fortification. Gradually, a strong defensive building was assembled around me. The keep, the bailey, the moat. I remember the satisfaction to be gained from pressing my face to this imaginary wall – the unyielding granite, forged deep in the earth by volcanic forces of heat and pressure, these tight crystals, the coldness of the stone to the touch.* My diaries, reflecting on walking out of the forest without supplies, northeastern Amazonia.

On we went towards dusk, scrambling east along my compass bearing, driving ourselves on through the last thin smudges of light. Sometimes the ice murmured and sighed. As we fought onward, the sounds seemed louder, like the ghosts of those who had been taken before me. Tread carefully now.

And where exactly were we? I needed a bearing. I needed the reassurance of something friendly out there. To the south, the Dane Bering died in the cold; to the north, on Wrangel Island, three perished on Stefansson's expedition – although one had preferred in the end to take his own life.

> *'Do not be afraid, stand firm and you will see the deliverance that the Lord will bring today.'* Exodus 14:13.
>
> *'Fear not, wise one! Thou art not in danger; there is a way to cross the ocean of this life beset by death. That way I shall reveal to thee . . .'* Sankaracharya, founder of the Adwaita School of Vedanta Philosophy.

'It's important that I keep watching the lead dogs,' I thought, 'see if they can smell water on the breeze.' I wondered if I might smell it myself – salt, the sweet smack of algae in the air. I listened for the sounds of water, the struggling of ice in the current, but there was only a faint breeze in my ears for now. At dawn I hoped to see the Diomede Islands. The stars splayed a soft white light over us; the ice threw back a green one. 'A cold, clear night, the sort that favours new ice,' I thought. There was not a murmur of wind, and if I was lucky this too might favour the sealing up of any fissures in the ice, the cracks that must be somewhere ahead.

Studies show that the most 'lucky' of us tend to be those who:

(i) are good at discerning potential;

(ii) are quick to recover from misfortune – they bounce back;

(iii) have an unrealistic view of the world. They believe they are luckier than they actually are – and this belief brings about more success.

Light was glowing off the ice to the east: four o'clock in the morning. A new day. I watched the ice below my feet now with increasing concern. A short span of very new, slushy ice, perhaps fifty metres across, then, after a small boulder field of splintered, flaky ice, more of the same. Was this the edge? Was this the end? Or had I already crossed to the firmer ice of the Alaskan side? I dared not think so.

Over there, to the northeast, was that land or cloud? A white bluff seemed to rise through the far skein of ice. Not America yet, but perhaps the Russian island, Big Diomede? According to my most optimistic estimate, I was still sixty-five kilometres from America. I'd now deliberately strayed north, off my line of navigation, in the hope of taking a bearing off the Diomede Islands and had yet to meet open water. I wondered if that had been fortuitous.

We carried on going. Surely each dog, like me, was listening for water, what Ranulph Fiennes called 'the most dangerous sound in the Arctic'.

And it began to look like we might, just conceivably, reach America. We might be standing there, the eleven of us, on the pebbled shore of the New World. I had to stop myself: 'But hold on . . . Have you thought of how you and your dogs are getting back?' My dream had been to go just as far as the ice would take me. It had brought me this far, but for months there had never really been a very serious possibility that I'd actually scramble on to the far shore.

XL

One hundred paces forward, thirty sideways, then forward again. What was driving me now was fear as much as hope: the fear of water ahead or behind. And all the time the thought of those bears, worthy adversaries for any animal on our planet. They would make quick work of my little gang. It was another reason to keep moving: the less time our scent had to lay out on the ice shelf, the more likely we would be to get away with it. All the time I had one eye over my shoulder as I watched for a sign that we were being followed, a block of ice that had moved. I had to steady my nerve, remind myself that the dogs would know before I would.

The fifty-kilometre mark, at an optimistic guess. I was growing impatient waiting for a bearing. Was I being carried off course up the coast instead of east? The clouds would lift soon, and then I'd know. 'On we go, dogs.' Still I was able to believe I might actually cross the Bering Strait alone by ice, conceivably something never accomplished before. 'And why should they bother?' Bernard might have added.

Then, a mistake. One elementary mistake – having come so far together, the dogs and I, strengthened by the tundra we had passed through, overcoming so many doubts, the alcohol and the leakage of energy through despair. Immediately, I knew it was a costly error. Just how costly remained to be seen.

I had planned to scout ahead. Nothing unusual in that. I stood on my sledge, checking for any stray fox or hare that might flip past. I looked at the dogs. They lay passively, taking advantage of the rest. No twitching of ears, no sniffing of the air; nothing was exciting their interest. I walked off ahead, passing Top Dog. I remember his eyes following me. All was as normal. Maybe I bent to pat his head.

Soon I was among the ice rubble, trying to plot the next move forward. I brought out my map. At a point that I later decided was some two hundred paces from the dogs, there was a snow flurry. The wind licked around, and an eddy swept the dry hard flakes across my face. I was temporarily blinded. My map was snatched from my gloved hands, and when I opened my eyes to give chase to it I received another stinging blast of snow. I hunkered down a second, shielding my face with an arm as I tried to watch the map fly. But nothing, just a blast of whiteness.

When the worst was over and I looked downwind, it was to see my map flapping like a trapped bird where it lay caught against a brick of nearby ice. I ran at it. It fluttered away and fell again, just ten paces ahead. Then it snapped into the wind, soaring high, taking flight to America, and I turned back, retracing my prints to the place where the squall had overcome me.

I orientated myself more accurately. Both compass and sun said I was presently facing due northeast. But from which direction had I approached this particular point? I looked around for my tracks and found that all trace had been swept away. A first tremor of disquiet went through me. I made a mental note: '(1) Sun is already low. (2) You are already dehydrated. (3) You have lost control of events.'

But there was no need for alarm yet. I set about doing what you are meant to do on such occasions; it was a well-rehearsed procedure. I marked my position by taking off my canvas smock. I counted out two hundred paces and began arcing around, looking for signs of the dogs and calling to them. 'Is this the only type of dog in the world that does not stand up when its master calls?' I wondered, slightly amused at my silly predicament.

Ten minutes later, I found dog tracks. Everything would work out. I looked around, and I was impressed to see just how much work I was putting into this venture to cross the Strait. There were prints all over the place: mine, the dogs', the creases left by the sledge. I traced my progress: it was remarkable how we'd probed the weaknesses in these ice ridges, foraying in and around, circling about, seizing on clues to this labyrinth.

The temperature was above zero again. I noticed that my reindeer boots were becoming damp, water rising from the seal-skin soles. I grew slower, tramping up and down, seeking footholds. 'Look,' I told myself, 'you may be dehydrated and want to rest, but your life depends on finding those dogs.' The situation was getting more serious now. Two hours must have gone by. My thoughts skipped ahead, seeking something to hold on to. If things didn't go well, would I make it to Lavrentiya by myself? Better forget about reaching one of the Diomede Islands, an as yet unknown distance away and the ice up to the north an unknown quantity altogether. Whatever route I do take, the emergency stove will be crucial.

But first things first. The priority remained finding the dogs. And that meant facing up to the truth, because there was surely only one explanation as to why I couldn't find the dogs: they had left me. 'And who could blame them,' I thought, not quite taking it in yet, sitting down as the sun dipped into the horizon and the light of the last rays fractured off the ice around and about. But the idea of such a betrayal began to sicken me. They were, in the end, only dogs, but it still mattered. Had not even one dog wanted to wait for me?

And now what would become of them? Sooner or later they'd be jammed in the pack ice. I imagined for a moment Jeremy and Basil slipping their collars, Frank biting through his harness, the dogs pulling off all manner of tricks to detach from the sledge and run for home. But no, this tribe wouldn't split up – and that would be their undoing. They'd tangle themselves up somewhere and die together.

I noticed that the breath caught on my fur collar was starting to freeze. The temperature was falling fast. Time to stop and think things through. In emergencies such as this, events have a tendency to spiral out of control. I dipped down behind some ice stacks, opened my survival kit, got out my torch and set about assembling my stove. 'I'll be able to think better after having had a good cuppa,' I thought. I would be able to take stock and begin the process of regaining control.

The polar adventurers Rune Gjeldnes and Pen Hadow spoke quietly to me in my living room about their tactics for outmanoeuvring the cold – karrimats, thermorests, neoprene face masks, balaclavas, throat guards. And for thwarting the dazzling light, goggles with yellow glass. Often it was a war against water, which is twenty-five times greater a conductor of cold than air. These calm men had strategized and schemed; they were humans who really *wanted to live. Their minds had been sharpened by so much proximity to death.*

Everything measured, always seeking control.
'How much chocolate should I take?'
'I suggest 150 g minimum a day.'
'Loo roll?'
'Two metres a day.'

I struck my first match. The stove lit, and I remember releasing a very protracted sigh of relief. The stove meant warmth and also being able to drink water. Snow was the only other option, and ingesting that in any amount would reduce my core body temperature.

Phuut! The stove went out. I tried to relight it. Nothing. I quickly checked the fuel jet. Dirty. 'Strange,' I thought. I'd given the stove a thorough clean out after the last emergency, and that seemed to have sorted it. Well, I'd have to clean it again – not what you want to do at a time like this, but needs must. I disassembled the stove, laying the pieces out on the ice. And then I noticed the petrol – it was dirty. That is, it was visibly dirty even in the twilight. 'The problem all along was with the emergency fuel, not the stove,' I thought. This was not my fuel. *My* fuel had been removed and replaced with old, low-grade Russian junk. Now wasn't the right moment to contemplate whether I was about to be the latest victim of the collapse of the Soviet system, but I allowed myself to give in to the temptation anyway. 'Had someone been so desperate that he had felt the need to steal a half litre's worth of decent petrol?' The answer, apparently, was yes.

I wondered if anyone would find the depot I'd left, complete with video tapes. As for the sledge and all the other equipment, in a couple of weeks the ice would be breaking up and it would drop either noisily or silently into the sea, there to lie subject to the Bering currents along with me, the dogs and all trace of this foolish enterprise.

I opened my emergency pack, counting out the rations – flapjack, pork scratchings. Then I began evaluating everything I had – spare compass, message pad . . . I prepared my foil sleeping bag. I sucked on a scoop of snow, followed by another, and then opened the pork scratchings and worked through half a packet. It was important to have energy right now – I needed to think things through, before I grew weak.

This is what life lived at its utmost feels like. It is at these rare times that modern man – most of us long since used to being sheltered from the elements – finds himself fully participating. Ready and fearful, I was consciously practising the art of survival. I could feel it, the adrenaline serving me, helping me deliver my fight or flight response. And to the instinctive was added my well-honed drill from the piece of paper in my kit. There was no need to get it out. I was already adapting to the world I was in, creating a house out of the ice, fashioning the snow into bedding. I was working on my goal of getting to Lavrentiya, trying to remain upbeat. In my mind, I checked through the list. I knew what I must do next – I'd done it enough times before.

I began working through the very few options I had open to me, sorting through the knowns, locating myself in the chaos of the ice and the wider scheme of things. Finally, I assembled what I had to work with. If I didn't find the dogs and sledge out there somewhere, the distance I would have to march to Lavrentiya, over crumpled and cracked ice, was, what, fifty, sixty kilometres? 'I will last four, five days – even a week if it stays warm,' I thought. 'But how far will I get in that time without water, wearing a fifteen-kilo reindeer suit, over pack ice? If the daytime temperature remains above zero, I'll be sweating all the way, but can safely drink snow. That's my best hope. But my reindeer suit is already damp from perspiration, and the moisture will conduct the cold. More dangerous are my boots: wet through. Tonight they might freeze solid, and my feet with them. To underline the point: if, at any time during the next few days' walk, the temperature drops even to just minus ten, I will die.'

How very lonely it was out here suddenly, without the dogs. But all was by no means lost. For heaven's sake, think of old Mawson, the one who walked for weeks out of the Antarctic so his body could be found.

So let's put the odds of me getting to safety without the dogs at one in four. Not brilliant, but something to work on – maybe I could raise them to one in three by guarding my resources well. If the weather stayed warm, survival was by no means out of the question.

It was too much to continue thinking about it right now. I'd had all the preparation in the world and yet I was still finding it hard to accept I'd got myself into this mess. But it was becoming clear: my best hope was that the dogs were stuck out of sight somewhere not too far away. I must start searching all over again. And, perversely, I had more chance of finding them now, in the dark – even a hundred metres away their eyes would reflect back the torch beam.

I got up. I wanted to know the answer for sure: had those dogs really let me down? Suddenly, that was more important than whether I would live or die. My dogs were companions and recently I'd come to see them as professional colleagues. 'No, they won't have left me,' I decided.

As I swung the torch beam around me, this gut feeling lent me further encouragement. 'Won't be long before ten pairs of eyes stare back from the night,' I thought. 'Can't have gone very far. Just a question of finding them. In five, maybe ten minutes I might be reunited with my supplies and dogs, and everything will be all right again. And when I do find them, the first thing I'll do is give the dogs their walrus rations.' I imagined the feeling of relief awaiting me – perhaps only a matter of seconds away now – as I caught first sight of them. I could picture Top Dog standing to greet me.

I moved the torch's ray back and forth over the ice. The light swept around me, systematically moving over grey ice with the smooth arc of a lighthouse beam. Sometimes it spun back at me, having caught a blade of ice; at other times the light was absorbed, fusing with humps of ghostly snow. Above, there was a smattering of stars, a smudge of cloud resting over the horizon. So many whites and greys, but no eyes shone back at me from the dark.

I turned back to my ice shelter. The world seemed to have gone silent for me now. 'It's not a question of them letting me down,' I thought. 'I let them down.' I worked my fingers and toes, keeping the numbness at bay, and tried to rid myself of that thought. If I got out of this there'd be time enough to blame myself.

I think we are in what might fairly be described as an extreme situation. My companions: two Torres Strait Islanders who know the four reef walls that make these waters so treacherous but who don't seem to be able to predict the weather. We are stuck on a rock, or reef, that is half the size of a tennis court. Although we still have a sea-faring canoe, it's not clear whether the waves will swamp us at high tide. The first day out from New Guinea was fine, the shifting waters turquoise and emerald; we saw dugong and even caught a giant turtle. With the help of other islanders we ate both. The next day, a gale blew up. First our food supplies were tossed overboard, then, almost unbelievably, our drinking water. I saw a sea snake tossed like rope in the foam.

Now we are shipwrecked, something that Captain Cook avoided more than two hundred years ago. We are living off limpets. Our

> *lips are swollen from the salt breeze. Our tongues are thickening. The eyes of my companions are red and haunted, as one would imagine Count Dracula's to be. I suppose mine are the same. We walk about like ghouls. I try to lift my heart by thinking of poetry.* 'Quid poetarum evolutio voluptatis affert,' *said Cicero – 'What pleasure the reading of the poets provides.' But it's more than pleasure; it transports us off this island of the living dead.* My diaries, marooned while crossing the Torres Strait between New Guinea and Australia.

My back was stiffening up. My head ached from dehydration and also the cold. But I was grateful I could still feel anything: feelings, even of pain, were good. I must keep moving my fingers and toes. I tried to think of a piano concerto I could pretend to play, and when that failed, any old tune that I could tap my fingers to. But this failed too because I needed a way out of here, and I knew I hadn't worked through all the possibilities. There was another option open to me, and it was one that I hadn't been able to face.

Here I was, a human being alone in the Arctic, and as such, I would die unless I found assistance in the form of my sledge first thing in the morning. But suppose I acted in a way more fitting to the Arctic. There were resources enough out here for bears and wolves; they did not die of starvation. Behaving as a human I would die, but as a wolf I might live.

I lay in this wilderness thinking of what it had come to. There was a chance of reaching help by myself, but there was a greater chance if I forgot about reaching Lavrentiya for now and thought only of tracking down the dogs. If I found the team, with the sledge, we might all live. If I found the dogs without the sledge, then I alone might live – by killing and eating the dogs like a wolf.

> *This above all else,* I thought: *the survivor must believe in his right to fight, to assert his right to replace others within the natural scheme of things. The dignity and justice of the bloody struggle upwards.*

> *'It may be difficult, but we ought to admire the savage instinctive hatred of the queen-bee, which urges her to destroy the young queens, her daughters, as soon as they are born . . . for undoubtedly this is for the good of the community; and maternal love or*

maternal hatred . . . is all the same to the inexorable principle of natural selection.' Charles Darwin, *The Origin of Species*.

Was I going to be the Siberian prisoner about to sacrifice his dog in the snow? My dream had led me full circle: I was a child again, excited by, yet fearful of, the force that I'd that day discovered each one of us has within – the compulsion to live. Tomorrow I might have to hunt down one of my own dogs and devour him like a beast.

'The decision can wait, at least just a moment,' I thought.

'I pointed to my watch and said, "We'll wait ten more minutes." Pertemba agreed. That helped us – it shifted some responsibility to the watch.' Pete Boardman, waiting below the summit of Everest for Mick Burke to join in the descent as the weather deteriorated.

The night came on. The temperature dropped, but only a little. I thought again of Darwin's murderous queen bee, how life seeks no justification for the blood it sheds. But would I do this, kill my own teammates? I weighed my duties. On the one hand, I had a duty to those who had entrusted their lives to me, the ten infant wolves. On the other, I had a duty to loved ones – perhaps a higher duty.

'. . . And gradually the thought arose, as I blundered on, day after day through the undergrowth, counting each pace, holding my compass out in front of me, that actually it would be very wrong of me to allow myself to die here in the jungle like this. Self-indulgent. My mum and dad were back in Britain waiting for news, and I had to do whatever it took to get back home – whether I liked it or not.' My diaries, regarding almost dying the first time (northeastern Amazon), aged twenty-three.

'Is that your decision, then?' I asked myself. 'You betray the trust of your poor colleagues? These creatures who've given up their lupine defences to serve man? My God, it isn't even as if it's the first time! What on earth *is* it about you, Benedict?'

And this inner voice tormented me like this through the long night, forcing me to justify my existence.

In the rainforest I came across a German hermit. He had made a home here, alone in the jungle with his dog. His existence hung by a thread. He patrolled the paths for fallen leaves, keeping the forest at bay. 'I cannot rest,' he'd say several times a day as he set out on another mission to defend the frontiers of his kingdom.

'So what happens if you fall sick?'

'Sick? What talk is this? I can't afford to be sick!'

'But malaria, a snake bite . . .?'

'In this unlikely *case, there is, of course, my larder . . .'*

He pointed to the brook that flowed through his camp. Beyond the mud bank I saw a piece of string, and at the end of it were his emergency rations: a quietly grazing tortoise.

'Surely you'd eat him only for a feast?' I said.

'On the contrary: only when I might die. It is my agreement with him.'

'Agreement?'

'Or should I say it is the tortoise's agreement with nature. He is granted life, but on condition that one day his life may be taken by something higher in the food chain. And I,' he added with what seemed to me was triumph, 'am higher in the food chain.' My diaries, the Orinoco/Amazon watershed.

I got to my feet. Now the first dull light came from the east. Soon it would be time to track the dogs. I sucked on some more snow. My teeth hurt with the cold – so much so that I felt the metal fillings might snap out of them. I exercised to keep warm, windmilling my arms as the light spread over the east, seeping in a creamy layer over the ice. I wondered if I might see Alaska today.

If we want to live, I reminded myself, *then we must live off others. It is the regrettable law of all higher things. Each day we pick off plants and animals and sometimes our own kind:*

At the dusty bus station hoodlums move in on me as I try to march with my rucksack to a bus. As they cavort around, I slow, seeing there's a huge man looming above me in a window seat. He wears no shirt, and he looks like the king of thieves. There's nowhere else to shelter, so I join him aboard. He doesn't look my way, but says, 'Don't allow yourself to be distracted by them, my friend.'

Thank God I've found an ally. What a stroke of luck! Who would have thought it?

But then he said, still without turning to me, 'Because these are only small fry. And I'm afraid I must prey on you now.' My diaries, Malindi, Kenya.

Dawn came, but I didn't welcome it. I met the day with dread. Then, very slowly, I stepped up to an ice block; slowly not only because I was weak and stiff, but because I knew that if I didn't see my dogs within the next few minutes then I might have to hunt them down, be the wolf I was meant to be protecting my ten little protégés from.

I looked out to the southwest, reassessing my whereabouts, and was surprised to find that I could discern exactly my route with the sledge. That was all very encouraging. Surely I should be able to work out where I'd left the dogs. Indeed, they should be right in front of me. But they were not there. 'Is this the end then?' I wondered.

It was as I turned back to my encampment in the ice that a movement caught my eye. It gave me a start. 'Watch out,' I thought, 'might not be a dog. Might be a bear . . .'

The movement – the clear, unambiguous movement of a living thing – was some fifty metres away, and I couldn't bear the hope of it. I moved forward cautiously, and what I saw as I came nearer was the face of a single dog. 'Top Dog,' I thought. I strained to see the black scars on his muzzle. 'He was the dog who stayed behind.' Then the realization quickly hit me: 'So am I going to have to kill *you*, of all dogs?'

However, as I got closer still, I saw it wasn't Top Dog but Flashy White. He was lying slumped, chin on the snow, watching me patiently. I wondered, puzzled. 'Why were you, the strongest dog, the one who stayed for me?' I closed my eyes and felt an upwelling of gratitude to this animal. And I knew then that I couldn't kill this dog. Not this one, nor any other.

I opened my eyes again and carried on towards the dog. My next thought was one of relief: 'Thank God. I'm not going to die alone.'

XLI

My initial view of the dog I called Flashy White had been obscured, for the next moment I saw that he was not alone but attached to the whole team. This was not where I had left them, and you could see the chaotic trail of the sledge. They had probably spent the night trapped between the ice blocks to the left, but now they were occupying an open space. Why here? The snow about them was thoroughly trampled. It very much looked as though they had given up waiting for my return and come to find me.

I got down on my knees and embraced Top Dog and Flashy White, as you might welcome any colleague back from the dead. Then, working back down the team, I hugged each of the others in turn. I opened the food sack immediately and fed the dogs. I sat among them, eating the raw walrus with them. I had the main stove going before long, and as I sat on my haunches I tried to adjust to the idea of having a chance of life again.

I knew already that I wasn't going any further across the Bering Strait. I had done what I had come to the Arctic for. That I had achieved it without reaching Alaska seemed something to celebrate. Making it to America could only ever be about pride in an unnecessary physical feat, and that pride was better placed wholly in my dogs.

Before leaving, I stood a while looking out towards Alaska. There was a smear of grey darkening the white line of the horizon. Was that America? Was that what the navigator Bering one day caught sight of through the clouds? I liked to think so. It was about 56 kilometres away by my best reckoning, and Russia 48 kilometres away. I was just about at the halfway point – conceivably. But the honest truth was that I might be a lot nearer or a lot further away. And even knowing the exact distance, I would never know precisely how close I had come to reaching the other continent. It might have been a day away, or if water lay across my path, an eternity. But it didn't matter; nor did the fact that the cloud I saw above the pack ice commonly indicates the presence of open water. I waited, savouring this moment as I stood without even a map somewhere on the dateline, mid-Bering Strait, with no one knowing I was here on this fragile spot. And more fragile each year: the Arctic as a whole seemed warmer each winter, a little more reluctant to freeze. 'Perhaps no one will ever again stand here so alone and isolated,' I thought.

I turned the dogs for home. I couldn't wait any longer, like a mountaineer who has reached a summit and knows he must immediately scuttle down before the winds change. And half a day later, when Russia seemed no nearer, I realized the enormity of the challenge still ahead of us. We were very far from safe.

There was no stopping for anything as we raced for solid ground. The dogs knew the mission was over. They were heading home, enthusiastic, noses to the scent they'd laid over the days before. We retreated along our tracks, willing Siberia to come closer and closer. I was very tired – and very scared now, seeing what I had risked.

There it was ahead on the horizon, the thin unflinching line of the cliffs. And watching it, I realized that this spread of permafrost, the Siberia that had killed so many, had become a sanctuary. It might yet kill me, but for now, it was my hope.

We traced our route out of no-man's-land. And as we wound nearer and nearer – no need to steer! – it seemed to me I was gathering in a safety line: the dogs, Yasha, my shattered file of survivors, the body of evidence that had sustained me. We each carry along with us so much to preserve our life force – compasses, maps, deities, and other survival gadgets. 'It would be cruel of Fate to do away with us now,' I thought as the solid cliffs drew nearer and nearer.

> *'For three days I have walked, I have been thirsty, I have followed tracks in the sand, I have pinned my hopes on the dew. I have striven to rejoin my kind, whose dwelling place on the earth I had forgotten . . .'* Antoine de Saint-Exupéry.

The sun was on my face, lending me unexpected encouragement. While I'd been thinking only of the ice ahead, behind me the spring had been advancing, spreading out over the tundra, the sun everywhere reactiving germs of life. As we edged closer, this simple thought filled me with pleasure: the tundra had been dangerous – hard, merciless; but now it was softening, retracting those claws. All of life lay ahead of me, and it felt very good indeed to come back out of the ice like this, thawing in the brightness. 'The company of the gods rejoice at thy rising,' I thought, remembering the hymn of the ancient Egyptians to their sun god Ra. 'The earth is glad when it beholdeth thy rays.' This was one of the best moments in my life: I had cared enough about wanting to live and had been rewarded; I was on the road back from the ice lands of Valhalla. But we all recognize this feeling, this return journey from despair. After grief, after tragedy, we continue our disrupted lives, rejoin the broken sentence, continue the song. We take our place back among the pack.

I closed my eyes, knowing I was returning to my kind.

'He didn't want to sleep he felt so happy.' On the safe arrival of Nansen at Frederick Jackson's expedition base, nearing the end of his 'thousand days in the Arctic'.

'We had pierced the veneer of outside things . . . We had seen God in his splendours, heard the text that Nature renders. We had reached the naked soul of man.' Shackleton on crossing South Georgia, knowing he'd reached help.

We pushed off from the rock, and when our little vessel reached safety in the form of Thursday Island, a whole squad of officials – policemen, customs, immigration, quarantine – all these uniformed men were there on the quayside. They seemed anxious to witness this event. They stared and pointed as we approached, dwarfed by a mighty battle-grey warship. Yet they don't know our full story: 'I have to ask, mate, have you been drinking alcohol?' It's our eyes – no doubt crazed and laced with crimson veins – but also because we slur when we speak and are wobbly on our feet. Adding to the colour of the scene, ants began piling off our canoe. Where they have come from we do not know. The officials began stamping on them. 'I think one got away,' said the policeman, drily, as hundreds ran for cover.

'Welcome to Australia,' the customs official said at last.

'Thanks,' I said. I seemed to be speaking on behalf of everyone – including the ants that I had unwittingly harboured. These busy

> *units of life now dispersed, following in the ant footsteps of countless thousands of others, most perhaps springing jubilantly ashore from driftwood. They disappeared, spreading out over the red-soiled terrain they would strive to make their home.* My diaries, after crossing the Torres Strait.

As we curled back towards the tundra, I watched the Russian cliffs lifting slowly from the ice, my chances of staying alive growing with each minute. My mind was again full of questions about this life I was to be given back: what was it in us, this life urge, so resourceful, so relentless?

> *'Bid them be cheerful and hopeful on account of what life yet has in store for them.'* William E. Chandler, Secretary of the US Navy, in a message to Greely and the other survivors.

Now I was coming to my depot. I could hear the water that dripped from the cliffs, darkening the black and tan rocks. It had been a close call: a couple more days and the sea ice would begin to split. But beneath me now was land, and all around me life was keen to express itself: as we sped by, soft green blades of moss and reddened sedge peeked through the snow.

I remembered the wolverine: 'And this thought above all else . . . Some instinctive urge, a life spirit, a primitive form of belief . . .' There was little more that need be said. All living things shared this same compulsion to advance across the universe, but in the case of man, it seemed, belief was everything – and there was no end to what we were prepared to believe in. I was reminded of the stanza from *The Rubaiyat of Omar Khayyam*:

> 'How sweet is mortal Sovranty!' think some:
> Others – 'how blest the Paradise to come!'
> Ah, take the Cash in hand and waive the Rest;
> O, the brave Music of a *distant* Drum!

Whatever we live for, it's only armed with purpose that we're able to march on into the blizzard, resisting the voice which urges us to lie down awhile and surrender ourselves to sweet sleep.

The soul also played a part in all this, many thought. I'd read that the Egyptians located it at the base of the tongue. I had New Guinean friends who insisted it was positioned in the liver. But who amongst us could ever completely unravel the human, pin him on a table, slit him open and reveal his full workings?

I watched my dogs run, this species that seemed to know us better than any other. They pounded along, drawing me out of the Arctic as the wind screeched and cried and quietly dropped. In time, would Top Dog be replaced by Basil? Maybe Basil would fail as leader and live an unremarkable life elsewhere in a dog team. Where any of us end up in the pack is not always to our liking, I supposed. We learn to accept our lot, hoping that we might somehow influence the outcome of things or that one day we'll be called upon to play a prominent role. We are leaders, we are foot soldiers. And whatever the disappointments of pack life, we find reassurance in the belief that we are valued by something greater than us. My comfort was that, for ten dogs in the Siberian winter of 2001, I had been that power.

Lorino was before us. It was still smouldering – that warehouse, burnt down in mysterious circumstances. I was all set to enjoy these last few metres of my journey, the glorious approach up the incline to Yasha's little wooden house, when a man ran out, stumbling and waving. 'A drunk,' I muttered. 'He's spoiling this moment. What a pity.'

'*Steeyr, steeyr*,' I called to Top Dog; my last command. He swung away to the left.

We were no longer moving now. The journey was over. I stuck the brake into the ice, jamming it into the tundra for the final time. I looked at Top Dog. He turned to look at me; he seemed to sigh with relief as he slumped to the snow.

I needed a second or two of quiet to absorb the idea that it was all over, that I was no longer having to strain to remain alive.

I heard the drunkard approach, the irregular pounding of his feet in the snow as they neared. Whether he was drunk or not, I was not ready for him.

'It's me!' he yelled.

'Go away,' I thought.

'It's me. *Alexei!*'

He hadn't been waving because he'd had a go at the vodka; he'd been hopping up and down, overexcited, wanting to get to his precious dogs.

'So sorry, Alexei, I didn't recognize you.'

'New sunglasses,' he said. I noticed his glance at the dog team. He was counting them. 'But you know, the dogs didn't recognize me either! They've forgotten me!'

'Not for long, I'm sure.'

'The dogs obeyed *you*, not me, Benya. This is the greatest possible compliment. You are their master. I am nothing to them.'

The comments were overly generous and I was drunk myself with exhaustion, but at that moment no other words from anyone in the world would have made me feel as content.

XLII

Alexei disappeared and a stranger kindly agreed to take my photo and capture the moment. I couldn't take it all in, not right then. But looking at the photo now, I can see how it was. There I sit before my sledge in my reindeer furs. Across my face is written the pride of someone who has safely brought something valuable back to where it belongs. Around me are my dogs. Flashy White stands slightly in front, guarding Top Dog from the photographer. Both have their eyes tightly closed. They are exhausted – the stress of leading their team to the far end of the abyss and back. To my left is Mad Jack; even at this late juncture I am having to keep him from Frank, who looks over to him, anxiously, from my right.

Yasha was running to me.

'I'm still alive!' I called out.

He squeezed me in his great arms. In his hand he had a bottle. '*Champanski!*' He must have had it waiting.

Suddenly, a boy was unloading my supplies and sitting astride my sledge. 'Alexei's son,' said Yasha. And with it came the horrible realization that the dogs and the sledge were no longer mine.

Later, as their harnesses were being undone, I had a quiet word with the team. I tried to console myself. I thought of the pleasure to be had each time the winter came around, imagining the dogs waiting to take someone out into the tundra. Top Dog would rise to his feet, stand while his harness was fitted, and then begin to run, leading the team out across the white stillness.

The dogs were peeled off, one by one, to join Alexei's A team. Bernard was the last. I gave him a squeeze as you might any old friend; he resisted. Dogs never do quite understand goodbyes. You might be gone a day or a week or a lifetime.

I walked away. 'I won't look back,' I thought. I was taking it badly. The dogs were safely back with their master; there was no place for me here any more. I felt cast out – cast out of Siberia, just as I'd found my place in it. Then, after only a few paces, I stopped. I could feel the eyes of the ten dogs on me.

'Enough,' I thought. 'Be satisfied.' I had almost lost my life and the lives of these dogs. But our lives had been given back to us by the Arctic and I could not, in fairness, ask for more. I carried on walking away from the dogs, taking that thought along with me. I walked faster, striding along in my colossal reindeer garment, out over the shrinking snows. I came now to the edge of town, to a ledge where the tundra lay before me in all its terrible vastness, and as I felt the spring sunshine alight again on my face, I smiled.

AUTHOR'S NOTE

A word on accuracy: the expedition adheres to my notes at the time, and also the video footage – which the BBC edited into the TV series *Icedogs*. I've disguised one character, but otherwise, although I have condensed, clarified and simplified, I'm not conscious of having exaggerated anything.

Since the events related here, Roman Abramovich has bought the English football club Chelsea and sold his Siberian oil company Sibneft for $13 billion, making him – some calculate – the world's richest man in cash terms. With President Putin's encouragement, Abramovich has now stood for a second term as Governor of Chukotka and been re-elected. Although continuing to receive overwhelming local support (not least because he continues to inject huge sums of his own money into the region) he remains cautious with regard to mainstream Russian politics – unlike the previous top oligarch, Mikhail Khodorkovsky. He, despite protestations of innocence, ended up being prosecuted for fraud and tax evasion, and was, in the traditional manner, dispatched to a prison camp in Siberia.

For me personally, this venture helped bring to a close a chapter in my life, one that began on my first major expedition when I found myself alone with a dog in the rainforest and struggling to survive. Although the book that followed, *Mad White Giant*, was one of a quartet written in deliberately different moods and didn't seek to offer a reliable record of that expedition – as the narrative style and whimsical cartoons made plain – it does give the right idea: this was a 'narrow squeak' of epic proportions, and all the more so as I'd departed on the venture aged just twenty-two. It seems to me that my desire to immerse myself in various inhospitable worlds in the two decades since – beginning with my undergoing the male initiation ceremony of a forest people in New Guinea – has come about in no small part because of this early trauma and a desire to come to terms with an environment that almost did me in. This tenth book of my travels, in which the fate of many dogs this time was wrapped up with mine, seemed to mark an end point, the closing of a circle – and perhaps it's just as well. As someone once said, 'You're a cat who's used up six of your nine lives.'

It was, of course, the subject of 'survival' which I aimed to explore on my journey through the Russian tundra. A final thought on this: at a gathering of adventurers recently I was told about a laboratory experiment in which a hundred or so rats were made to swim to the limit of their endurance, alongside one wild rat. Oddly, although perhaps the fittest animal, it was only the wild rat that gave up and died. Why? It seems that the laboratory rats were accustomed to being put through various trials by their human masters. They had learnt that if they hung on long enough things would work out for them. They'd even get a reward. In short, the laboratory rats were sustained by something akin to hope.

Although I can't be certain as to the details of the experiment, the story is, to me at least, a graphic reminder of the value of hope in our own lives. With my own project, I wished to investigate not simply the nature of the hope we find but how some amongst us are able to keep pushing onwards when there's apparently no hope at all.

I've already expressed my profound gratitude to the Chukchi guides Yasha and Tolia – I dedicated *The Faber Book of Exploration* to them – but would like to emphasize again here how they worked tirelessly and selflessly to keep me safe, in unimaginably tough physical and social conditions. Needless to say, the problems endured so stoically by the peoples of the Russian Far East, which are depicted in some measure in this book, are not of their own making. Hundreds of other individuals – Chukchis, Yupiks, Russians, Ukrainians and others – also looked after me in Chukotka, in settlements from Anadyr to Lavrentiya, doing their best to help the expedition along. They too have left me with many fond memories, only some of which are related here.

I'd like to thank Governor Roman Abramovich for his support and kind interest in the project; also Sergei Raityrgin, who put an enormous amount of time and effort into helping set up the expedition and secure permissions, and whose helpful office team lent us such encouragement. Thanks to Walter Donohue for all his dedicated work on me and the manuscript; to Ian Bahrami for such diligence with the proofs and Yana Toultchinskaya for advice on Cyrillic; and, before the expedition, to Brian Gillett, for such invaluable advice on sledge dogs and for fashioning the special ice spikes, to Tim Simpson for assembling the Arctic kit, to Peter Wadhams for advice on the Bering ice, and to Pen Hadow and Rune Gjeldnes for advice on the varied perils of the Arctic; also to Andrew Eavis, Chris Bonington and all those others I've quoted from my personal survival notes. These and other background notes I've supplemented and updated, but sometimes they date back many years, and I apologize to anyone I might have inadvertently paraphrased without due acknowledgement.

I am deeply indebted to John Hesling for steering the project through and lending unwavering personal and professional assistance before, during and after the expedition, as it underwent its various trials and emerged as the *Icedogs* programme. I'd especially like to thank Rachel Foster for her heartfelt and conscientious support and advice, always given so selflessly and with such integrity; my thanks also to Chloe Pettersson and, of course, the very patient and trusting BBC Executive Producer and friend Bob Long, the person who gave me the opportunity to record my expeditions with a video camera. The programmes he brought to fruition for the first time allowed millions to witness the ups and downs of authentic, testing journeys via their television sets. Finally, I'd like to mention Lenka Flidrova, who has been so patient with me over the last two years.

SELECT BIBLIOGRAPHY

Amundsen, R. *The South Pole: An Account of the Norwegian Antarctic Expedition in the Fram, 1910–1912*, London, John Murray, 1912.

Barrow, J., *Voyages of Discovery and Research within the Arctic Regions from the Year 1818 to the Present Time*, London, John Murray, 1846.

Bauer, J. M., *As Far as My Feet Will Carry Me*, London, André Deutsch, 1957.

Beardsley, M., *Deadly Winter: The Life of Sir John Franklin*, London, Chatham Publishing, 2002.

Bogoras, W., *The Chukchee*. Jesup North Pacific Expedition 7. Leiden, E. J. Brill, 1909.

Brody, H., *The Other Side of Eden: Hunters, Farmers, and the Shaping of the World*, London, Faber and Faber, 2002.

Conrad, J., *The Heart of Darkness*, first published 1902. London, Penguin, 1994.

Cook, J., *The Journals*, Ed. Philip Edwards, from the Hakluyt Society 1955–67. London, Penguin, 1999.

Darwin, C., *The Origin of Species*, London, John Murray, 1859.

Dawkins, R., *The Selfish Gene*. Oxford, Oxford University Press, 1976.

Fitzgerald, E. (trans.), *The Rubaiyat of Omar Khayyam*. Mumbai, Jaico Publishing House, 1948.

Fleming, F., *Cassell's Tales of Endurance*, London, Weidenfeld and Nicolson, 2004.

Haafner, J., *Travels on Foot through the Island of Ceylon*. London, Phillips and Co., 1821.

Hayes, I., *The Open Polar Sea*. London, Sampson Low, Son and Marston, 1867.

Hedin, S., *Crossing the Taklamakan: My Life as an Explorer*. New York, Boni & Liveright, 1925.

Hooper, W. H., *Ten Months among the Tents of the Tuski*. London, John Murray, 1853.

Hough, R., *Captain James Cook*, Hodder and Stoughton, London, 1994.

Huntford, R., *Nansen*. London, Duckworth, 1997.

Jennings, M., *The New Complete Siberian Husky*. New York, Macmillan, 1992.

Jones, S., *Almost Like a Whale*, London, Doubleday, 1999.

Lorenz, K., *Man Meets Dog*. Boston, Houghton Mifflin, 1954.

Machiavelli, N., *The Prince*, trans. George Bull. London, Penguin, 1961.
Margulis, L. and Sagan, D., *What Is Life?* Berkeley, University of California Press, 1995.
McKinlay, W. L., *Karluk: The Untold Story of Arctic Exploration*. London, Weidenfeld and Nicholson, 1999.
Moorhouse, G., *The Fearful Void*. London, Hodder and Stoughton, 1974.
Mymrin N. I. (Ed.), *Traditional Ecological Knowledge of Siberian Eskimo: The Bowhead Whale*. Provideniya, Chukotka, 1999.
Nansen, F, *Farthest North*. London, Constable, 1897.
Nuttall, M. (Ed.) *Encyclopaedia of the Arctic*, New York, Routledge, 2005.
Rawicz, S., *The Long Walk: The True Story of a Trek to Freedom*. London Constable and Robinson, 2000.
Saint-Exupéry, A. De, *Wind, Sand, Stars,* Harmondsworth, Penguin, 1993.
Salisbury, G. and Salisbury, L., *The Cruellest Miles*, London, Bloomsbury, 2003.
Schley, W. S. and Soley, J. R., *The Rescue of Greely*. London, Sampson Low, Marston, Searle and Rivington, 1885.
Schrödinger, E., *What Is Life? With Mind and Matter and Autobiographical Sketches*. Cambridge, Cambridge University Press, 1992.
Schweitzer, P. P., 'The Chukchi and Siberian Yupik of the Chukchi Peninsula, Russia.' In: *The Cambridge Encyclopaedia of Hunters and Gatherers*, Eds Richard B. Lee and Richard Daly. Cambridge, Cambridge University Press, 1999.
Scott, R., *Scott's Last Expedition*. London, Smith, Elder and Co., 1913.
Seneca, *Letters from a Stoic*. Harmondsworth, Penguin, 1969.
Shackleton, E., *South: The Story of Shackleton's Last Expedition 1914–1917*. London, William Heinemann, 1919.
Stark, F., *The Valleys of the Assassins*. London, John Murray, 1936.
Stefansson, V., *The Friendly Arctic: The Story of Five Years in Polar Regions*. London, Macmillan, 1921.
Vakhtin, N., 'Endangered Languages in Northeast Siberia: Siberian Yupik and Other Languages of Chukotka.' In: *Bicultural Education in the North: Ways of Preserving and Enhancing Indigenous People's Languages and Traditional Knowledge*, Ed. Erich Kasten, pp. 159–173. Münster, Waxmann Verlag, 1998.
Van der Merwe, P., Preston, D., Feeney, R. E. and McKernan, L., *South: The Race to the Pole*. London, National Maritime Museum, 2000.

INDEX

Figures in italics indicate captions. 'BA' indicates the author.

Aborigines, 168, 169, 170, 188
Abramovich, Governor Roman, 16, 17–18, 25, 27, 104, 180, 206, 257
Adelaide, 169
Africa
 and the domesticated dog, 73
 man's spread from, 235
Ain Mallaha, Israel, 73
Alaska, 7, 24, 25, 29, 32, 33, 34, 43, 44, 221, 248
 land bridge to Siberia, 72, 94
Aleuts, 35, 94
Alex (Chukchi fisherman), 155–6
Algeria, 73
All Alaska Sweepstakes, 79
Allen, Benedict
 arrives in Anadyr, 20
 battles against the wind, 148–50
 bitten by Mad Jack, 228
 childhood attraction to expeditions and Siberia, 4–5, 7–9
 decision to have faith in the Chukchis, 44–6
 dreams of journeying with dogs across the Bering Strait, 15
 feast at Uelkal Cultural Centre, 119–20
 final preparations, 56–8
 finds his team, 247, 248
 first serious run with his team, 87–9
 frostbite, 90, 92, 103, 159
 in West Papua, 10–11
 knee injury, 158, 159, 171, 200
 loss of his map and the dogs, 239
 Mad White Giant, 257
 meets Gena and Alexei, 36–40
 meets his dogs, 67–70
 starts his journey across the Strait, 221
 survival list, 57–8, 161–2, 164–5, 167, 170, 242
 taken over a cliff by his team, 1–3, 157–60, 161
 takes passengers on a solitary trip, 103–4
 talks to schoolchildren in Konergino, 130–31
 tells Yasha of his intentions, 191–2
 The Faber Book of Exploration, 258
Allen, Katie (author's sister), 8–9
Altai range, 16
Amazon region, 10, 210, 245
Amazon River, 166
Amazonia, 236
American Coast Guard, 24
American–Soviet agreement (1989), 33
Americans, and Cold War, 29
Americas

animal settlement, 94
colonization, 72
third and final phase of migration to, 35
Amundsen, Roald
as the first modern adventurer, 229
cancelled attempt on the North Pole, 79
depots, 143, 144, 147
experienced, 146
markers, 143
Nansen's protégé, 95, 124
on dog harnesses, 81
on dogs' friendships, 125
on dogs' obedience, 124
personality, 142, 144
rations, 144
realizes the value of dogs, 73
sacrifices his dogs, 140, 141, 142
sledges, 144
survival of, 16, 73, 143–4
uses Greenland Eskimo dogs, 95, 143, 145
Anadyr, Chukotka, Russia, 20, 22–6, 28, 39, 41, 51, 56, 60, 61–2, 63–4, 69, 80, 88, 98, 100, 103, 154, 224
Anadyr River, 79
Anaviapik (an Inuit), 114
Anchorage, Alaska, 79
Andes, 166
Andre (a Russian in Lorino), 205, 214
Andrée, Salomon August, 186
Andropov, Yuri, 139
angyapik (leather open boat), 32
animal faithfulness, 167
Anquallyt ('sea people'), 32
Antarctica, 95, 141, 229
Arctic
BA achieves his goal, 248
BA's aim, 159–60
dangers of, 60–61, 63, 93
offers something special, 11–12
Peary's Eskimo dogs in, 95, 141
role of women, 102
survival without food or water, 16
Arctic Circle, 4
Arctic Ocean, 6
Association of the Peoples of the North, 33
Athabaskans, 34
auklets, 18
aurora (northern lights), 132–3, 158, 163
Aztec empire, 189

Back, George, 6
Baffin Bay, 7
Balto (a famous sledge dog), 79
Barabbas (Nansen's dog), 94
Barisan highlands, Sumatra, 57–8
Barrow, John, 6–7
Bartlett, Captain, 93
Basil (a member of BA's dog team), 75, 80, 83, 87, 93, 98, 99, 105, 136, 138, 140, 142, 147, 161, 174, 199, 207, 223, 240, 252
BBC (British Broadcasting Corporation), 56, 184, 232, 257
Beardmore Glacier, 146
Beechey Island, 163
Berezovsky, Boris, 18
Bering, Vitus, 43, 51, 160, 236, 248
Bering Bridge, 72, 94
Bering Island, 43
Bering Sea, 18, 29
Bering Strait, 25, 26, 28, 92
amphibious vehicle in, 22
BA achieves his goal, 248
BA envisages his journey with dogs, 15
BA turns the dogs for home, 249
and Cook, 14, 18, 21, 44, 48
crossed by stray reindeer, 45
depot, 232, 241, 251
described, 30
Dezhnev's travels, 43
Flashy White is found, 247, 248
Gena's suggested routes, 38
ice levels, 17, 39, 54, 65
loss of BA's map and dogs, 239
marine biodiversity, 18

narrowing of, 153, 174
Shparo's expedition, 24–5, 38, 39, 41, 42, 43
spread of Eskimos and Aleuts, 35
start of BA's journey, 221
transit route for migrating birds and sea mammals, 32
visa-free access, 33
Beringia plain, 94
Bernard (a member of BA's dog team), 98, 99, 105, 109, 115, 125, 126, 137, 209, 212, 216–17, 231–4, 238, 254
Bjaaland, Olav, 143
Bjelkiers, 95
Black Sea, 206
Blot (a member of BA's dog team), 74–5, 76, 80, 99, 105
Boardman, Pete, 245
Bogoras, Waldemar, 108
Bolshevik Revolution (1917), 33
Bolsheviks, 7
Bonington, Chris, 197, 221
Borneo, 56, 153
Bowers, Henry 'Birdie', 146, 229–30
Brahe, William, 168–9
Branson, Sir Richard, 104
Brazilian Amazon, 207–8
Brody, Hugh, 34, 114
Buchan, Captain David, 5
Burke, Mick, 245
Burke, Robert O'Hara, 167, 168–70
Burton, Sir Richard, 167

California pine cone, 177
camels, 189–90
cameras, 56, 184, 231, 232
Canada, 7, 33, 34, 125
Canadian Red Cross, 68
Canela, La (the 'Land of Cinnamon'), 166
Canidae, 72
canned goods, 162
cannibalism, 5, 163
Cape Crozier, 229
Cape Sabine, 121
Castro, Fidel, 206
Central Park, New York City, 79
Chalbi, Kenya, 56
Chandler, William E., 251
Chechnya, 29, 65
Chelsea FC, 257
Cherry-Garrard, Apsley, 143, 147, 229
Chesterfield nightspot, Moscow, 59
China, 32
Chukchi Peninsula, 13, 18, 19, 33, 35, 44, 94, 107, 214
Chukchis, 29
bone carvings, 31
Cook meets (1778), 21
dependence on the Russians, 40
dogs, *see under* dogs
fights with Eskimos, 224
history of, 32–3
internal navigation system, 110–111
living in Anadyr, 22
masters of the Arctic, 14–15
reindeer-herding nomads, 9, 14, 32, 33, 201–2
and Russian technology, 155–6
sledges, 125
spirituality, 31, 107–8
tents, 31, 35, 48, 201–2, 203
their homeland, 13
trade with Eskimos, 35
Chukotka, 51, 60, 126
Abramovich as Governor, 17–18
climate, 13
dependence on the dog, 14, 15
described, 20, 28, 227
ecology, 18
geography, 13, 18
history, 32–3
Russians in, 22, 33
in Soviet days, 22–3
Chukotka Autonomous Region, 33
cicada, 177
Cicero, 244
clappers, whale-bone, 35
clothing, 31, 35, 53, 55, 56, 65, 66, 68, 85, 124, 144, 227, 242

clubs, 35
co-operation, 222
Coca River, 166
Cold War, 29, 33, 180
Columbus, Christopher, 43, 210, 226
Colwell, Lieutenant, 121, 122, 123
Committee of Assistance of Peoples of the North, 33
compass, 57, 232, 236, 239, 241, 249
Congo River, 167
conquistadors, 166
Cook, Captain James, 20, 47, 243
  on Chukchi dogs, 14, 32
  describes Chukchi Peninsula, 18
  encounter with the Chukchis (1778), 21
  explores the Bering Strait, 14, 18, 21, 44
  ordeal with walrus meat, 111
Cooper's Creek, Australia, 167, 168, 169
Cortés, Hernán, 162, 167, 188
Cossacks, 14, 32, 77
Crean, Tom, 142
Crimean war, 196
crustacean, 18

Darling River, 168
Darwin, Charles, 177
  The Origin of Species, 244–5
Davis, Captain John King, 210
Davis Strait, 48
de la Billière, Edward, 207
dehydration, 239, 244
Dennis (a member of BA's dog team), 104, 105, 113, 147, 159, 171, 172, 193, 204, 225, 234
Dezhnev, Semyon, 32, 43
Diamond, John, 194–5
Diomede Islands, 29, 38, 43, 235, 236, 237, 240
Discovery (ship), 44, 95
dog boots, 55, 84
dog team
  Alexei discusses the team, 212
  arrival in Lorino, 252–3
  BA is bitten by Mad Jack, 228
  BA meets his dog team, 67–70
  BA's last command, 252
  begin to obey BA, 179
  begins to become BA's team, 138
  consolidation as a team, 199, 205
  disappearance of the team, 239
  feeding, 77–8, 80, 173–4, 194, 231, 248
  first assessment of, 74–6
  first outing, 80–83
  first serious run, 87–9
  found by BA, 247, 248
  naming completed, 104–5
  returned to Alexei, 254–5
  takes BA over a cliff, 1–3, 157–8, 161
  trust, 50, 140, 225
dogs
  and Amundsen's success at the South Pole, 73
  Amundsen's understanding of, 143, 144
  BA meets his first Chukchi dog, 36
  Bjelkiers, 95
  Chukchi dogs as the greatest sledge dogs, 13
  Chukchi dogs as one of the oldest of all dog breeds, 95
  Chukchi dog's specialism, 14
  compared with wolf pups, 73–4
  described, 47
  dog teams as hardened professionals, 2
  domestication worldwide, 72–3
  eaten by wolves, 101
  Eskimo, 9, 13, 14, 69, 81, 95, 141, 143
  Evgeni's dogs, 49–50
  female, 117
  as food, 32, 141–4, 208, 209, 244, 245
  harnesses, 81, 95
  lead dogs, 86
  life expectancy, 86
  love of the tundra, 117
  Malamutes, 79, 96

as a means of transport, 71, 73
novices and dog teams, 81
official Soviet dog (Leningrad factory breed), 15
Samoyeds, 95, 96
Siberian huskies, 79–80, 95, 96
support on hunts, 71
and wolves, 73–4, 101, 116, 117
Dostoevsky, Fyodor: *From the House of the Dead*, 110
drums, 31, 48

East Asia, 34
East Siberian Sea, 18
Eavis, Andrew, 195
Egyptians, Ancient, 250, 251
eider
common, 148
king, 148
El Dorado, 166, 198
Elison, Sergeant, 120
Ellesmere Island, 121, 198
Endurance (ship), 167
Enmelen, 152
Erebus (ship), 7, 162
Escobar, Pablo, 195
Eskimos, 22, 29, 34–5, 93, 165
bone carvings, 31
diet, 143–4
fights with Chukchis, 224
and Franklin's last expedition, 163
hostility to expedition members, 7
journeys across the Strait, 223
relocated by Russians, 224
sea-hunting technology, 32, 35
sledges, 125
their dogs, 9, 13, 14, 69
trade with Chukchis, 35
see also Inuit community
Estonians, 33
Eurasia, 29
Evans, Petty Officer Edgar, 144
Evans, Lieutenant Teddy, 142, 145
Even group, 32
Everest, Mount, 217, 245
fan hitch, 125
Farr, Martyn: *The Darkness Beckons*, 196
Fatty (one of Yasha's lead dogs), 80–83, 87–90, 96, 99, 218
Fawcett, Colonel Percy, 226
Feeney, Robert, 146
Ferdinand, King of Spain, 226
Fiennes, Ranulph, 190, 237
First World War, 8
fish, 18, 35, 60–61, 107, 155
flares, 113, 116, 132, 231
Flashy White (a member of BA's dog team), 80, 87, 93, 96, 100, 101, 104, 105, 112, 118, 137, 139, 147, 157, 158, 172, 174, 179, 193, 199, 212, 226, 247, 248, 254
Flinders, Matthew, 5
Forell, Clemens, 214
foxes, 137, 151, 224, 230
Fram (ship), 93, 94, 95, 141, 165
Frank (a member of BA's dog team), 96, 97, 99, 105, 115, 124, 137, 154, 199, 212, 228, 240, 254
Franklin, Lady Jane, 7, 133
Franklin, Sir John, 4–7, 15, 16, 47, 48, 51, 133, 144, 160, 162–4, 165, 170, 180, 235
frostbite, 90, 92, 103, 116, 120, 159, 193
frostnip, 90
FSB (Federal Security Service), 215

Gena, *see* Inankuejas, Gennadi
George III, King, 44
Gerof, Demetri, 95, 145
Gibson Desert, Western Australia, 188
Gillett, Brian, 207
Gjeldnes, Rune, 240
glaciation, 94
Gobi Altai, Mongolia, 190
Gobi Desert, 110
Goosak, William, 79
Goss, Pete, 190
Gray, Charles, 168, 169, 170

Greely, Adolphus, 120, 121–3, 166, 186, 229, 251
  Three Years of Arctic Service, 123
Greenland, 33, 34, 81, 95, 125
Gregory, Augustus, 168
Gula, Roman, 101
Gulags, 1, 8, 10, 51, 52, 208, 214
Gulf of Anadyr, 102
Gulf of Carpentaria, 168
gulls
  glaucous, 148
  herring, 148
guns
  arrival of, 32
  and bears, 116, 220

Haafner, J., 214
Hadow, Pen, 116, 221, 240
al-Hallaj, Mansur, 121
hares, 218, 223, 235
  Arctic, 109
  tracks, 159
harpoons, 31, 32, 35
Hayes, Isaac, 81
Hedin, Sven, 186, 226
Hepburn, John, 6
Herald (ship), 48
Herzog, Maurice, 197
Hesling, John, 99
  in Anadyr, 62
  and the dog team's first outing, 82
  and the dogs, 68, 74, 76, 80, 83
  film producer, 59
  in Moscow, 59
  and Tolia's drunkenness, 77
  told of author's intentions, 216
Himba people, 211
Hood, Robert, 6
Hooper, William, 47, 125, 180
Hope Challenge, 24
Hopeless, Mount, Australia, 169
Hudson Bay, 5
Hudson's Bay Company, 33

Iban people, 208
ice spikes, 55
Icedogs (TV series), 257
Iceland, 176
Iditarod dog race, Alaska, 55, 79, 207
igloo, *see nynglyu*
Igor (at Provideniya museum), 185, 191
Inankuejas, Gennadi (Gena), 28, 42, 53, 212
  appearance, 36
  drops out of the venture, 56
  education, 37–8
  and new ice, 19, 37, 213
  personality, 36, 38
  rendezvous with BA, 26, 36–40
  and Shparo, 39–40
international border, 29
International League for the Rights of Man, 52
International Women's Day, 103, 104
Inuit community, 33, 34, 114
  see also Eskimos
Ivan (BA's contact in Russia), 20, 76, 100, 103, 108, 128, 206, 211–12, 216, 217
  and Alexei, 66–7
  in Anadyr, 23–6, 61
  appearance, 17
  behaviour in Provideniya, 182–5
  behaviour while in Loreno, 205, 211–12, 215
  clarifies the author's plans for Yasha, 191–2
  contacts Gena, 19
  drunken evening in Moscow, 59–60
  finds tyre tracks in the tundra, 133
  and first outing of author's dog team, 80–83
  his ugly phase, 173
  and International Women's Day, 103, 104
  in Konergino, 130, 131
  in Lavrentiya, 29, 30, 31, 34, 36–9, 66, 67, 68
  panics, 149
  personality, 17, 22, 41–2, 46, 130, 171
  shoots a wolverine, 131

and a spirit ritual, 107
supports the Chukchis, 44–5
in Uri's flat, 91

Jackson, Frederick, 250
James Caird, The (whaler), 167
Janáček, Leoš, 110
Javari River, *210*
Jennings, Michael: *The New Complete Siberian Husky*, 79
Jensen (dog handler), 81
Jeremy (a member of BA's dog team), 105, 106, 107, 109, 115, 125, 137, 138, 154, 161, 217, 223, 234, 240
Job (Nansen's dog), 93, 94
Joel (of the Niowra people), *211*
Jones, Steve, 178

Kalahari Desert, 57, 189
Kamchatka, 32, 43, 44
Kandengei village, Papua New Guinea, 187
Kane, Elisha, 81
Kataktovik (Bartlett's Eskimo companion), 93
kayak (closed leather canoe), 32, 35, 107, 124, 127, 223
Kazak herders, 16, 39
Kellett, Captain, 48
kettle, 161
KGB, 215
Khodorkovsky, Mikhail, 257
Khrushchev, Nikita, 52
King, John, 168, 169
King William Island, 7
kittiwakes, red-legged, 148
Konergino, 126, 129–33
Koryak, 32
kulaks (village heads), 33
Kursk (submarine), 60, 211

Lady Franklin Bay, Ellesmere Island, off Greenland, 121
Landells, George, 168
Larkin, Philip, 194
Lashly, William, 142, 145
Lasse (Amundsen's favourite dog), 144
Lavrentiya, Chukotka, 28, 29, 31, 34, 42, 47, 63, 65, 66, 78, 216, 217, 218, 228, 240, 242, 244
Lena River, 18
Lenin, Vladimir, 7, 23, 52
Leonid (a Chukchi in Yanrakkynot), 200–201
Livingstone, David, 162, 167
Liza (Yasha's cousin), 100, 102, 106, 107, 108
Lloyds TSB, 186
London, Jack, 10
Long (Lady Franklin Bay Expedition survivor), 121
Lorino, 36, 38, 100, 102, 142, 153, 192, 200, 204, 217, 252
Luda (Yasha's cousin), 100, 102, 103, 106, 107, 108–9, 114
Lyg'oravetl'an ('real people') *see* Chukchis

Maasai, 188
McClintock, Francis Leopold, 7
McGee, Eddie: *No Need to Die*, 189
Machiavelli, Niccolò, 198
McKinlay, William Laird: *Karluk*, 93
Mad Jack (a member of BA's dog team), 88, 89, 96, 100–101, 105, 112, 115, 124, 125, 129, 137–40, 154, 199, 212, 223, 228, 234, 254
Magadan, 52
Mahlemuits, 13, 96
Malamutes, 79, 96
Malindi, Kenya, 246
mammoth, 94
man-hauling, 141, 142, 146
Margulis, Lynn, 177
Markovo, 69, 77, 79
marriage, Yupik, 35
mastodon, American, 94
matches, 57, 161
Mato Grosso, Brazil, 226
Matses Indians, *210*
Mawson, Douglas, 208, 209, 242

Meares, Cecil, 95, 145
Mech, David, 101
Medellin cartel, 195
Melbourne, 168, 169
Menindee, Australia, 168
Mertz, Xavier, 208, 209
Messner, Reinhold, 198
Mexico, 189
Michel (Native American guide), 5, 6, 112
Misha (a reindeer herder), 151–2
mollusc, 18
Momwina nation, 10, 11
Mongolia, 32, 56
Moore, Commander, 48
Moorhouse, Geoffrey, 190, 197
Moscow, 29, 41, 59, 211
  airport, 196
Muckpah (an Inuit), 114
murres (guillemots), 18
Muttley (a member of BA's dog team), 104, 105, 113, 147, 159, 204, 212, 225, 234

Namibia, 211
Nansen, Fridtjof, 81, 93–4, 95, 124, 128, 165, 234, 250
Natasha (of Anadyr), 25, 26, 61, 63, 160
Native American guides, 6
Natufian people, 73
Naukam, 224
Nenana, Alaska, 79
Nenets people (Samoyed), 81, 95
Neshkan, 53, 68
New Guinea, 57, 161, 162, 170, 188, 243, 258
New Guineans, 251–2
new ice, 19, 37, 213, 236
Nicholas II, Tsar of Russia, 7
Nietzsche, Friedrich, 12, 210
Niger River, 188
Nikolai (sheriff of Konergino), 131–4, 135
Nikolayevsk, Siberia, 95
Ninnis, Lieutenant Belgrave, 208
Niowra people, *211*
Nome, Alaska, 79
North Atlantic, 176
North Pole, 5, 71, 79, 81, 95, 165, 186, 198, 217
Northeast Passage, 43, 44
northern lights, *see* aurora
Northwest Passage, 5, 6, 7, 21
Novoye Chaplino, 35, 193, 197
Nunligran, 154
Nunyamo, 223, 224, 232
nynglyu ('igloo'), 35

Oates, Captain L. E. G., 142, 144, 145, 187
Obini nation, 10, 11
Observer, 195
Ogre, The, Pakistan, 196
Old Suggen (Nansen's dog), 94, 234
One Ton Depot, 146–7, 229
Orellana, Francisco de, 165, 166
Orinoco/Amazon watershed, 246
Ottoi, Alexei, 74, 81, 89, 96, 99, 136, 204, 234
  personality, 28, 37
  appearance, 38, 212, 217
  BA replaces him as alpha male, 100–101
  discusses the dog team, 212
  drops out of the venture, 56
  greets BA on his return, 252–3
  helps BA prepare for his solo journey, 216
  his dogs are returned to him, 254–5
  positioning of dogs in the team, 94, 96
  rendezvous with BA, 37–40
  seal hunting, 213
  and Shparo, 40
  unable to teach BA about his dogs, 66–7
owl, snowy, 156

Pablito (Matses Indian), *210*
Papua New Guinea, *211*
Park, Mungo, 188

Parry, Edward, 6
Pasteur, Louis, 177–8
Patagonia, Argentina, 167
patriarchal clans, 35
Peary, Robert, 95, 141, 143, 198
Pegtymel River, 107
penguins, 145
Persia (later Iran), 196
Peru, 153
Peter the Great, 43
petroglyphs of River Pegtymel, 107
petrol, 57, 106, 161, 241
Pierre Saint Martin, Pyrenees, 195
Pizarro, Francisco, 166
Pizarro, Gonzalo, 165–6, 167
Pizza restaurant, Anadyr, 26
Plan C, 163, 164, 170, 228
Pleiades, 132
Plover, HMS, 47, 180
Point Hope, Alaska, 24
polar bears, 151–2, 216, 229, 244
  Hadow on, 116
  illegal hunting of, 185
  and Shparo, 43
  spring migration, 115
  tracks, 132, 223
  and Yasha, 91
Pole of Hope, 18
Pond Inlet, Baffin Island, 114
ponies, Scott's, 141–2, 143, 145, 146
Pontianak (female demon), 208
Prince William Sound, 44
Prokofiev, Sergei: *Peter and the Wolf*, 223
Provideniya, 102, 174, 180–81, 193
ptarmigans, 109
Putin, Vladimir, 18, 215, 257
Putumayo, Colombia, 195

queen bee, 244–5
Quito, Ecuador, 166

Ra (sun god), 250
Rae, Dr, 48
Raityrgin, Sergei, 21, 24, 25, 38, 61
Ramsay, Fox Maule, 79
raven, 31, 107, 108
Rawicz, Slavomir, 208
Red Square, Moscow, 30
reindeer, 108, 137
  Bering Strait crossed by stray reindeer, 45
  decline of herds, 33
  domesticated, 33
  herds forcibly collectivized, 33
  pastoralism, 32
  slaughter of herd members, 152, 203
  uses of, 202
  wild, 33
  and wolves, 138–9
Resolution (ship), 44
Richardson, Sir John, 6, 48
Ross, Sir James, 48
Royal Geographical Society, 196
Rubaiyat of Omar Khayyam, The, 251
RUSAL, 18
Russian Far East, 13, 18, 21, 51, 258
Russian Federation, 33
Russian mafia, 29
Russians, and Cold War, 29

Sagan, Dorion, 177
Sahara Desert, 186, 190, 197
St Lawrence Island, 35
St Peter (ship), 43
St Petersburg, 131
Saint-Exupéry, Antoine de, 186, 249
Samoyeds (dogs), 95, 96
Samoyeds (people), 13, 95
Sankaracharya, 236
Sarah (lead dog of Yasha's team), 98–9, 108, 118, 204, 209, 216, 217, 231
Sarawak, 208
satellite phone, 56–7, 216
Savolainen, Peter, 72
Schrödinger, Erwin, 177
Scott, Doug, 196–7
Scott, Sir Robert Falcon, 141–2, 187
  amateurism, 229
  ambitions, 229
  choice of dogs from Nikolayevsk, 95, 144

collection of geological samples, 144, 229
death of, 16
depots, 146–7
inexperience, 146
lack of success with ponies, 141–2
lack of understanding of dogs, 145
man-hauling, 141, 142, 146
markers, 146
puts his trust in men, 142
rations, 146
realizes too late the value of dogs, 73
sledges, 145
starvation, 142, 143, 146
survival of the ideal, 229–30
Scott Polar Research Institute, Cambridge, 16–17
sea birds, 18
sea mammals, 35, 108
seals, 35, 85, 108, 127, 145
bearded, 32
and bears' spring migration, 115
common, 32
dissection of, 181
hunting, 213
meat, 67
ribbon, 32
ringed, 32, 129, 180
spirits, 224
and Tolia's dogs, 128
Seneca, 195–6
Seppala, Leonhard, 79
Serengeti, 203
Sergei (fixer), 21–2, 22, 28, 36, 39, 40
Sergei (in Lavrentiya), 30, 31
Seward Peninsula, 35
Shackleton, Ernest, 145, 146, 167, 209, 210, 250
shamans, 14, 33, 34, 40, 107–8
Shambles Depot, 146
shovels, 55
Shparo, Dmitry, 24–5, 38–40, 41–3
Shparo, Matvey (Dmitry's son), 24, 41, 43, 44
Siberia
BA's first day in, 20–26
Bering's explorations, 43
land bridge to Alaska, 72, 94
used for punishment, 7, 257
Siberian huskies, 79–80, 95, 96
Sibneft, 18, 257
Sierra Madre Occidental, Mexico, 189
Simpson, Joe, 188, 198, 208, 218
Sireniki frontier base, 35, 172, 179, 192–3
skidoos, 133, 134
sledges
Amundsen's, 144
repair of, 173
Scott's, 145
traditional, 124, 125
snacks, high-energy, 161
snipe, 128
snowmobiles, 106, 108, 118, 125, 128, 131–4, 136, 193, 199
snowshoes, 55, 56, 59, 84, 99
Solzhenitsyn, Alexander: *The First Circle*, 10
soul, the, 251–2
South: The Race to the Pole (ed. Pieter van der Merwe *et al.*), 146
South Australia, 168
South Georgia, 167, 250
South Pole, 71, 73, 95, 124, 141, 142, 143, 146, 229
Soviet Union
Cold War, 29
fall of, 33, 235, 241
fur-trading agreement, 80
industrial projects (from 1940s), 33
modernization programme, 33
official Soviet dog (Leningrad factory breed), 15
spears, 35, 44, 73
Speke, John, 167
spirits, 31, 34, 91, 107, 108, 119, 155–6, 181, 191, 192, 200, 224
spontaneous generation theory, 178
Stalin, Joseph, 7, 10, 52, 227
Stanley, H. M., 162, 167, 188
Stark, Freya, 196
steam engines, 162

Stefansson, Vilhjalmur, 92, 93, 236
Steller, Georg Wilhelm, 43
stoves, 55, 57, 113, 150, 161, 232, 234–5, 240, 241, 248
Stuart, John McDouall, 168, 170
Sumatra, 57–8, 153
Surtsey Island, 176
survival kit, 57, 161, 170, 228, 240
survival list, 57–8, 161–2, 164–5, 167, 170, 242
survivors file, 170, 185–6, 194–9, 207–211
Susi (Livingstone's servant), 167
swallows, 108
Swenson, Olaf, 80, 96

Taklamakan Desert, 186, 226
Tanya (Yasha's daughter), 206
tents, 106, 161, 230
  skin, 31, 35, 224
  yarangas, 201–2, 203
Terror (ship), 7, 162
Thames River, 162
thermodynamic equilibrium, 177
Thermodynamics, Second Law of, 177
Thesiger, Wilfred, 198
Thomson, Joseph, 188
Thursday Island, 250
Thurstrup (driver), 79
Tibetan Pleateau, 167
Togo (a famous sledge dog), 79
Tolia, 56
  appearance, 66, 69
  on bears' spring migration, 115
  choice of lead dogs, 99
  and dog commands, 67, 68, 74, 82
  first outing of BA's dog team, 82
  and first serious run of BA's team, 88, 89
  his dogs, 127, 128, 139, 172, 174, 204, 205
  meets BA, 66
  partying in Markovo, 77
  and the spirits, 91, 107
  in Uri's flat, 84, 85, 90, 91
  on Yasha, 126
Top Dog (team leader, BA's dog team), 104, 105, 109, 112–13, 115, 118, 136, 137, 138, 140, 142, 147, 152, 157, 158, 161, 172, 199, 204, 212, 221, 223, 225, 226, 229, 234, 238, 243, 247, 248, 252, 254
Torres Strait, 244, 251
Torres Strait Islanders, 243
trajetas, 195
trans-Siberian railway, 33
transmitter, 57, 216
trees, rarity in Chukotka, 18
Trent (ship), 5
tripe de roche (a lichen), 4, 6, 15, 112
Trontheim (a Latvian), 95
Trotsky, Leon, 52

Uelen, 38, 91
Uelkal, 106, 118, 119–20, 127, 129
Ukrainians, 22, 33
Ulabrand (Nansen's dog), 94
Ural mountains, 18
Uri the Kazak, 64, 83, 84–5, 90, 91, 96, 106, 113, 119, 126, 128, 134, 135, 136
Uvs, Mongolia, 208

Valentia (museum owner, Lavrentiya), 31, 34, 36, 119
Valya (Yasha's daughter), 206
Vanya (a Chukchi in Provideniya), 180, 181, 185, 193, 199, 200, 235
Velázquez, Diego, 189
Vermont, 79
Victor (helicopter pilot), 60, 65, 68, 69, 77, 80
Victoria, Australia, 168
Vikings, 43
Vladimir (in Lavrentiya), 30–31, 218
Vladivostok, 95
Volodyr (poet in Anadyr), 26, 27, 63

Wadhams, Professor Peter, 16, 38
walrus, 32, 35, 39, 108, 155
  meat, 2, 53, 55, 67, 68, 78, 80, 110,

111–12, 126, 137, 173, 174, 194, 212, 216, 220, 223, 248
Weddell Sea, 167
Wells, H. G., 185
West Papua, 10–11, 153
whales, 85
beluga, 21
bowhead (Greenland), 32, 107, 199
grey, 32
killer, 31, 35, 108, 117–18
meat, 224
whale-bone arches, Yttygran Island, 181–2, 199–200
whale fat as dog food, 49
whistle, 57
WHO (World Health Organization), 62
wildlife in Chukotka, 18
Wills, William John, 167, 168–70
Wilson, Edward, 229–30
Wiluna, Gibson Desert, Western Australia, 188
Wind of the Bad Spirits (southerly wind), 126
Wind of the Good Spirits (northerly wind), 126
wolverine, 131–4, 226
wolves, 71, 72, 108, 137–9, 218, 223, 224, 230, 244
dogs as part of wolf diet, 101
Eurasian grey, 73
North American grey, 73
pack behaviour, 101
and sledge dogs, 116, 117
territorial markers, 140
tracks, 140
wolf pups compared with the modern dog, 73–4
women, role in the Arctic, 102
Wrangel Island, 93, 116, 236
Wright, William, 168, 169

yaks, 208
Yanrakkynot, 199, 200
Yapishka, Sergei, 41–3
yarangas (tents), 201–2, 203
Yasha
accompanies BA to the start of his solo journey, 216–19, 220–21
appearance, 69
argument with Ivan, 182, 183
and BA's first solo trip, 103–4
celebrates BA's return, 254
choice of lead dogs, 98, 99
depression on arrival in Lorino, 205–6
and dog commands, 68, 74, 82, 86, 96–7
encounter with a mother bear, 91
feeding the dogs, 78, 80
feels that BA doesn't know his dogs' characters, 192, 200
finally sees BA and his dogs as a team, 205
first outing of BA's dog team, 82, 83
and first serious run of BA's team, 87–9
guides by memory or instinct, 110
his dogs, 75, 76, 98–9, 108, 115, 118, 135, 149, 174, 204, 205, 216, 218
on killer whales, 117–18
loss of a tooth while harpooning walruses, 90–91
loss of all his dogs, 86
on love of the tundra, 117
meets BA, 66
partying in Markovo, 77
rescue of four of his dogs, 149
seal hunting, 213
shapes a snow bear, 220
and the spirits, 91, 107
told of BA's intentions, 191–2
in Uri's flat, 84–5, 90–91
warns BA against favouritism, 93, 140
Yeltsin, Boris, 18
Yttygran Island, 199
Yupik, Yupigyt, 33, 35, 108

Zeenoviyev, Vitali, 23
Zeenoviyeva, Tatiana, 22–3